The elements of social theory

The elements
of social theory

Barry Barnes

University of Exeter

UCL
PRESS

First published in 1995 by UCL Press

UCL Press Limited
University College London
Gower Street
London WC1E 6BT

The name of University College London (UCL) is a registered
trade mark used by UCL Press with the consent of the owner.

British Library Cataloguing-in-Publication Data
A catalogue record for this book is available from the British Library.

Library of Congress Cataloging-in-Publication Data are available

ISBN: 1-85728-203-5 HB
       1-85728-204-3 PB

Typeset in Times Roman.
Printed and bound by
Biddles Ltd, Guildford and King's Lynn, England.

Contents

Preface

This book is an attempt to identify those fundamental themes and ideas in social theory that currently possess the most plausibility, and hence deserve the most attention in future research and the greatest trust when theory is applied. The outcome will be clear and evident in what follows. However, the enterprise itself involved a review and evaluation of basic ideas and assumptions in a number of different theoretical traditions. This quickly made it apparent that, although most of these different traditions are rightly regarded as incompatible with each other, they are all none the less of great value as sources of theoretical insight, and all indubitably necessary for what might be called an education in theory. It has been necessary to work through these traditions in order to formulate the finished argument of this book, and their fundamental characteristics and claims are set out and analyzed here accordingly. This ought to make the book of use in the teaching of sociological theory, perhaps for students who are taking their studies further after an initial introduction to the subject. In Britain, I hope it will help to complement the much more widespread approach of learning theory via theorists. In the USA, it will not represent a neglected approach to theory in the same way, but here too it may be that its strategy of concentrating on fundamentals will give it a distinctive value.

Some readers, particularly those already well versed in social theory, may wish to read the book selectively. There is no reason why they should not; it is even possible to begin with the second part, using the index to refer back where necessary. However, the book offers a positive argument that builds cumulatively from one chapter to the next and this needs to be kept in mind. Parts of this basic argument have appeared in earlier publications; in particular, some themes of Chapters 3 and 4 are prefigured in a paper in *Sociological Review* (Barnes 1990), and the key argument of Chapter 5 is given in *Sociology* (Barnes 1992). The general sociological approach builds upon that adopted in an earlier book on *The nature of power* (Barnes 1988) and the way the approach is illustrated and exemplified in the present text is designed to avoid overlap with the examples given prominence there. The treatment of social institutions and distributions of self-referring knowledge in that book may also be found useful in that it complements and serves to expand the scope of the argument of the present work.

The wide range of materials covered by the book has led me to call on the help of a large number of friends and colleagues, all of whom deserve thanks for the unstinting assistance they gave. Colleagues in my department at Exeter University all deserve acknowledgement, but I particularly need to mention those who read parts of the manuscript: Grace Davie, Tia DeNora, Paul Keating, Steve Loyal, Greg Martin, Bob Snowden and Bob Witkin all provided valuable comments and criticisms that helped me to improve the text. Thanks are also due to Andrew Travers, John Vincent and Steve Reicher. Friends and former colleagues at Edinburgh University also played an important part in the evolution of the book, and I would like to mention particularly David Bloor, Colin Bell and Colwyn Trevarthen. Randall Collins must also be thanked, both for specific comments on an earlier version of Chapter 5 and for more general inspiration; and so too must Peter Abell for his kindness in finding time where there was none, in order to read and comment on Chapter 1. Finally, I want to thank Mary Guy, who also performed miracles with time in her invaluable work on the production of the manuscript.

BARRY BARNES, EXETER UNIVERSITY   January 1995

Introduction

Sociological theories come in many forms and are directed to many different ends. Much the most widely read theories, however, at least in Europe, are those that serve as the basis for commentary on the nature of present-day industrial societies and on how they are likely to develop and change. At the same time, these "macro" theories are the ones that give rise to the greatest amount of dissatisfaction and elicit the strongest criticisms. Macro theorists are notorious for confusing the future they would like to see with the future that can plausibly be expected, to the extent that many outsiders have come to discount their work as worse than useless as a basis for an understanding of social change. And indeed theorists themselves frequently acknowledge that this is so. Most of the pivotal events of the century, up to and including 1989, have evoked laments for the failure of theory, while Marxists, who have been a major force in the European tradition of macro theory, treat it as in crisis just so long as the capitalist system is not. This recognition of failure does at least acknowledge an obligation to orient theory to actuality, to attempt to explain our present state and predict how it will change, and to evaluate the success of such attempts. Other theorists appear to have given up on this kind of activity altogether, and to have reconciled themselves to following along in the tracks of change, offering discourses for its *ex post facto* rationalization – diverse discourses to meet the needs of all the different sources of demand that arise in the academic market places of competitive capitalist societies. Perhaps it is this development in particular that has led to the complaint that sociological theory is no longer any such thing, that what now exists is ersatz theory, a substitute for theory, a hotchpotch of critique, philosophy, taxonomy, history, the biography of theorists, practically anything, in fact, save theory itself (Mullins 1991).

1

In these circumstances, it is not surprising that some sociologists see the way forward as involving a turn away from theory and a renewed appreciation of the merits of empiricism. Certainly, there are virtues in empiricism, and many theorists have been far too involved in reconnoitring the road to paradise to give proper heed to them. But a policy of retreat from theory should not be pressed too far. Even those sociologists with the greatest respect for "the facts" recognize that in isolation they offer us nothing. If facts are the pearls of a field of enquiry, they must none the less be threaded on a rope of theory before they are capable of assuming a shape or defining a direction and thereby creating expectations of any kind. The formulation of links and connections between particulars is what theorizing is. Where there is no theorizing, there is no sociology. What is generally recognized as the literature of sociological theory is merely an outcrop of a great array of loosely connected theoretical orientations incarnate in the practice of the field as a whole: its references to socialization and enculturation, norms and values, classes and interests, kinds of actions, mobility and stratification, and so forth, involve the use, if perhaps in an unusually abstract way, of concepts that are found everywhere. The difficulties of macro sociological theory are thus, for the most part, the difficulties of the field of which it is a part, exposed to view in a particularly cruel and brightly lit way, dissociated from the particular achievements that stand to the credit of most of the specific substantive fields in sociology.

Evidently, the need is not for a turn away from theory but for continued efforts to improve it and thereby the field as a whole. There are always those who wish to believe that sociological theories, like all other theories of voluntary human behaviour, are part of an impossible project. But no plausible argument on behalf of this view exists. And in its absence the mere fact that a tradition of theory has a poor track record is no reason for its termination. With patient work, theory could come good any century now. The single criticism that can validly be levelled against practically all macro sociological theorists is that they have been in too much of a rush.

Needless to say, improvements and reconstructions of theory cannot be carried out in the course of its use in theoretical commentary. This would be rather like trying to reconstruct theoretical physics whilst designing a nuclear power station. Large pronouncements about the nature of modern societies and their institutions, even if for many they count as the acme of sociological theory, are in fact just applications of its basic concepts and ideas, and amongst the most problematic and least clear-cut applications at that. To know theory only at this level is to have no practised autonomy with respect to it, to be unduly dependent on it or perhaps even upon particular exponents of it. In order to grasp what sociological theory can offer, its strengths and weaknesses, its present failings and future possibilities, it is necessary to move away from secondary applications and to focus upon its basic form. This is what the present book seeks to do. It is the result of digging into the literature that carries theory along at this fundamental level, looking through the resources available therein, tentatively checking different approaches against some substantive materials, trying to gain a sense of what holds promise and what does not. It has involved an examination of basic theories in a number of different theoretical traditions, most of the traditions, in fact, currently sustained in the social sciences: this indeed is why, given that (ideally) all the different social science fields should be theoretically integrated and continuous with each other, the title speaks of "social theory" rather than "sociological theory". None the less, the book has been written with sociology predominantly in mind, and the main purpose of the book is to present an account of the basic form that theory ought to take in that field. The book is designed to convey a coherent conception of this basic form, to set out the grounds for regarding that particular conception as a plausible one, and to show that it is applicable to substantive problems.

Since this positive conception emerges only slowly as the book proceeds, it may be useful to give a preliminary indication of what it consists in. An important part of it is simply a reaffirmation of the platitude that human beings are, of their nature, social creatures. There is impressive empirical evidence for this conjecture, which ought perhaps to be regarded as a central dogma of sociology, a claim that the field should keep, at all times, at the forefront of its thought. The particular version of the dogma to be offered here holds that human sociability is deepseated and pervasive. It will not do for macro sociological theory to conceive of it simply as a source of constraint and restriction on the individual, a way of accounting for her actions as conforming actions, and for social order as an harmonious, conflict-free system of such actions. Rather our sociability should be conceived of as a continuing, profound, mutual susceptibility, which finds expression in aligned cognition, shared language and knowledge, and indeed in the existence of all manner of powers, skills and capacities that can be readily combined and co-ordinated with those of other people. Our sociability is what allows us to achieve an intelligibly ordered social life through and as the collective use of all these powers. Thus, rather than restricting us to, or confining us within, a given social order, our sociability is what facilitates its production and allows its continuing reconstitution and recreation.

To insist that we are social creatures and to treat this as a matter of profound and pervasive significance is to announce a strongly anti-individualistic sociological theory, and just that will be forthcoming. However, rather than rejecting the individualistic contribution to social theory, the strategy here will be to begin with it and work through it. It constitutes an immensely impressive body of work, systematic, lucid, exemplary in its self-criticism, which any account of theory needs to address and evaluate. And here there is an added incentive, in that the limitations of individualism point the way forward for the positive argument. Thus, as far as this argument is concerned, it is particularly important to address the claims that separate individuals are unable to act collectively (section 1.4), or to conform to rules or norms (section 2.4), or even to know what rules or norms specifically imply (sections 2.4, 4.3).

Those readers wishing particularly to follow the positive argument may wish to take special note of references to the problem of collective action, since they will serve as a marker of the progress of that argument. The problem, also known as the free-rider problem, is introduced in section 1.4 as a notorious problem for individualistic social theory: collective action manifestly exists, but according to individualism it should not. Subsequently, however, the problem is used more generally as a touchstone of a good social theory. In particular, it is argued that the existence of collective action will not be accounted for by any theory that deals in independent individuals. Independent calculative individuals will not act collectively, but neither will the socialized individuals of functionalism: neither moral individuals, nor individuals oriented to norms or rules, nor individuals predisposed in any other way will solve the collective action problem so long as they operate separately. For collective action must continually be monitored and adapted to circumstances, aligned and realigned with what others are doing, and it is not possible to predispose an autonomous individual mind so that it may adapt and realign actions in the way that is required. However, it is then argued that interacting, non-independent, mutually susceptible individuals may do what independent individuals cannot. Continually communicating with each other on the basis of a body of shared knowledge and culture, constantly influencing each other through symbolically mediated evaluations, operating as a collective in thought and calculation, they are able to formulate, encourage and perform actions for their collective good, and to monitor, modify and adapt those actions so that they remain oriented to that good. And, having made this case in the first part of the book, the problem of collective action remains at the centre of interest in the second as the argument is evaluated and illustrated in the course of a substantive discussion of social formations.

The picture of the human condition to be presented in what follows is a reasonably simple one, and one that is already to be found at work here and there in various contexts in the social sciences. Yet it is not routinely encountered in macro social theory, even as an approach to be criticized and rejected. Perhaps this is because of the strongly anti-individualistic character of the picture. For all that it is often hostile to the individualism of economic theory, macro sociological theory is suffused with individualistic forms of thought, many of which are hard to reconcile with what is to be put forward here. There is, for example, a widely accepted policy in macro theory of separating off "instrumental" and "economic" actions, and treating them as "non-social", for all that they are knowledge based and co-ordinated with other actions on the basis of shared knowledge. Secondly, there is a tendency to understand "genuinely social" actions, such as actions oriented to norms, or moral principles or ritual requirements, by privatizing them, as it were, and making them wholly a matter between the individual performer and the particular norm, or principle or rite in question. Thirdly, this tendency to privatization may be exacerbated by an essentialist treatment of concepts, beliefs and ideas (possibly related to the fact that, for theorists, these are items of intellectual property). If ideas and so forth are conceptualized as essences, then it is easy to think of them taking up residence in individual minds and the encounter between individual and society occurring wholly at an ideal level, without the continuing mediation of other people, which will be identified as crucial here.

This is not a book about particular sociologists. None the less, it is interesting to ask whether the tendencies just described might not be the consequence of a neglect of Durkheim in the practice of macro social theory. He is the seminal figure above all others who insists upon a comprehensively sociological approach and offers protection against lapses into individualism. Yet, although his place on a pedestal goes unchallenged, his role in the practice of macro theory, particularly in the English-speaking world, is less than it should be. There is still a residual reserve, in this context, at Durkheim's acceptance of the *sui generis* reality of collectives and collective phenomena. The proper response to this is not to deny the serious problems and difficulties of the Durkheimian position, but rather to notice that they are no more formidable than the problems of an individualistic alternative. Why, for example, should it be improper to attribute thought, inference or calculation to collectives, but not to individual persons? Certainly, the sound waves and light rays that carry messages between the component brains of a collective are more accessible to investigation than the neuronal transmissions that are said to fulfil the same role within a single brain. We should not infer the superior merit of individualistic metaphysics and epistemology from the mere fact of their popularity.

Durkheim was one of the great social theorists, but many of the currents of influence flowing from his work have passed around rather than through the main body of social theory. He has been important to interactionist theorists whose "micro sociology" has always stood at a distance from the major trends of sociological theory itself. He has been an inspiration to social anthropologists in their studies of culture and belief. His work on knowledge and classification has been built upon in the sociology of knowledge, even as sociological theory generally has avoided it. Now that sociological theory is coming to recognize the pressing need for a general understanding of social interaction, and of the knowledge and culture it sustains, it is likely in due course thoroughly to reassimilate Durkheimian approaches that for so long it has tended to neglect. This book could conceivably be read as an attempt to imagine the fundamental form that theory might come to take as a result of such a reassimilation, although this is not a point that is laboured in the text itself.

The positive argument offered in this book requires a movement through most of the theoretical traditions of social theory. Hence, it has been possible to provide a review of key ideas in these traditions, so that the book may serve a range of purposes in the context of sociology, without adding inordinately to its length. It could even be that there are positive virtues in the strategy that has been followed. Certainly, the thought that the book might perhaps be used on theory courses of serious intent, taken together with the fact that sociologists tend on the whole to work within rather than across theoretical traditions, has encouraged an attempt to deal with issues in the simplest possible terms, and to avoid adding to the already considerable difficulties of fundamental points of theory by an unduly complex or abstract presentation. Only in the two codas is this approach modified in favour of something that, although substantially more demanding of background knowledge, is none the less both looser and more allusive. But a coda normally follows the completion of the argument of a work, and by convention here it is forgivable if the line is blurred by a certain amount of noise. The codas, let it be clear, are in the way of optional extras.

Although it seeks to avoid unnecessary complication, this is not a book to use in a first encounter with sociological theory. Some initial familiarity with the literature, and particularly with the ideas of the seminal sociological theorists, will be useful background. However, this is not a book about theorists. It is a book about theoretical ideas in which theorists make appearances, just as ideas make appearances in books about theorists. Theorists are mentioned to ease the task of understanding for those who may know them, and to give some indication of where the reader might turn for further reflections on the relevant theoretical issues. No attempt is made to identify the "best" theorists, or to direct attention only to the most recent contributions to the field, or to become involved in currently celebrated debates or confrontations. Above all, this book must not be looked to for accounts of what this or that theorist "really said" or "really meant". Excavation of that kind is a wholly different task from that engaged in here: it requires the exacting methods of the historian and limitless drafts of time. Fortunately, in so far as the distinction can be drawn, it can be theoretically productive to misunderstand theorists as well as to understand them correctly.

Finally, it must be acknowledged that in a book such as this, which both reviews a number of possible theoretical positions and presents a particular one, there is an inevitable internal tension between what is ideally required by these different tasks, between balance and advocacy. But there is a specific feature of social theory that substantially diminishes the problem, to the great good fortune of all who write on the subject. This is its very low credibility. There is no need to be on guard in this field, as there may be in others, lest a clearly formulated opinion is confused with a fact or a truth. The social theorist need not trouble to cast off any significant accumulation of unwanted authority. The need for caution, reserve and a tentative presentation is less than acute, since the reader is going to take for granted that these are intrinsic to theorizing in any case. Not even those who lack a training in deconstruction are likely to be adversely affected by the absence of these elements of style and expression. Thus, in this context, the economical idiom of confident assertion may be adopted, secure in the knowledge that it is harmless and that, by stating what is the case, a text automatically inspires, as well, the thought that it may not be the case after all.

Part I

Traditions of social theory

In the context of social theory, there are many ways in which the resources of tradition may be described as so many distinct traditions. What follows represents just one of many such possibilities. Some theorists would draw attention to a Marxian tradition and thereby bring together and relate materials that are cited separately here. More profoundly, many theorists see social change as the central concern of sociology, not the persistence of pattern and order in social life that is identified as the key concern of those traditions of social theory discussed in what follows. What I hope will emerge, however, as the discussion proceeds, is that persistence and change are but different sides of the same coin, and that to understand one is to understand the other.

1

Individualism

1.1 Postulates of individualism

> . . . during the time men live without a common power to keep them
> all in awe they are in that condition which is called warre; and such a
> warre is of every man against every man. . . . It is consequent also to
> the same condition, that there be no Propriety, no Dominion, no *Mine*
> and *Thine* distinct; but only that to be every mans that he can get; and
> for so long as he can keep it. And thus much for the ill condition,
> which man by meer Nature is actually placed in; though with a possi-
> bility to come out of it. (Hobbes 1651)

The most challenging way of responding to Hobbes is to take him literally and attempt to envisage his state of war. Does it preclude all social
relationships? What of linguistic relationships: are linguistic communication and the sharing of knowledge and ideas precluded as well? And
where might people be found living in this "natural" condition, if indeed
it is a condition in which people conceivably could live? These, however, are large questions, too large for our immediate purposes. It will
be better to start with a narrower, more conventional approach, one that
recognizes that Hobbes' account of the state of nature is designed not to
inspire a search, but rather to make peace and order in society the focus
of curiosity, and to introduce an individualistic account of how they are
sustained. This has become the standard mode of use of Hobbes in the
context of modern sociological theory.

Hobbes poses a problem of social order deriving from the conflicting
wants of individual human beings and their mutual distrust, and he offers
a solution based on the common fear of coercion by a single sovereign

power. Hobbes' solution is no longer widely accepted, but his individualistic formulation of both problem and solution remains of great importance. Individualism continues to be a thriving theoretical tradition today, and is in many ways the least problematic of all the traditions of social theory. Our immediate awareness of social life is awareness of individuals. We watch individuals doing things, take account of them as we do things ourselves, try to guess what they are likely to do as we work out our own future plans. And when we gather data as social scientists it is usually data about individuals; indeed it is not obvious what else there is, in the last analysis, to observe, besides the activities of individuals and the products of that activity. Thus, it is perfectly plausible to conjecture that it is through observing individuals, and theorizing about the basis of what they individually do, that we shall come to an understanding of social life and social order, that a society is the aggregate of all the separately engendered actions of its individual members.

There are many kinds of individualism and the term means different things in different contexts, but for present purposes it will suffice to look at the predominant form of individualism in current theory. This is the form of individualism, particularly favoured in economics, that takes as its point of departure "the two well-known a prioris of self-interest and calculative rationality" (Reisman 1990: 10). In specifying calculative rationality and self-interest this approach seeks to identify the ways in which individuals remain independent of each other and stably internally constituted, as they engage in the fluctuating circumstances of social life. Individuals are to be treated as independent reasoning and information-processing systems with independent ends or objectives. To this extent individuals are unaffected by other people or indeed their environment in general, even though in other ways they may be profoundly affected by both, and obliged to take account of both. To this extent individuals stand as so many independent sources of action. This crucially simplifies the task of understanding entire systems of actions: if the actions are separately produced, then they are amenable to deductive modelling and aggregation by quantitative methods. These are very much the preferred techniques of most current individualistic theorists, and it can indeed be asked how far individualistic postulates are adopted not in response to evidence but in order to facilitate and simplify the application of these mathematical techniques.

Certainly, individualistic theorists tend to agree not only in their theoretical point of departure but in their methodology. They favour a deductive approach to social theory, and their work serves to exemplify the merits and problems of that approach. They start with simple postulates about the behaviour of individual human beings, and the overall outcome of that behaviour in any given context is then deduced from the postulates. In the form of individualism that concerns us here, four postulates are generally taken as fundamental. Human beings are presumed to be:[1]

- independent
- rational/calculative
- goal-oriented
- egoistic or self-regarding

The assumption of independence is the most important of all. The entire individualistic approach is based upon the conviction that actions are produced by agents whose objectives and decision-making procedures are stable, intrinsic characteristics independent of the immediate context. Individualism expects individuals to take account of their environment and of the actions of other individuals in it, but not to change their nature or intrinsic properties in response to them. Individualism wants to use the rationality and the objectives of individuals as givens with which to explain other things, not as variables that are in need of explanation themselves.

Individuals are assumed to be rational and calculative (and hence knowledgeable, since knowledge is required for calculation), in order to account for their ability to imagine the consequences of possible actions prior to choosing which they will actually perform. There are, however, different accounts of what is involved in being rational and calculative.

The assumption that individuals have goals (often referred to as "wants" or "desires" by individualists) is made in order to explain why they should choose one course of action rather than another. It is commonly assumed that the wants of individuals can be ranked in an order of priority or preference and that individuals act optimally to realize their preferences. It is also generally assumed that preferences and their rank ordering are fixed and stable. "The assumption of stable preferences . . . prevents the analyst from succumbing to the temptation of simply postulating the required shift in preferences to 'explain' all apparent contradictions to his predictions" (Becker 1976: 5).

Finally, it is commonly assumed that the wants and desires of individuals relate to their own benefit rather than the benefit of others, that individuals are egoistic and self-regarding. This, however, is the least important of the four postulates, and is often set aside. The crucial features of the individualistic perspective in social theory can be sustained without an assumption of egoism. The mathematical apparatus of individualism needs independent stable objectives or preferences, but the apparatus still operates whether or not they are egoistic ones.

In a nutshell, individualism assumes that an agent in a social situation will operate as follows: she will independently take stock of the situation; rationally calculate in the light of what she knows how each available action is liable to affect that situation; note which action is likely to be the most effective in furthering her goals; and enact that action accordingly. Where the individual is egoistic, goals will be self-serving and actions will be self-interested. Such a hypothetical individual, because it is commonly postulated in economic theories of human behaviour, is sometimes referred to as manifesting "economic rationality". Where the need arises, she will be referred to here accordingly as an ER individual.

In a society of ER individuals, all actions are individually calculated, rational, goal-oriented and (usually) self-regarding. Individualism implies therefore that all the actions actually found in social situations are of this kind, and seeks to predict the overall patterns of action we are likely to find in social situations given that every individual action is indeed of this kind. Unfortunately, however, there is no way of predicting from the basic postulates how individuals will act if they are brought together, as it were, as so many separate bodies in an unspecified environment. Plausible predictions are possible only if individuals operate in a context wherein their choices are heavily constrained by *externalities* of some kind. In the context of much current individualistic social theory, external constraint is provided artificially; ER individuals appear as players in games invented by theorists. The rules of the games are assumed to constrain the players, and rational playing strategies are inferred. Real human beings are believed to be involved in situations analogous to the games, so that a game in the theory will serve as a model of real human behaviour. For example, a game in which rational individuals exchange goods may be taken as a model of the economic life of real human beings. The rules of the game may be taken as analogous to the legal rules surrounding economic life, and the nature of the theorized ER individuals as analogous to the nature of the real human beings exchanging goods. Predictions about real activities of exchange then become possible by considering the theoretical game of exchange.

This approach to social theory is a familiar and oft-encountered one. It is commonplace in economics, as we have already noted. And it is also an important component of modern political theory and sociological theory, wherein it exists as game theory and rational choice theory.[2] For all that, however, there is no doubt that, of the social science disciplines, sociology is the least sympathetic to this individualist approach. Indeed, most of the seminal figures in the tradition of sociological theory have uncompromisingly opposed it. For Emile Durkheim, opposition to individualism was part and parcel of the business of establishing the discipline of sociology. Much of Talcott Parsons' theoretical work was devoted to establishing the insufficiency of individualism. The Marxian tradition, until the advent of "rational-choice Marxism", has been predominantly anti-individualistic. Max Weber, although a "methodological individualist", initiated a tradition of sociological theory that emphasized the insufficiency of theories based upon "economic rationality".

It is because of this that the crucial importance of individualistic assumptions in sociological theory is often overlooked. The seminal theorists actually rely upon individualistic kinds of explanation. What these theorists say is that the individual is not *just* an independent calculative egoist, which is to acknowledge that the individual is this some of the time, or to some degree. Thus, in the work of Talcott Parsons (1937, 1951), the individual human being is depicted as in a state of tension between the egoistic urges inherent in her nature and countervailing pressures originating in society and its moral order. Parsons holds that social order is possible only when egoism is sufficiently overridden by countervailing pressures, but equally he acknowledges that egoism is always incompletely overridden, that "rational" egoistic actions are always encountered in any society, and indeed that such actions are necessary parts of social life and essential to any understanding of the course of social change. The same actions play crucial roles in the theories of all the founders of sociology, constituting much of the realm of the profane for the early Durkheim, lurking in the domain of the economy in both Marx and Weber. Nor are they any less significant in current work. In the theories of Jürgen Habermas, for example, they are present among the "non-social" instrumental actions, oriented wholly to technical success, that play a leading role in his vision of modern capitalist societies (Habermas 1984: 285).

It is crucial to recognize the role of individualism and of the theoretical construction of the ER individual in the mainstream of sociological theory. If there is anything lacking in this construction it will have implications not just for economics or for fields such as game theory but for the core of sociology as well. As some applications of the individualistic approach and its characteristic methods are explored in what follows, and a sense of its limitations and deficiencies is thereby eventually evoked, this point needs to be kept firmly in mind.

1.2 Co-ordination

The powers and possibilities of ER individuals are of great sociological interest. What are they capable of doing? What games are they able to play, and how will they play them? Will they do the kinds of things that real people do in real social situations? Many kinds of action are generally agreed to be performable by ER individuals. Even Durkheim and Parsons allow them to act directly upon the physical environment to further their goals, and to play, within given systems of enforceable rules, the games of exchange studied by economists. But these are far from being the only capacities that ER individuals possess. Another extremely important one is that of *co-ordination.*

Imagine a number of individuals acting simultaneously, with each able to choose between alternative actions. Many combinations of actions will be possible. Imagine now that all individuals agree which are the best and worst combinations, and that they all want one of the best possible combinations to be produced. In this sense, all the individuals may be said to have the same interests. They all share an interest in *co-ordinating* their actions so that a best overall combination is the outcome. ER individuals should be good at co-ordinating their actions. As each individual seeks the same outcome, there should be no serious obstacle to its achievement even in a society of egoists.

Difficulties may none the less arise in achieving co-ordination. Consider two individuals seeking to lift a piano onto a platform. To lift the piano, a concerted, synchronized, all-out heave is essential. So the pair set a radio by the piano and agree to lift at the instant of two o'clock. They each grasp the piano, draw breath, tense muscles, and await the signal. Alas, one of them then cannot remember whether it is the first or last of the six forthcoming pips that signifies two o'clock. And as she seeks to recall the crucial missing information, it occurs to her to ask whether after all the other party may not also be in difficulty on the same matter. About to explode into action, united in a common goal, alike in their interests, a problem of co-ordination none the less arises for the two participants. Should they manage to heave in concert, whether at the first pip or the last, success will be theirs. But should they act just ever so slightly out of phase, one at the first pip, the other at the last, the result will be likely hospitalization and an unmoved piano.

Individualistic social theories, and in particular game theory and decision theory, make use of formal representations of the general problems they study. The problem of co-ordination just described can be represented as in Figure 1.1. Note how, for the purposes of formal representation, the two individuals must be treated as playing a game wherein only two alternative actions are allowed; they cannot be modelled as they would exist in a real world situation where any number of actions would be open to them. Each individual must take either action A (lifting at the first pip) or action B (lifting at the last pip). Four combinations of actions are possible: in two they lift together and in the other two out of phase. Both individuals give the possible outcomes the same order of preference. They both want to achieve a concerted lift and avoid an out-of-phase one. Lifting together, either on the first or the last pip indifferently, is the first preference; lifting out of phase is likewise, for both, the second preference. It is because there are two equally good routes to co-ordination, via the first pip and via the last, that a problem exists. Precisely because both possibilities are equally good there is no knowing what the other individual is going to do, even if that other is an ER indi-

(a)

I_1 \ I_2	Acts at pip 1	Acts at pip 6
Acts at pip 1	1.1	2.2
Acts at pip 6	2.2	1.1

(b)

Individual$_1$ \ Individual$_2$	Acts A	Acts B
Acts A	$P_{I_1} P_{I_2}$	$P_{I_1} P_{I_2}$
Acts B	$P_{I_1} P_{I_2}$	$P_{I_1} P_{I_2}$

Figure 1.1 Co-ordination. (a) Example in text. (b) General form of diagram (P_I = rank of preference of individual I).

vidual. A guess will be necessary, with only a 50:50 chance of success.

The kind of co-ordination problem of which this is an example is the product of inadequate knowledge. Shared goals and interests in themselves do not narrow the possibilities of action sufficiently. Further narrowing must be achieved by agreement, but for that shared knowledge and shared understanding are necessary. To recognize that this is the nature of the problem is to see how to solve it. The creation of further shared knowledge and shared understandings suffices. Were the two individuals in the above example to become professional lifters of heavy objects they would readily develop reliable routines of co-ordination, based on shared knowledge. Sufficient shared knowledge to make the required co-ordination possible is all that is necessary here, because the individuals want to co-ordinate. Because they have common goals and interests, ER individuals can trust each other here. Indeed, they can trust each other to seek the possibility of co-ordination as well as to enact it when it is recognized. And the former may actually be invaluable in securing the latter.

Schelling (1960), whose writings on co-ordination are seminal, offers a number of examples of this kind. Consider two individuals who lose each other in the course of a walk. The mist-laden country is largely featureless, but just one sharp tor or summit is marked rising from the land, on a map otherwise largely empty of information. The individuals need to reunite. The tor is the only "special" point nearby, the only place uniquely defined in their shared knowledge (the map). Each knows that the other wants to reunite. The only plans or strategies for co-ordination must involve the tor. The simplest plan would be to meet at the top, something readily achievable, even in mist, by walking upwards. Why not go to the top in the hope that the other will go as well? The reasoning is thin, but there is nothing better. Just because there is nothing better it may be that it is good enough. Recognizing that there is no better thing to do, both individuals may proceed to the top – and meet. Schelling calls the tor the *prominent solution* to the co-ordination problem, and suggests that its adoption is likely simply because it is prominent. Where the important thing for people is that they agree on *something*, and what is agreed on is secondary, then prominent solutions figure large because they are things that *can* be agreed upon.

It is plausible to imagine that, if our two individuals were to repeat this walk, they might say at the start: "If we lose each other, we'll meet at the tor." With co-ordination problems, solutions evolved on one occasion tend to be used on further occasions. Forms of solution are laid down in the social stock of knowledge and future social action becomes more co-ordinated in consequence. This is a profoundly significant social process. It may be, for example, that it is currently at work in Britain in our voting behaviour. Do you wish your local MP removed? Is this more important than how precisely she is replaced? Then the candidate for the party in second place at the previous election offers a prominent solution, a place around which to co-ordinate voting. And, in so far as the vote around this position grows in one election, so it may attract more votes at the next.[3]

When large numbers of individuals solve co-ordination problems, the resulting patterns of activity involve the following of *conventions*, and it is in the interest of ER individuals to continue to follow such conventions. Examples include our continuing to drive on the left (right), our use of the VHS video format, our referring to Greenwich Mean Time (or whatever other time). What is characteristic of these examples is that it is in our interest to conform to them just in so far as (nearly) everyone else does so. There is no intrinsic merit in driving on the left rather than on the right, but it is a matter of life and death that we drive on the side that others drive on. The intrinsic qualities of VHS were apparently inferior to those of competing now-defunct video formats, but the advantages of purchasing the most-purchased format, and the skilful initial establishment of VHS as the prominent candidate, led to its achieving a virtual monopoly.[4]

Conventions in the precise sense set out above are ubiquitous in all societies, and the ability of ER individuals to create and sustain them is of great theoretical significance. Yet the importance of work on co-ordination has only quite recently been properly emphasized in discursive sociological theory; and in this context there is still a need for greater appreciation of its value as a theoretical resource.

Many problems associated with power can be clarified by thinking of them as co-ordination problems. Consider the example of the two individuals lifting the piano. Neither individual separately possesses this power. Only when they act in a relationship with each other, whereby their actions are co-ordinated, is this power created: the power to lift a piano. And it is similarly the case generally that through co-ordination individuals become able to do more; their capabilities increase; their powers multiply. This is a neat and simple way of displaying the inadequacy of the old *zero-sum* conception of power. The zero-sum conception assumed that the gain of power by one agent implied a corresponding loss of power by another agent or agents. It implied that powerful agents were necessarily exploiting others by depriving them of power.

The zero-sum conception can appear very plausible and persuasive. For whatever reason, we sometimes have difficulty with the notion that power can be generated "out of nowhere" as it were, simply by ordering our actions so that they are co-ordinated. There is a tendency to regard power as something almost material, a substance that has to come from somewhere and reside somewhere. Power produced by co-ordination seems to come from nowhere, which we find hard to acknowledge. Marx noted the tendency to redescribe such power as something substantial, something that was "always there".

> The productive power developed by the labourer when working in co-operation is the productive power of capital. This productive power of associated labour is developed gratuitously, whenever the workmen are placed under given conditions, and it is capital that places them under such conditions. Because this power costs capital nothing, and because, on the other hand, the labourer himself does not develop it before his labour belongs to capital, it appears as a power with which capital is endowed by Nature – a productive power that is immanent in capital. (Marx [1883] 1974: 349)

Modern capitalist societies are very highly co-ordinated indeed. Their powers, their capacities and capabilities, are massively amplified by this co-ordination. Their productive output, which reflects the exploitation of these powers, is vastly increased. What gets done through co-ordinated actions is orders of magnitude greater than what could get done without co-ordination. Moreover, individual interests in retaining overall co-ordination, always present, always strong, are especially strong in modern societies, where individual actions are bound up into co-ordination with the actions of a diverse range of others to an unusual degree. All this must help to account for the stability of the key institutional arrangements of these societies.

This is not to say that the status quo is, for most individuals, the best of all possible worlds, or even that there is no alternative that most people could agree upon as preferable. It is merely to note the high conversion costs of a shift even to a thoroughly practical utopia, if an initial loss of co-ordination is involved. In the face of ever-increasing individually borne conversion costs, the attractions of putting up with the inherited social and political order, rather as we put up with VHS, are correspondingly enhanced. Patterns of social change that retain co-ordination are another matter of course; these are routine and familiar in modern societies, so much so indeed that they are often incarnate in what we refer to as the status quo.

1.3 Co-operation

In looking at the problem of co-ordination we considered individuals with identical interests. They evaluated the possible combinations of their actions identically: the rank order of preferences of one was the same as that of the other. They both sought the same state of affairs and their problem was simply to achieve it: the problem was one of knowledge and communication.

There may also be circumstances in which two individuals evaluate combinations of their actions differently, in which different rank orderings of preferences appertain and the best combination of actions for one person is not the best for another. This does not necessarily imply conflict; it may make sense for both individuals to settle for second-best. Where they have conflicting interests, individuals may stand to gain by co-operating to realize their interests to the limited extent that is possible. But such co-operation may actually be prevented by the rational pursuit of self-interest itself. Acting according to self-interest can actually be what prevents the optimal satisfaction of self-interest. An example is the best route to an understanding of this counterintuitive point.

Consider two soldiers, both ER individuals, guarding a road. Each sits in a pill-box, one on each side of the road, equipped with a machine-gun. Along the road come the enemy, several truckloads, well-equipped and formidable. None the less, with two machine guns and strong positions it is almost certain that the defenders can prevail, that the enemy can be forced to turn around and flee. Moreover, the defenders are stiffened by the thought that should they themselves turn tail and run they would very probably die, overtaken by the mobile enemy before they could reach safety. For them to stay and fight is clearly preferable to their making a run for it.

Unfortunately, these are not the only combinations of action that are possible. What if one of the pair stays and one runs for it? Then she who stays will surely die, while she who runs will surely escape, under the cover of the other's fire. Here is where interests conflict. Each would prefer the other to stay while she herself withdraws. And tragedy ensues

I_1 \\ I_2	Run Don't co-operate	Stand Co-operate
Run Don't co-operate	Very probable death 3.3	Certain death 1.4
Stand Co-operate	Certain escape 4.1	Very probable escape 2.2

Figure 1.2 Co-operation. I_2's preferences stated and their ranking emphasized.

from this conflict of interests. For it leads to both soldiers running to their probable deaths, when if they had both stood firm they would almost certainly have survived.

The situation is represented in Figure 1.2. Note again how the formal representation converts the situation into a game wherein only two actions are possible, running and fighting, and hence only four combinations of actions. Consider the viewpoint of either soldier as she weighs all the possibilities and seeks her best strategy. One possibility is that the other soldier stays. In this case it is best to run for it; for this ensures certain survival, which is preferable even to the very good chance of survival associated with fighting. The other possibility is that the other soldier will flee. In this case it is also best to flee; for very probable death, however unattractive, is none the less better than the certain death entailed by standing and fighting on alone. Accordingly, the best strategy is clear and unambiguous, established by impeccable and completely secure reasoning: whatever the other does it is best to run away. So the soldier runs, and her companion, being no less rational and self-interested also runs. And they both very probably die.

Because they were rational and self-interested, i.e. because they were ER individuals, the two soldiers acted in a way that was very probably fatal. Had they acted irrationally, and stood fast, they would almost certainly have survived. Had each acted altruistically, giving priority to the life of the other, then similarly each would have almost certainly saved her own life. Not only did their self-interested actions produce the worst outcome *overall*; it was an outcome far worse for each *individually* than the outcome if both had acted against self-interest. Being rational calculators, both would no doubt have welcomed the presence of an external Hobbesian power to force them to act irrationally (or rather to use the threat of force to convert irrational into rational action and hence make it performable).

This is an example of what is everywhere known as the *Prisoner's Dilemma*, and is also sometimes described as the problem of two-person co-operation.[5] The standard analysis of the problem is entirely uncontroversial. It serves as a striking example of how individual rational calculations can combine to produce unfortunate suboptimal outcomes, and its formal simplicity makes it one of the key memorable exemplars of individualistic social theory, one of its most valuable cognitive resources.

Let us stress our interest in *both* participants by referring to the *Prisoners' Dilemma*. The participants in a Prisoners' Dilemma are doomed to disaster by their own rationality and self-interest. This is what diverts them from a co-operative response to their situation, one that would make the best of their situation and provide both of them with a superior outcome. And because rational self-interest is the cause of their problem it cannot be looked to as the basis for its solution. It is sometimes thought that the problem of co-operation faces only individuals who are unable to communicate, but this is not so: because each individual has a best strategy independent of whatever the other individual does, communication with the other cannot be helpful. How is this so? Would not an agreement to stand solve the problem? Is it not uncertainty about the intentions of the other that causes the problem? There is no problem of uncertainty here. To run is always the best strategy. If an agreement is made then it is rational to break it. Between ER individuals such an agreement would lack force. In Hobbes' words: "covenants, without the sword, are mere words, and of no strength to secure a man at all" ([1651] 1968: 223).

The problem of two-person co-operation is insoluble for ER individuals. Playing the game just described, they must always let each other down. Individual rationality requires that they don't co-operate, that each *defects*. On the face of it, this is bad news for individualism. People with different interests do seem to be able, in practice, to co-operate, and it is hard to imagine how an ordered society would be possible if they did not. If co-operation is not rational then it would appear that individuals are not ER individuals. However, great care is needed in relating any abstract model to real situations. Real situations may fail to refute a model because they are not situations of precisely the same kind as those presented in the model itself.

Robert Axelrod (1984) has suggested that many actual historically situated problems of co-operation may be soluble, because they are not one-off events as implied in the account above, but encounters that may recur, perhaps many times. When the possibility of later encounters is taken into account, participants may be more inclined to co-operate in their present encounter. Co-operation may thus be possible between ER individuals after all.

Consider two ER individuals who know they will encounter each other again and again over a long period of time, and will repeatedly have the opportunity to co-operate. The two individuals know that they will be playing a long sequence of Prisoners' Dilemma games. Taking each game in isolation they know that defection (D) is rational and that co-operation (C) cannot be beneficial. The prospect of a long string of mutual defections beckons. Much better would be a sequence of mutual co-operation. But how to achieve it? Think of two competing shops sharing the market in a remote village. Every morning they set their prices. Co-operative pricing, say with 20 per cent margins, would allow them a good income. But if either were to set such a price the other would gain from setting a lower price to capture the available market. To co-operate allows exploitation: it allows the other to defect and gain thereby. How then might mutual co-operation day after day be achieved, instead of relentless competition wherein day after day prices in each shop are cut to the bone?

In Prisoners' Dilemma both individuals prefer mutual co-operation, CC, to mutual defection, DD. A long series of CCs is accordingly vastly preferable to a series of DDs. If there were a means of inducing it, would it not be rational and self-interested to make use of that means? Perhaps the encounters themselves could be so used. Perhaps the first games could be played, not to win, as it were, but to set up the later games as a series of mutual co-operations.

In Figure 1.3, consider a long sequence A, of mutual defections, and a similar sequence B, the beginning of which is unknown but which continues as a series of mutual co-operations. For either individual, B may be preferable to A, however B begins. Accordingly, if the initial encounters in B could be used to secure the later CC series, i.e. could be used to teach and induce the other player to assist in producing the later series, then it would be rational so to use them. The immediate pay-off from the initial encounters could be ignored; any costs from those encounters could be treated as investments in the future. The encounters would no

23

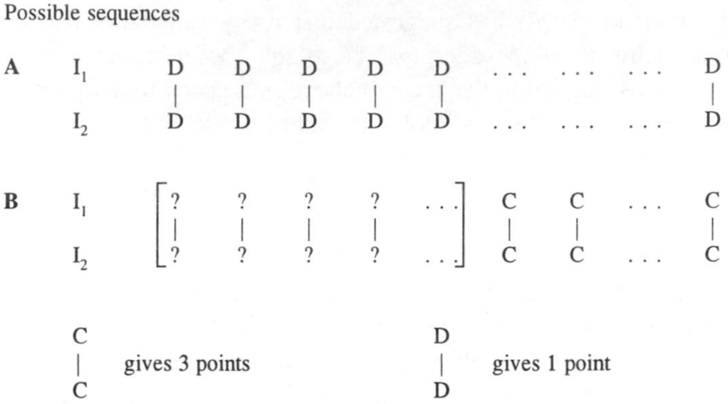

INDIVIDUALISM

Possible sequences

A   I₁   D   D   D   D   D ... ... D
        | | | | | |
   I₂   D   D   D   D   D ... ... D

B   I₁   [? ? ? ? ...] C C ... C
   I₂   [? ? ? ? ...] C C ... C

C | C gives 3 points   D | D gives 1 point

Figure 1.3 Repeated co-operation in Axelrod's game.

longer be the encapsulated events modelled by the Prisoners' Dilemma game, but events with consequences extending indefinitely into the future and pay-offs accumulating slowly over time.

How, though, might a sequence of mutual co-operation be induced? It is necessary to demonstrate to the other player that co-operation is in her interest. Defection must be discouraged, and co-operation encouraged, by real incentives and sanctions. Axelrod indicates a simple strategy for doing exactly this in the course of the actual series of encounters itself. The strategy is that of *tit-for-tat* reciprocity, wherein one acts in any given encounter in the way that the other player has acted in the previous one. Once the other player has learned that what she does determines what is subsequently done to her next time, she will infer, rightly, that co-operation is her best strategy and a sequence of mutual co-operation will ensue. The initial cost of the teaching will soon be recompensed.

Notice, however, that the argument here will be valid only in specific circumstances. It does not claim that co-operation is rational in any series of repeated encounters, or in any sequence of imagined games. It requires, for example, that the reward for co-operation is relatively large compared with that obtainable by defection, that future reward is not vastly less desirable than immediate reward, and that knowledge of the future can be relied upon so that the rewards co-operation will bring can be trusted to arrive in due course. For this reason Axelrod always uses a *particular version* of the Prisoners' Dilemma in his work, so that invalid generalizations of his claims are discouraged (Fig. 1.4).[6]

I₂ $\overset{I_2}{\underset{I_1}{\diagdown}}$	Defect (D)	Co-operate (C)
Defect (D)	(D D) 1 1	(D C) 5 0
Co-operate (C)	(C D) 0 5	(C C) 3 3

Figure 1.4 Axelrod's game. Numbers indicate points gained by an individual in an encounter, and not ranked preference.

It is important to recognize as well that the structure of Axelrod's argument is not that of secure deduction, like that associated with one-off co-operation. Axelrod relies on conjectures about *inductive* learning, about how an individual will learn from experience. His argument is actually a contentious one, particularly amongst game theorists who set great store by formal, deductively secure reasoning. This is a useful reminder that what constitutes valid reasoning by ER individuals is highly controversial.[7]

When Axelrod himself presses the claim that tit-for-tat reciprocity is a potent and rational strategy for securing co-operation, he does so not in the main by elaborating formal models but by presenting empirical evidence – albeit evidence of a slightly strange kind. The evidence derives from a computer simulation of two-person interaction. A number of game theorists and social scientists were invited to submit strategies for an individual to use in repeated two-person interactions of the Prisoners' Dilemma kind. The strategies were expressed as computer programs and set against each other in a series of repeated "encounters" generated by the computer. The computer thus simulated a number of individuals engaged in repeated "two-person" encounters, with each individual using a different strategy. "Nice" co-operative strategies faced "nasty" unco-operative ones, and each other, in all possible pairings. Taken overall, the strategy of tit-for-tat reciprocity produced a greater pay-off than any alternative. To use Axelrod's terminology, it "won" the "computer tournament".

Axelrod made the detailed results of his "tournament" available to participants and others in their fields and invited the submission of new, or revised strategies, or the resubmission of existing strategies, for a second joust. Once again tit-for-tat won. Learning about two-person co-operation through repeated experience did not result in the emergence of a superior strategy: making the "players" better informed merely reinforced the position of tit-for-tat as the best strategy.

Axelrod's computer tournament supported the thesis that co-operative strategies are rational even more strongly than it supported the specific strategy of strict tit-for-tat reciprocity. Overall, in these simulations, co-operative strategies paid off better than unco-operative ones: "nasty" strategies were less profitable than "nice" ones. Tit-for-tat reciprocity was a "nice" strategy that never obtained a greater pay-off from a sequence of encounters than its "opponent", and sometimes obtained a less good pay-off. Yet, like most "nice" strategies, it did better overall than unco-operative strategies, because these generally produced disastrous pay-offs when they encountered each other.

In the simulations, successful strategies were co-operative but only if co-operation was reciprocated. They obeyed four key rules. First, they were "nice" and began with co-operation. Second, they none the less responded to exploitation (defection) by immediate cessation of co-operation: they "retaliated" immediately. Third, they responded to renewed co-operation by immediate renewed co-operation of their own: they "forgave" immediately and did not "bear grudges". Finally, they avoided complexity of response: they were simple for the "opponent" to understand. Tit-for-tat itself was all of these things. Apparently, it was close to the ideal combination of the four key rules.

Yet again, however, it must be emphasized that Axelrod did not "prove" the rationality of tit-for-tat reciprocity in Prisoners' Dilemma encounters. Nor did his results demonstrate the superiority of the strategy in actual social situations, where circumstances, and the range of other "strategies" encountered, could be radically different from those simulated in the "computer tournament". What matters most for present purposes, however, is not the precise scope of Axelrod's claims or the rigour of his arguments, but the form and the *prima facie* plausibility of his basic thesis. Systematic and long-lasting co-operative relationships may, on the face of it, be possible between pairs of ER individuals, even when their interests are in opposition. Co-operative relationships of this kind can be argued to be "rational". Along with production, exchange and co-ordination, two-person co-operation may perhaps be consistent with the postulates of individualism.

26

1.4 Collective action

If continued co-operation is possible between two ER individuals with opposed interests, might it be possible analogously between larger numbers? The basic arguments advanced by Axelrod can indeed be extended to some extent. Suppose there are three people who do best overall by engaging in repeated co-operation. Any defector may be pressed back into line by either or both of the other two, for reasons analogous to those set out earlier. And, similarly, in other very small groups it may perhaps be that ER individuals will continue to secure co-operation from each other. However, as groups become larger and larger, the incentives to co-operation become weaker. In very large groups the benefit of any individual act of co-operation or defection is very widely spread, and likely to be negligible for any particular individual. Nor is a single individual in a position to affect the future actions of very large numbers of others in the way that she affects a single other in Axelrod's example.

The problem of co-operation in very large groups is more often referred to as the problem of collective action, or the free-rider problem. It is analogous to the Prisoners' Dilemma problem, and the analogy may be emphasized by thinking of it as a problem of co-operation between an individual and a group. Consider an individual deciding whether or not to purchase a catalytic converter to purify her car exhaust and contribute to the provision of unpolluted air. Clean air may be counted a benefit by all the members of a group, and indeed every member may count it a benefit well worth the cost of a catalytic converter for her car exhaust. Yet it may be that no member would rationally decide to purchase such a converter. For such a purchase would not in itself provide clean air. Only a number of purchases by nearly all the members of the group would provide that. Every individual converter makes a negligible difference to the air. Hence any ER individual is bound to reason that clean air is best left for everyone else to provide, that it is best to free-ride on the actions of others, reaping their benefits but making no contribution to their costs. And hence no individual at all will purchase an exhaust converter, and clean air will not be provided.

Clean air is an example of a collective good. The overall cost of the provision of such a good may be far less than its overall benefit, once provided. The individual's portion of the overall cost may be far less than the benefit that individual receives from provision of the good. Provision may be good for the group *and* for each individual in it separately.

I Individual \ Group G	No action Don't co-operate	Fit catalyst Co-operate
No action Don't co-operate	3 Vile air	1 Clean air free
Fit catalyst Co-operate	4 Vile air and lose £100	2 Clean air for £100

Figure 1.5 Collective action.
Cost of exhaust catalyst = £100.
Numbers are I's preferences.

Yet the good will not be provided by ER individuals because the incremental benefit from an individual's contribution to its provision is not enjoyed exclusively by the contributing individual but is spread over all group members alike. Since the benefit is enjoyed whether or not it is "paid for", individual self-interest is not coupled to the provision of its cost. A collective good like clean air may, overall, be as profitable an investment as an individual good like a bottle of whisky, but ER individuals would invest only in the latter; as to the former, if other group members do not provide it then the individual is helpless to provide it in any case, and if others do provide it then it is best to free-ride on what they are doing and save the cost of contributing to it (Fig. 1.5).

Wherever the costs of a project are borne individually, but its benefits are indivisible and enjoyed collectively, a problem of collective action arises. Why should an ER individual contribute to the costs of such a project when it is rational to free-ride instead? Defence is a standard example here, oft cited because it is extremely difficult to convert the collective good of security into a divisible, or private good; but as we shall see there are many other important examples. Similarly, where the costs of a project are borne collectively, and individuals cannot avoid them, yet the benefits are enjoyed individually, a problem of collective action arises. Examples are pollutions of all kinds, overexploitation of common resources, and overpopulation: these are all collective bads that ER individuals have no inducement to eliminate.

Evidently, collective goods may be of enormous value. Yet very large groups of ER individuals will not freely provide them, either on a one-off basis or, through the means suggested by Axelrod, on a continuing or repeated basis. Nor has any alternative mechanism been suggested by which large groups of ER individuals might be induced to act freely for their collective good. It is indeed generally accepted that, if the postulates of individualism are correct, genuine collective action of this kind is *impossible*.

Note that the fundamental reason for the existence of the problem is not that ER individuals are *self-regarding* but rather that they operate *independently*. The postulate of egoism can generally be set aside without a solution to the problem thereby coming any closer. One does not buy a catalytic converter for one's own gain, but neither does one buy it for the good of others, that is, if one is rational. To make a negligible difference to the air benefits nobody. To expend resources for no clear gain, when one might use them instead to benefit others in some straightforward, unproblematic way, is scarcely a rational expression of altruism. Thus, even if individuals could be suffused with a utilitarian morality, collective action would remain highly problematic: consequentialist moral reasoning will not serve to generate actions that are of no consequence. In a world where the adverse side-effects of independently calculated actions are being perceived as of ever-increasing importance, and environmental pollution by productive processes is becoming a significant concern even of sociological theory, this is a point that needs emphasis.

Genuine collective action by ER individuals is impossible. And indeed individualists assert that this is what we find empirically, that there is indeed no genuine collective action and that action resulting in the collective good can be induced only by the threat of coercion or the prospect of private loss or gain. People must, for example, be forced to pay the taxes essential for the provision of the services they require; be induced to take account of the speed limits designed to ensure their safety by the potential impact upon their wallets of doing otherwise.

The *locus classicus* of the individualistic approach to the free-rider problem is Mancur Olson's (1965) *The logic of collective action*, which suggests that very large groups will typically be unable to act for their collective good precisely because of their size; they will remain "latent" groups liable to be dominated by smaller groups that, again by virtue of their size, can act collectively. Where large groups apparently do act collectively, appearances are likely to be deceptive according to Olson. If workers join trade unions or professional associations, look out for the *selective benefits* like health insurance or legal protection that come with membership. If individuals join the armed forces at times of war, look to the coercive force of the state, as either that which pushes or that which makes them jump first, to avoid being pushed.

How far *prima facie* cases of collective action can actually be explained (away) by these devices is a matter of great theoretical importance. Many sociologists judge them to be a wholly inadequate response to the empirical evidence. Nor are they altogether plausible when judged within an "economic" framework. If people are induced to act collectively by the offer of selective benefits, i.e. private goods, how is it that a competing source does not offer the private goods more cheaply? How can trade unions retain their memberships by offers of health insurance or discounted motor cars in a competitive modern economy: are unions to be regarded as the most lean and efficient suppliers of these goods? Again, if it is coercion that makes people act collectively, by paying taxes for example, or enlisting in the army, how is the source of coercion sustained? Part of the accepted answer in the context of modern societies is that governments are voted in with coercive powers, but voting itself (notoriously) is collective action, so that references to coercion by government merely achieve a temporary abatement of the collective action problem and can in no way be said to solve it.

Yet many theorists, in several social science disciplines, remain wedded to Olson's basic approach. And this is highly desirable, because the problem of collective action raises crucial questions not just for individualism but for all varieties of social theory. Prior to Olson, and, it must be admitted, to much the same degree since, sociologists have cited group actors of many and various kinds in telling their stories of social change. Organizations have pursued their objectives; ethnic groups and religious sects have coexisted or conflicted; professional and occupational groups have defended their interests; conforming majorities have conformed to the laws that advance their collective benefit, while deviant groups have deviated; social classes have stirred into action and then decided it was not worth the trouble after all. (And references to groups and organizations are perhaps the least worrying manifestations of this tendency. There are still more problematic collective actors to be found here and there in the literature of sociological theory: capitalism, technology, patriarchy, have all been treated at times as potent agents with their own interests to further.) In denying the possibility of collective action, individualism serves as an invaluable call to order. If routine references to collective actors and collective action are to continue, then there should be a proper theoretical basis for them, an account of how the solidarity implied by such references is actually engendered. This is one reason the problem of collective action is given some prominence in this book. For an individualist, the incidence of collective action inspires a search for private benefits and selective incentives. But for other theorists it points to the need to account for social solidarity, and thereby raises genuine sociological problems.

1.5 An evaluation of individualism

Both supporters and opponents should be willing to recognize the distinctive virtues of the individualistic approach to social theory. Its focus is the least problematic of all the varieties of social theory: it speaks directly of individual human beings and their manifest behaviour. In order to understand that behaviour it postulates that human beings are identical in being independent, rational, goal-oriented and (in most versions) egoistic. All its theorizing flows from these postulates, for the most part in a deductive or pseudo-deductive way, which gives the theorizing a particularly lucid and accessible quality, making it easy both to understand and to criticize. The joints and connections in the theory are readily inspected; the auxiliary arguments that link the theory to particular situations are easy to distinguish from the main structure. The theory is readily visible as a model, separate from and problematically related to any actual situation it is used to interpret or understand.[8]

Individualism can claim empirical relevance as well as the formal virtues of clarity and simplicity. It offers a plausible basis for understanding how individuals use and manipulate physical objects and processes, how they engage in exchange, in interpersonal co-ordination and co-operation. Indeed, ER individuals might perhaps generate an entire social order with actions of all these kinds available to them, particularly since co-ordinated and co-operating ER individuals will be in a position to coerce others, and induce a great variety of additional actions through the threat of coercion. However, efforts to justify individualism by systematic presentation of empirical evidence are notably rare in the literature, and there is widespread recognition that it faces problems at this level. We have already noted that it cannot account for collective action, unless it takes the empirically implausible position that authentic instances of such action do not exist. But empirical studies of two-person co-operation are no less problematic. They reveal behaviour in Prisoners'-Dilemma-type situations as far more co-operative than "rationally" it ought to be. And even the paradigm actions of purchase and exchange of goods are typically carried out "irrationally" as a matter of empirical fact (Garfinkel 1967: 68–9). Nor are the results of experiment any more favourable than those of observation: social-psychological studies of individual behaviour serve not to confirm but consistently to cast doubt on the validity of individualism. Indeed, the most plausible inference from the evidence is that individualism is false.[9]

The reason that this evidence is not systematically reviewed here is that, curiously, it seems to have caused little controversy. Individualist theorists seem perfectly willing to concede that their postulates and actual human behaviour diverge. They tend to justify individualism not by challenging the evidence that calls it into question but in other ways. One is to assert that individuals much of the time, in many circumstances, behave as ER individuals. Another is to suggest that the "rationality" defined by the postulates represents how individuals "ought" to behave, so that the postulates provide the basis for a normative not a descriptive social theory. Another way is to insist that useful models can be constructed from the postulates; since the models "work", there is, so it is said, no need to worry about the truth or falsity of the postulates. Yet another way is to find virtue in the models even when they fail to "work".[10]

It is commonplace to note that individualism is an ideology much favoured in modern democratic capitalist societies. And it is tempting accordingly to account for the cheerful insouciance of some individualist theorists, as they develop their ideas in the teeth of so much evidence, by reference to this fact. But this would be unjust. Indifference to the truth or falsity of theoretical assumptions is widespread in the social sciences, and defended by sociologists of many different inclinations. A typical formulation is Stinchecombe's: "I have been a longtime advocate of an eclectic or toolkit version of social theorizing, that a sociologist should be prepared to use one theory when that theory works, another theory when it does not" (1992: 200). This indeed is now very much the dominant approach: confronted with empirical findings, take from the shelf the theory that best accords with them. Individualistic theory is picked from the shelf frequently, and the activities it has been used to describe and explain have come to be known as "economic" activities. Other activities, lacking point or rationality or egoism, are labelled "social" or "political" actions and are dealt with using different theories. Moreover, the different theories are now kept separate in distinct social science disciplines, and phenomena awkward for one theory to deal with are posted to another address, to be rationalized by a different theory. This perpetuates the status quo of the range of existing institutionalized theories and drains empirical findings of any theoretical significance. Every theorist may be confident that, whatever the field and the theoretical tradition to which she has committed herself, there is a little piece of "society" reserved for her, a little set of data that will allow her theory to work: it is a comfortable and even-handed arrangement.

The alternative to such eclecticism is to seek theoretical unity. When coins are tossed, sometimes they land "heads" and sometimes "tails". It is useless to deploy two theories here, one for each kind of outcome, and to choose whichever "works" in a given case. It is useless, that is, if one's aim is more than that of shovelling words over the coffin of a dead event. What is needed is one theory to make sense of both kinds of event, not two distinct theories. It is scarcely a justification for either one of such theories that it "works" half the time.

Indeed, it is important to bear in mind that a model remains open to question even when it works all the time. Too much emphasis on the "success" of models, rather than the plausibility of their assumptions, can be inimical to the development of theory. Even when a model is completely successful it remains a model: it may still be false; alternative models may well be capable of equal success in the same context. Consider those activities that involve the exchange of goods and services. There is a widespread impression that individualistic social theory works well in modelling them. Let us assume, strictly for the sake of argument, that individualism does indeed work in some sense here. By no means does this imply that individualism is giving a correct account of what is going on. The possibilities of different models and theories still need to be considered, and indeed sociologists are at last beginning to offer such alternatives (Molotch 1990, Davis 1993, Carrier 1995). But even in economics, where individualistic modes of thought are ubiquitous, it is possible to find alternative perspectives on exchange. Thus, according to one economist, rational economic exchange is not ubiquitous but exists specifically in societies where "the individual is urged to secure maximum value for money" and "self-interest becomes the social norm, even duty" (Hirsch 1977: 82). And according to another, specifically regulated contexts are necessary, wherein market competition and exchange are "supported by the moral, economic and physical sanctions of collective action" (Commons 1959: 713).[11]

That any given set of actions may be given many different theoretical rationalizations is a very important general point of theory, but it is particularly worthy of emphasis in relation to market exchange. This is because individualistic rationalizations of exchange are often accompanied by glosses that treat markets and free exchanges therein as somehow "natural", as forms of rational action that will arise once obstacles and impediments to them are removed. Actual markets are often better understood as collective political accomplishments created by regulatory activities and the careful fashioning of appropriate systems of legal sanctioning. Individualistic accounts of exchange might be better understood not as descriptions but as ideals, patterns of desired behaviour that inform attempts at social engineering.[12]

Be that as it may, because specific actions may always be successfully rationalized in more than one way, it is misconceived to evaluate a theory by reference to its "success rate" or any similar criterion. It is usually better to look to the difficulties faced by a theory and what promise exists of their being overcome. In so far as the identification of the difficulties facing individualistic theory is concerned, there is no better resource than the literature of individualism itself, which spotlights them with ruthless effectiveness. But, in its evaluation of these weaknesses, that literature is guilty of a certain optimism, of a failure to acknowledge that some of the weaknesses are fundamental and not amenable to cures or palliatives.

Two fundamental difficulties in the individualistic approach have special salience for what is to follow here, and both are acknowledged in the context of individualism itself. The first is that represented by the existence of collective action; it has already been discussed in some detail because the fundamental problem represented by the existence of such action is stressed in individualistic theory itself. The second is the problem of specifying the relevant aspects of the environment in which individuals act; this problem is also acknowledged in individualistic theory, but it is none the less insistently backgrounded by use of models, games and formal presentations, wherein the social environment is arbitrarily simplified, the physical environment may fail to appear at all, and cardboard figures choose between given alternatives on the basis of a fixed set of already ascertained facts.

What is thereby avoided is a problem of knowledge. In order to act as ER individuals we have to be knowledgeable. But knowledge and knowledgeability cannot be taken as givens. When real individuals enter into contexts of exchange or co-operation, their knowledge is not given and unproblematic. Much of it has to be learned.

The problem then arises of how far learning is rational action. It arises in the most acute form in the case of the new member, just arrived in the world with very little cognitive baggage at all, about to acquire language, knowledge and culture *ab initio*. Fundamental difficulties arise if a new member is treated as an ER individual. Consider an ER baby, lying in its cot facing its new world of threat and opportunity. Will it consult its preference schedule and reflect: "Well what should I do now? A restful nap perhaps, or a spot of healthy foot-kicking for muscle development. Or perhaps a cry for mother, to do a bit of language-learning. Hang on a minute! How can I be thinking this when I haven't any language yet to . . . ?"

New members are incompetent members. They cannot be rational in quite the way that existing members perhaps are, because rationality requires mastery of a repertoire of symbols and reference to a body of knowledge, neither of which new members possess. The activities of new members, therefore, and in particular their learning activities, pose a special challenge to an individualist social theory with which they are *prima facie* incompatible. Unfortunately, "toolkit eclecticism" has been the commonest response to this challenge: learning and knowledge acquisition have been handed over to specialized fields. It seems often to be assumed that rational action occurs after these processes are completed.

Individualism should not bracket off in this way the problem of how we acquire knowledge, because it is not just associated with *initial* knowledge acquisition. It arises whenever individuals engage in means/end-oriented action. If we are to act rationally to further our ends, we need empirical knowledge in order to calculate the likely consequences of how we act. But existing empirical knowledge is always and invariably incomplete. This raises the awkward problem of whether to act on the basis of what is known or to learn more about the situation first. To act in ignorance is on the face of it irrational, but to act on the basis only of complete knowledge is scarcely any more rational, for this entails never acting at all. When then should the switch be made from learning to action?

This problem is well recognized by individualists as an intractable one, although they normally refer to it as a problem of *information*. Associated with every action are information costs, the costs incurred in securing the information on which the decision to act is based. But "full information" in an indefinitely complex real world would take infinite time to acquire and be infinitely costly. Any actual representation of that world can only provide incomplete information, capable of further elaboration at a cost. It follows that action must always be based on less than "full" information.

What then is the "optimal" amount of effort to put into information gathering, the "appropriate" level of information to seek? There is no way of knowing, because there is no way of assessing the gains of information gathering in advance. This, incidentally, is similarly true of all the processes involved in *being rational* – not just of information gathering, but also of classification, inference, symbolic manipulation: their value, if any, is assessable only *ex post facto*. Hence, nobody can ever know, when they stop information gathering and proceed to act, that they have stopped at the best point.[13]

Evidently acts of learning, classification and inference, the actions involved in knowledge acquisition, raise pervasive problems for individualism, problems associated with activities of all kinds. It would seem that individuals must act in a certain sense arbitrarily if they are to act at all; what is routinely identified as rational action begins to look as if it is conventional action. On a strict construction, and with a rigorously specified definition of rationality, we might perhaps deduce from the problem of information costs that all human actions are irrational. This would imply that ER individuals should abandon individualism. But, then again, it would also imply that there are no ER individuals.[14]

2

Functionalism

2.1 Functionalism and system integration

Functionalist social theory was for a long period the dominant form of sociological and anthropological theory, and its possibilities have been explored in great detail in those fields. Many sociologists are inclined to believe that everything worth saying about functionalism has already been said, and to express that view in a way which implies that functionalism is as dead as a dodo. But whatever is worth saying about functionalism bears repeating, for it is the most misunderstood and misused of social theories. And it remains in any case clearly alive; in the work, for example, of Luhmann and of Habermas. Moreover, functionalist forms of thought have penetrated so deeply into the culture of the social sciences that they are often employed without being explicitly recognized as such, so that an understanding of their strengths and weaknesses remains necessary even if they are no longer as widely advocated and defended as once they were.

Functionalist theories in the social sciences seek to describe, to understand and in most cases to explain the orderliness and stability of entire social systems. In so far as they treat of individuals, the treatment comes after and emerges from analysis of the system as a whole. Functionalist theories move from an understanding of the whole to an understanding of the parts of that whole, whereas individualism proceeds in the opposite direction. The two kinds of theory conflict in their methodological implications and their epistemological rationales.

From a functionalist perspective, the key feature of "society" considered as a unified system is its orderliness and relative stability in the context of a changing environment. The system is held to persist as a pattern that resists disturbance and endures over long periods of time compared with the duration of specific social encounters or interactions. Indeed, to recognize the pattern one has to look at "society" over a comparatively long period of time, for the pattern is in the social processes themselves, as it were, constituted out of cycles of movement and change. The usual vocabulary for capturing this point refers to social systems being in "dynamic equilibrium"; the intended analogy is with natural systems that remain equilibrated even though their constituents are constantly changing – systems like the body, or the weather, or an eco-system. A social system may be thought of as a pattern through which people pass, rather as chemical substances pass through a plant, and constitute it as they pass.

If "society" is indeed a system in dynamic equilibrium, if it is stable and orderly in this sense, to this extent, then the key question is why this is so. And the standard answer, which defines the functionalist approach to society, is that the equilibrium of the whole derives from the operation of its parts: each part of the social system, each particular social institution, "functions" in a way that, given how all the other institutions are "functioning", contributes to the persistence of the whole.

We need an example at this point of a "functioning system" and how it "functions". The familiar case of a central heating system will serve very well. Consider the system represented in Figure 2.1. Water is heated in the boiler and propelled by the pump into the radiators; heat is

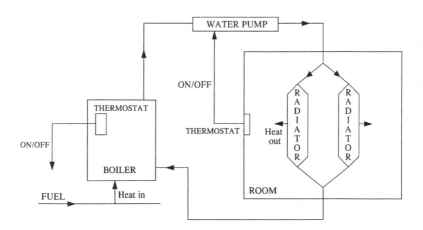

Figure 2.1 A central heating system.

transferred from the radiators into the room and the temperature of the room rises. So far we have a simple heat transfer device that will make the room hotter and hotter over time. However, there is a thermostat in the room, which operates at a certain temperature to switch off the pump; at this temperature there is *feedback* from the room to the pump. This results in further feedback to the boiler: with an inoperative pump the water in the boiler gets hotter and hotter until the boiler thermostat switches off the fuel supply. Subsequently, as the room cools, the room thermostat switches the pump back on, hot water is drawn from the boiler once more to raise the temperature of the room, the boiler thermostat switches the fuel supply back on, and the heating cycle starts again.

Central heating provides an admirably pellucid example of a functioning system. It is a whole comprising connected interacting parts. Constantly in the course of change, it none the less remains in a dynamic equilibrium around a given state, in this case a given temperature. The equilibrium is resistant to disturbance and can be sustained in the face of considerable environmental variation. This resistance derives from two features of the system: feedback and redundancy. Feedback, the existence of two-way causation in the system, makes it resistant to external environmental disturbance: if the weather gets hotter the thermostat spends more time in the "off" position; if cooler, the system remains on for more of the time, so that in both cases room temperature is unaffected. Redundancy, the existence of duplication of system parts, makes the system resistant to internal disturbance, to damage to its own constituents: if one radiator is blocked, water may move through the other; if one gas-jet is blocked, gas may still burn at another. Redundancy has the interesting consequence that no part of a functioning system may be "functionally necessary", and that any part may be destroyed or removed without the equilibrium of the whole being affected. This point is often overlooked.

As a simple mechanical system it is possible to give a causal account of the operation of the central heating. The action of the pump causes heat to flow into the room; the heat causes the switch in the room thermostat to cut off the electricity, which causes the pump to stop; the alternation of hot and cool water in the radiator causes the radiator to expand and contract; and so on. The possible causal relations are innumerable. It is also possible to give a functional account of the same system. The function of the boiler is to generate heat; the function of the pump is to move the heat to where it is needed; the function of the thermostat is to regulate the supply of heat so that neither too little nor too much arrives at the radiator; the function of the radiator is to transfer heat into the room; and so on. In comparison with a causal account, a functional account is far more selective. Many connections are missed out. The arrival of the hot water causes the radiator metal to corrode, but this would not be mentioned as a function of the water pump. The operation of the boiler produces CO_2 emissions, but this would not be mentioned either. A functionalist account mentions only those operations, and those consequences thereof, that help us to understand the equilibrium of the system. The heat produced by the boiler is *essential* for the maintenance of a stable temperature, whereas the CO_2 produced is *incidental* to that; thus, heat production is functional, whereas CO_2 is not. The functional account draws our attention to the part of what the boiler does that is essential to maintain the equilibrium of the whole system.

Notice, however, that this is not all that a functional account does. There are many ways of describing the equilibrium state of a central heating system. The radiator is alternately getting larger and smaller as it expands and contracts with small temperature changes. The thermostats are regularly clicking on and off. The pump is being maintained at 40 per cent output. But we make no mention of these things. We choose to describe the equilibrated system as a constant room temperature system. Why? Because this is the aspect of the equilibrated system that interests us. The provision of a constant room temperature is the *purpose* for which a central heating system is designed. The dial on the thermostat, available for us to adjust, is the sign and symbol of that purpose. The functional account shows how, in maintaining a dynamic equilibrium, the parts of the system combine to realize that purpose. It makes visible those features of the system most relevant to the purpose, thus expediting such actions upon the system as improvement and repair. It offers us a vision of the system of maximum practical value. In addition, from a formal perspective, it offers us an account of some *explanatory* value. For, in understanding the functions of the parts of the system, we thereby genuinely understand, to some extent, *why* they are there. No doubt the system designer had a mind to how they functioned when she included them in the system; in that sense they are there *because* of their function.

Let us now consider functionalist accounts of social systems and their constituent institutions. Consider the impossibly simple arrangement in

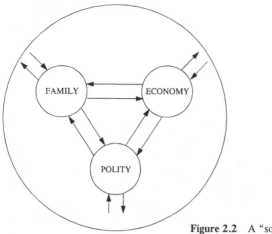

Figure 2.2 A "social system".

Figure 2.2. Within and between the three institutions identified in the figure, much will be going on. Like the central heating system, this simple "social system" will form a highly complex empirical state of affairs of which any verbal description, whatever its length, will be incomplete. What do standard sociological accounts of its functioning draw attention to? Conventionally, such accounts list the "functions" of the various institutions. They might describe the function of the economy as the production of goods and services essential to the operation of the other institutions and hence the system as a whole. The function of the family may be to engender and socialize persons for incorporation into the system as competent performers of economic and political tasks. And the functions of the polity could be maintenance of the system boundary and provision of the supply of coercion needed in the other parts of the system. Ideally, such accounts would go on to describe how, because there is two-way causation, feedback can occur so that even in a changing environment the institutions may continue to relate to each other harmoniously and coherently as part of an equilibrated whole.[1]

These descriptions are recognizable as parodies of standard sociological accounts of the functions of key social institutions. They will serve as a reminder of the nature of these accounts. What is their value? In what way do they significantly add to our knowledge? The standard answer is that they identify as functions just those things done by the individual institutions which are necessary for the equilibrium of the system as a

41

whole, and that in doing so they explain the existence of the institutions within the system and the particular form that they have come to take within the system. There are many questions that can be raised in relation to this standard account, but two are crucial. What is being referred to as "the equilibrium of the system as a whole"? And why is an institution and/or its operation explained if it is shown to be functional for system equilibrium? In the case of the central heating system there are clear answers to the equivalent questions. Although the equilibrium of the central heating system could be defined in innumerable ways, we actually define it by temperature stability because that is the stability we are interested in, the purpose that the system has been explicitly designed to serve. And if something contributes to temperature stability it will to some extent be explained thereby, since the designer will have incorporated it into the system for that very purpose. In the case of the central heating system there is a dial on a thermostat to register a purpose, and a designer cognizant of that purpose who invented the system around it. But in the case of a social system there is no equivalent of either of these things. And without them the relevant notion of equilibrium remains problematic and the possibility of functional explanation is absent.

It is possibly for these very reasons that functionalist sociologists have avoided the analogy between social systems and functioning mechanical systems, and stressed instead the analogy with organic systems, and particularly the human body. The separate parts of the human body interact with each other so that the body overall remains equilibrated in changing conditions, where "equilibrated" has a clearly specifiable, empirically straightforward sense. Yet there is no designer of the body and no extrinsic purpose that it is clearly intended to serve. The human body does have a number of known feedback loops that stabilize it in changing conditions: if the heart beats "too" rapidly, messages find their way back to it to slow it down; centres in the carotid arteries send corrective feedback to the heart, which keeps the blood pressure to the brain within set limits. However, much of the stability of the body is observed but unexplained. The temperature of the body, for example, oscillates within narrow limits around 37°C in a state of dynamic equilibrium, and yet there is no visible thermostat to account for this. How the equilibrium is achieved still apparently remains something of a mystery.

Here lies an attraction of the organic analogy.[2] An organism such as the human body remains in a stable state of dynamic equilibrium, a state of homeostasis, even as its external environment changes. We do not know why it does so, in the sense that we know why the central heating system does so. None the less biologists and physiologists see the organs of the human body as functioning to sustain homeostasis. And they routinely *explain* the operation of these various organs in terms of their functions for the organism as a whole. Hence, it is open to sociologists to offer functional explanations of institutions, and to defend them by claiming that they are just as scientific as biological functional explanations of the parts of a living organism.

It is important to notice, however, that functions are not generally accepted as explanatory even in biology or physiology. References to functions are ubiquitous in these fields, and generally recognized as useful, but there is also widespread recognition that function does not in itself explain. To say that an organ exists because of what it contributes to the whole system is to risk the charge of teleology, of explanation by purpose in a system that knows no purpose; this has long been fought against as an illegitimate anthropomorphic form of explanation.

It is worth stressing also that functional accounts of the human body long preceded the rise of modern "scientific" medicine and biology. For centuries the body was regarded as an equilibrated system, and many accounts were offered of how individual organs contributed to its normal operation and its overall stability. But the concepts of normality and stability that were employed here were highly specific ones related to clear pragmatic concerns: the "normal" body was the body in a state of health. And even now, in physiology and medicine, functional accounts of the organs of the body largely remain accounts of how they contribute to *health*. Just as the functionalist account of the central heating system makes the system visible in a way that facilitates improvement, adaptation and repair, so the functional account of the human body in the context of medical and biological science has facilitated the maintenance of health and the identification and cure of pathologies. The import of this for a functionalist sociology is that the model for its theory is not a paradigm of scientific explanation at all, but a pragmatically valuable form of *description* that involves specific moral and evaluative assumptions.[3]

2.2 Functionalism as ideology

A number of traditions of social theory have described themselves as functionalist or structural-functionalist. Perhaps the best known is the one derived from the work of the US sociologist Talcott Parsons, which provided for a long period the dominant theoretical paradigm in sociology in the United States.[4] These traditions, and especially that associated with Parsons, have often been criticized for a conservative bias: it is claimed that they were developed as much to justify as to describe and explain the existing social order. Certainly, a theory that directs attention to equilibrium, and regards a high level of integration of parts as necessary in anything sufficiently ordered to be recognizable as a social system, might appeal as a legitimating resource for reactionary political views. Any reader of the functionalist literature will want to keep in mind the possibility that her attention is being directed toward selected aspects of "the social system", and that her reason is being presented with arguments that are neither exhaustive nor watertight, as part of a project of justification. It must also be kept in mind, however, that all theories encourage selective attention; they are bound to do so because empirical phenomena are invariably too complex and rich in information to be addressed without selectivity. Equally it has to be recognized that, even if functionalist sociology has a conservative bias, it may none the less be making valid claims and may serve as a valuable complement to theories reflecting other biases and involving different kinds of selectivity. Whether (a version of) functionalism is valid is not purely and simply a matter of whether or not its advocates are purveying persuasive justifications of the status quo.

It was noted earlier how functional accounts of the human body preserve a vision of its normal stable operation, where "normality" is an ideal conception of the body in a state of health. The notion of health is at once descriptive and evaluative. It can be specified empirically to a great extent; it also represents what is desired and sought after. To speak of the functions of individual organs in maintaining health is to speak of the good things they do. Functionalist discourse in biology and medicine is, we might say, deeply "ideological". We are not routinely troubled by this because most of us share the "ideology". The "unscientific" practice of conflating evaluation and description, even in a "science", goes largely unremarked in so far as most people have no desire to dissent from the evaluations. The "normal" human body can be a reference to what is natural and what is desirable simultaneously without major difficulties arising.

If we refer to the normal state of society, however, the reference is generally to what actually exists, without any implication of desirability. Some of us are for it, others not. What is normal in the sense of being familiar may not be regarded as normal in the sense of being desirable. Thus, it is most important in the context of the social sciences that the status quo, the existing system, is understood wholly and entirely as an empirical state of affairs, something that just happens to be in place. Similarly, a claim about how an institution functions ought to be understood simply as a claim about how far it happens to stabilize or reconstitute that state of affairs.

Functionalist sociological theory would not formally dissent from this. None the less functionalists, and especially those in the long-dominant tradition initiated by the theories of Talcott Parsons, have not satisfactorily sustained a strong distinction between what is and what ought to be, and indeed have often tacitly encouraged an illegitimate movement from the one to the other. The status quo may indeed be described as normal and natural: it is normal in that it usually appertains, and natural in that it is an empirical phenomenon. But it is also a part of our moral discourse to refer to what is normal and natural as opposed to what is abnormal and unnatural: heterosexuality is sometimes recommended over homosexuality, or monogamy over polygamy, using these terms as rhetorical resources. Unless the move is actively opposed, remarks on what is normal and natural come readily to be heard as assertions of what is desirable, and accounts of what is functional or functionally necessary in relation to such things as justifications. This is precisely what the orthodox functionalist tradition in sociology has not merely failed to avert but frequently encouraged. It is a tradition that has invited us to think of how to maintain a healthy social system rather as we seek to maintain a healthy body, and to think of the existing system as the paradigm of a state of health.

Talcott Parsons' (1956) essay on the functions of the modern family is one of several familiar examples here. Anyone who has made use of this celebrated essay will know how easily it is read as a justification of "the modern family", and of the "functional" differentiation of tasks between the male and female roles that is characteristic of it. And anyone familiar with the criticisms that the essay has inspired will be aware of how many of them attack the idea of the modern family as "a good thing", and how few criticize functionalism *per se*. Indeed, many of Parsons' critics are themselves functionalists in their approach, which is not to imply, however, that the critical attack upon this essay has not been entirely justified.[5]

Given the existence of examples of this kind it is not at all surprising that functionalist sociological theory has so often been dismissed as irredeemably conservative. However, even if writers in the main traditions of functionalist theory deserve to be criticized in this way, it is mistaken to extend the criticism to functionalism *per se*. Theories and ideas are not inherently value-laden in the relevant sense. There is, after all, nothing inherently attractive about stability or equilibrium. A totalitarian nightmare may also be a stable, persisting social system. An executed criminal, swinging on the end of a rope, will, as Schelling remarks somewhere, eventually come to rest at a point of equilibrium.

The example that makes the case here is, of course, that of Marxist social theory. Some variations on this theory are formally almost indistinguishable from orthodox functionalism, given only that they speak of "capitalism" rather than "the social system" and that they invert the evaluations of the orthodox view: for Marxists, the status quo is not a "healthy" state but a "pathological" state. Thus, when Marxists identify institutions functioning in a way that sustains the status quo, as for example the "ideological state apparatus" is often alleged to do, the institutions stand condemned not justified. Where there are "contradictions" (Marxism) or "strains" (orthodox functionalism) in the system, where the parts of the whole are not in harmony so that the system is malfunctioning and its persistence is threatened, that is a source of hope not regret. David Lockwood's (1964) succinct account of why functionalist accounts of social system integration may be important in Marxist theory is seminal here.

As social theorists, if not as moralists, orthodox functionalists and Marxists have an identity of interest. They are alike interested in the conditions of stability and change for any given social and institutional order. Their pragmatic concerns are to this extent the same. A theory of system stability is, after all, *ipso facto* a theory of instability as well: a source of insight into the integration of a system is also a clue to the conditions that could lead to its disintegration, differentiation or change. Indeed, a functional description is likely to interest any group that is exercising power or aspiring to do so, any group, that is, with reason to look upon the social system as an instrument (Rueschemeyer 1986).

This is to reiterate that a functionalist description of a social system may have pragmatic utility, just as such descriptions of central heating or the human body may have. Any general evaluation of functionalist social theory needs to acknowledge this. A functional description may highlight stabilizing causal interactions between the parts of a social system, as those operations of the parts that are of specific pragmatic interest. Functionalist theorists in the orthodox and in the Marxian traditions both seek to do this: no doubt a consistent anarchist would wish a plague on both their houses.

It is also the case, however, that no form of functionalist theory in the social sciences has succeeded in confining itself entirely to pragmatically applicable description. Most of them run such description together with explanatory speculation and evaluative judgements. Some involve a hidden agenda, so that persuasive argumentation or even persuasive misrepresentation are made to masquerade as empirical description and scientific explanation. Because of this in particular, functionalist theory has long failed to realize whatever promise it might have had as a form of holistic theory, and the case that it should be abandoned altogether in favour of pedantic analyses of the causal interactions between and within the parts of a social system has gained in plausibility.

Functionalism, however, is too deeply engrained in the modes of thought of the social sciences for its abandonment to be a realistic possibility. Much of interest will continue to be written in a problematic functionalist idiom. It will have to be read, but read with due care.[6] One invaluable means of addressing a significant but suspect and difficult body of theory is to go equipped with particularly simple and transparent exemplars of its application. Exemplars of this kind can be more informative than even extended abstract accounts and can yield considerable insights. They deserve greater use in sociological theory. This is one reason the discussion of functionalism began with an account of a simple mechanical system. Many of the standard problems of functionalist sociology are analogous to more tractable problems in that simpler context; problems of functional necessity, for example, and of functional alternatives. Consider the central heating system again. What happens if we remove a radiator? Much or little may happen: the room may or may not get cooler and vary more in temperature, but all we can plausibly predict is that the pump will stay on longer than before. What happens if we replace the radiators with a fan-operated output? Nothing significant need happen. What happens if we remove the thermostats? The system probably boils over or explodes. Evidently, when changes to a functioning system are imagined, very little can be inferred purely and simply from the fact that a part has a function in sustaining the persistence of the whole; close study of the details of the system is needed to make sensible predictions. This is something that is worth keeping in mind when the whole is a social system. It is arguable that no existing functional analysis of a social system is accompanied by sufficient empirical detail to give it any pragmatic value.

2.3 Normative functionalism and the problem of social integration

So far we have considered whether and how the "functioning" of the various parts of a social system may secure the persistence of the whole. David Lockwood (1964) characterizes this as the problem of *system integration*, in contrast to the problem of *social integration*, which asks how and why individuals in the system produce the actions necessary to its existence as a system. This valuable contrast identifies two related but distinct problems for sociological investigation. On the one hand, there is the problem of how the parts of a social system, the constituent institutions, operate in relation to each other; on the other hand, there is the problem of how a social system, constituted of institutions, is enacted by individuals.

Clearly, there is a limited extent to which levels of system and social integration can vary independently of each other. Crucially, however, for there to be system integration and system persistence at all, there must be a minimal level of social integration. For a social system to exist it must be enacted; for it to be enacted individuals must enact it; for individuals to enact it they must relate to each other and to their environment in an appropriately orderly way. If functionalism is to provide a fully convincing account of a social system, it must provide, or show itself to be consistent with, at least a prototype solution to the problem of social integration.

Functionalists themselves have generally recognized this, although they have not always agreed on the best solution. And indeed there are many solutions compatible with a basic functionalist approach as it has been described so far. It is even arguable that the problem could be solved by the ER individuals discussed in Chapter 1. Once a few such individuals co-ordinate their actions and learn to co-operate, they may be able to coerce other ER individuals and exercise power against them. The possession of power may allow them to press everyone into the pattern of a functioning system of social institutions, a system that, in the course of reproducing itself, produces a continuing surplus for the enjoyment of those within it who are able to treat it as an instrument.[7]

The mainstream of sociological functionalism, however, does not recognize the possibility of a purely individualistic solution to the problem of social integration. It offers an entirely different view of the nature of the individual human being and of her relationship with the social system. The development of this view was largely the work of Talcott Parsons. It is Parsons' account of social integration that makes his functionalism (and hence the mainstream of sociological functionalism that has followed his lead) so distinctive and important. Lockwood (1964) refers to it as "normative functionalism", in allusion to its central claim that social integration is achieved through the sharing of values and norms.

Only the basic form of Parsons' elaborately developed position need concern us here, and that basic form will be so familiar that little more than a reminder of it is required. According to Parsons, the "social system" is composed of institutions that in turn are composed of statuses and roles. Associated with any status are expectations of appropriate behaviour in relation to other statuses. These expectations have the character of rules or norms. When the occupant of a status acts in conformity with an associated norm, she performs the role associated with that status. Performance of all the various roles in the system enacts it as a manifest functioning social system.

In an equilibrated social order, in Parsons' account, the norms have become organized to constitute and sustain that equilibrium, and action that conforms to the norms contributes to system maintenance. It is evident that action of this kind exists. Yet, because it is system oriented, it cannot be understood as a direct expression of the wants or interests of so many independent individuals. Nor will Parsons accept that aligned or co-ordinated individual interests could produce such actions, either directly and freely, or indirectly by the coercion of others. Parsons follows Durkheim in insisting that the alignment of individual interests cannot be more than transient, and hence cannot account for the persistence of social systems, which is observable over very long periods of time in radically changing circumstances.[8] Conformity to norms, the key to system enactment and system stability, must be sustained, according to Parsons, *over and against* the promptings of rational self-interest. The key problem of social integration is to understand how conformity to norms is secured given that it goes against "rationality". For his answer Parsons looks to the process of socialization. In the course of socialization the child does not just learn the competences necessary to conform to norms but becomes oriented to norms as moral rules. Norms are *internalized* by the individual; they become part of her moral conscience and thus of her very self, so that conformity with the norms gives satisfaction and deviation from them becomes a cause of pain. As a consequence, an inner pressure to conform to norms acts in opposition to the urges of self-interest, to the extent that a sufficient amount of normatively regulated (and hence "functional") action is available. Parsons (1964, 1967) cites Durkheim and Freud as the major preceding theorists to offer an account of this kind.[9] And Freud's image of the ego as subject to the conflicting pressures of the asocial id and the socially sensitive super-ego does indeed seem to offer not just precursor concepts for Parsons but a structural analogy as well. Egoistic urges and implanted norms conflict in Parsons' account much as id and super-ego conflict in Freud's: "there is an element of super-ego organization correlative with every role-orientation pattern of the individual. . . . the internalization of a super-ego element means motivation to accept the priority of collective over personal interests" (Parsons 1951: 150).

We should note in passing the reference to "collective" interests here. The enactment of norms evidently furthers collective interests as it continues to constitute the system of institutions. It is wholly typical of Parsons that he should more or less equate system persistence and the collective good in this way, and it is part of the reason he has been so strongly criticized for a conservative bias in his theorizing. What it means for our present purposes is that conformity to norms is the only solution to the problem of collective action available in Parsons. Implanted norms, which cannot be changed at the discretion either of individuals or of collectives, have to account for action to further collective interests, which evidently do change and sometimes change rapidly and radically.[10]

Let us, however, return to the main issue of how norms operate. Parsons suggests that they can be specified as "super-ego elements" and thus as components of the psyche. This permits him to account for the enactment of norms with a theory of socialization that separately implants the impetus so to act into every individual mind. His account of the socialization of the individual is thus at the same time an account of the privatization of the social. The result is that Parsons' theory has many analogies with individualism. Instead of postulating an individual with one kind of urge – that to egoistic behaviour – he postulates as a key unit of his theory an individual with two urges – that to egoism and that to the enactment of what is indicated by an internalized norm. Much of the behaviour of the individual is accordingly what one would expect of an ER individual in the same circumstances, with the same wants or interests. When egoism tramples over "super-ego elements" or is unopposed by any such elements, an individualistic account stands. And, indeed, many of the daunting problems of individualism discussed in the previous chapter remain in Parsons' theory.

Moreover, it is not merely that individualism and its problems persist in relation to deviant egoistic action. Even where "super-ego elements" prevail so that complete conformity to norms is observed, an individualistic component remains in Parsons' theoretical account. For when a majority of a collective are moved to accept and support a norm, they seek to enforce it by sanctions, and unsocialized or weakly socialized individuals, indifferent to the norm but moved by the sanctions, will often themselves enact the norm out of self-interest. Thus, in any given functioning social system it will be impossible to say how much normatively regulated action represents a direct response to the promptings of "super-ego elements" and how much represents the expedient conformity of, in effect, ER individuals. None the less, Parsons insists that the existence of internalized norms, of "super-ego elements", must always stand as the final explanation of conformity. For without internalization there is no incentive either to conform to norms or to sanction others into doing so. Expedient conformity must always be a secondary consequence of "genuine" acceptance of the norms. This is a crucial claim of his theory.

Enough has now been said about the basic form of Parsons' theory, but it is perhaps worth repeating that in the theory norms are not direct causes of actions, but rather causes of guilt or pain should such actions not be performed. Parsons needed only to account for the existence of a supply of conforming actions, not to account for everything done in a given society. And he took great care to present his theory as a "voluntaristic" one, not one that involved determinism at the level of action or behaviour itself. Parsons was anxious not to imply that the future path of a society could be predicted from its existing system of norms, or that, having internalized a set of norms, persons then lacked choice in what they did.

As far as the first point is concerned, there was no real need for anxiety. Social norms are not going to make the future completely predictable, however they relate to social actions. *Acting* in conformity to a norm merely entails *behaving* in one of the innumerable ways that so conform. Norms can never be sufficient causes or complete determinants of what is done, since conformity to a norm merely involves the performance of one of a whole class of possible conforming behaviours. Thus, it may be normative to avenge a murdered relative with the death of an enemy; but whether one uses a 5-inch stiletto or a 5-megaton nuclear device is consequential for how life goes on.[11] Oddly, this simple point about norms and rules is often forgotten by theorists, and their reluctance to treat norms as causes of action is sometimes intensified by the excessive "determining power" they attribute to them.

As far as the matter of choice is concerned, however, Parsons rightly foresaw the possibility of his being read as a determinist, who denied the existence of free choice. Because conformity to norms is doubly reinforced in his theory, both by internalization and by sanctioning from other individuals, it predicts very high levels of social integration as the typical condition of most social systems. Parsons stressed, accordingly, that, although his theory was indeed a predictive one in that sense, it was at the same time a theory wherein individuals chose how to act in situations where they faced conflicting pressures. If the pressure to conform to norms increased, more choices would be conforming choices; if it decreased, more egoistic choices would be made. But action would none the less remain a matter for genuine choice in either case.

Without necessarily criticizing this account, it is none the less worth asking what work is done by the concept of "choice" within it. On the one hand, we may say with Parsons that individuals choose to conform to norms and that, as the pressure to conform increases, more conforming choices will be made. On the other hand, we may say that as the pressure to conform increases it will overcome more and more egoistic urges and cause more and more individuals to yield to the stronger pressure and conform. Either formulation will account for observed conformity. No fact of the matter indicates which formulation is the better. It is a matter of choice, as it were, which is used.

Parsons believed that theories that relied wholly upon references to egoism and self-interest, because they explained human action entirely in terms of a biological force or power, would "reduce" the individual to the status of a natural object. But he did not oppose this reductionism with a discussion of the irreducible unpredictability of action, the transcendent freedom of the will and the unfathomable mystery of the human condition. Parsons wanted both freedom and predictability. And so, instead of denying the power of the urge to egoistic action, he added a second, opposed power, and characterized the condition of the individual caught in the middle as one of choice, even though that concept had no theoretical work to do. The point of making mention of this is, of course, that what Parsons wanted continues to be wanted by many theorists today. On the one hand, they wish to have something to say about why some courses of action are more likely than others. Hence they make reference to circumstances, or pressures, or rewards, or deep psychological tendencies or orientations. On the other hand, they wish to continue, out of politeness, to refer to human action with the language of choice and freedom. Thus, a solution to the problem represented by Parsons' voluntarism would be of as much interest today as it was in the lifetime of Parsons himself.

2.4 Social norms

Although Parsons expected participants in social systems routinely to produce both egoistic and normatively regulated actions, it is his account of the latter that has been important and influential. And it must be recognized that this account, by stressing how, everywhere, action will be found oriented to norms, values, rules, laws, conventions and so forth, has been of great service in the development of sociological theory. Indeed, just how the relationship of norm and action is to be understood remains one of the basic problems of sociological theory generally.

Parsons' own answer to the problem also continues in use even though the normative functionalist approach with which it was associated is no longer generally favoured. The crucial feature of Parsons' account is its stress on the internal relationship between the acting individual and the norm. We are to imagine a norm existing as a subjective element in an individual mind, a "super-ego element", internalized with memorized formulations and examples of what it means, or requires, or consists in. We have to assume that on the basis of this information it is clear what the norm implies for future actions, that the individual will know how to act in conformity with the norm next time. If what the norm requires is not apparent to the individual then she cannot be prompted by it and cannot orient her actions in relation to it. Only if its implications for action are clear can a conforming or deviant action be chosen, only in that case can inner satisfaction or inner pain be experienced as the consequence of an act.

There is, however, an important body of argument that holds that norms cannot be followed in this way, and, more generally, that norms cannot be followed by an isolated individual.[12] In order to get a preliminary sense of what might be amiss with an individualistic view, think of a number of "Parsonian actors" following an internalized norm. Will "the norm" just provide very rough and ready indications of what to do, vague precedents on which to base the next action? If this is so, will not individuals conform in different ways so that their practices eventually diverge and they lose co-ordination with each other and even cease to understand each other? Or, alternatively, will the norm specify exactly what is to be done? If this is so, then how does all the necessarily elaborate and complex information required get packed into a "super-ego element" that can be installed in an individual mind?

If norms are internalized, they must be internalized as a finite amount of stored information. But if the norms themselves must then maintain conformity and co-ordination in the collective, they must operate to fix and specify appropriate behaviour in innumerable indefinitely complex future situations. However one conceives of internalized norms, this will prove to be impossible. Take a simple example, say the dietary norm of vegetarianism. How will an independent individual follow it? A fixed amount of information implanted in advance will not tell her what is to count as a vegetarian diet in all future situations. To "follow the norm" in future situations will require actions that differ in detail from existing, familiar paradigm cases, and how far these actions are "different from" or "the same as" standard cases of vegetarian fare cannot be specified in advance for each and every future case, whatever it might be. Consider that the dates imported for the manufacture of culinary sauces commonly show a significant percentage of insect content, and that flours and meals are similarly permeated with problematic material. Consider too that the boundary between the animal and vegetable realm is contestable at the level of scientific taxonomy. Of course, these are ridiculous irrelevancies as far as an evaluation of vegetarianism as *custom and practice* is concerned, but it is just that which reveals the difficulty of understanding such practice as separate individuals steered by what a norm or rule "really" implies. The example helps, as almost any example would help when reflected upon, to override the habit of thinking of norms, rules or laws as having clear and fixed implications for all particular cases. There is a temptation to imagine we have been issued with an instruction book, like those that come with electrical appliances, to tell us how to follow a given norm. But there is no such book and, if anyone attempted to write one, a text of endless length would ensue from the failed attempt to cover all future possibilities.

How then do we manage to follow norms and rules? What is involved in actual rule-following behaviour? The problem, as we have noted, is one of the enduring issues at the centre of sociological theory and is addressed in several important book-length studies.[13] It will be necessary here to proceed on the basis of a ruthlessly simplified and schematic account, leaving the notes to point in the direction of something better. When an individual seeks to follow a norm or rule, she acts in a way learned by familiarity with previous accepted instances or examples. The intention is to act in proper analogy with those examples. Let us take it as our starting point, then, that to follow a rule or norm is to extend an analogy. To understand rule-following or norm-guided behaviour in this way immediately highlights the formally open-ended character of norms, the fact that they cannot themselves fix and determine what actions are in true conformity with them, that there is no logical compulsion to follow them in any specific way. Every instance of a norm may be analogous to every other, but analogy is not identity; analogy exists between things that are similar yet different. And this means that, although it is always possible to assimilate the next instance to a norm by analogy with existing examples of the norm, it is equally always possible to resist such assimilation, to hold the analogy insufficiently strong, to stress the differences between the instance and existing examples. If norms apply by analogy then it is up to us to decide where they apply, where the analogy is sufficiently strong and where not.[14]

Let us make use of this image to highlight three crucial points about how individuals follow norms. First of all, the individual will be *formally* unconstrained by the norm she intends to follow: she must act in analogy with standard, existing examples, but any action can formally speaking be made out as analogous to any other.[15] Secondly, the individual will none the less be contingently affected by her knowledge of earlier examples of conformity to the norm. As a result, she will see some actions, as a matter of fact, as like the standard examples of conforming actions, and others as unlike. Indeed, conformity to a norm may be experienced much of the time as an obvious, matter-of-course affair – just the unthinking enactment of routine.[16] The drill sergeant may call "attention" and the body may move just as it has before, in routine analogy with previous movements, without reflection or hesitation.[17] Thirdly, however, such a routine, automatic response by an individual will in no way imply that the norm has been correctly followed; for individuals may extend analogies differently, even blindly and automatically extend them differently, and how a given individual acts may appear as incorrect to others. It can always be asked whether what she does routinely in relation to a norm is done correctly. The former does not define the latter. The individual will have to take into account how other people act in evaluating how she herself has routinely acted. The implications of social norms are not decidable privately and separately by each and every individual.[18]

If the argument seems unduly abstract here, consider the case of a panel of judges concerned to apply the law. Perhaps they must decide whether an admitted bodily contact does or does not constitute an assault. They will have available an account, perhaps even a video, of the contact in dispute, and knowledge of earlier recognized cases of assault. Formally, there is no way of saying whether the analogy between the current instance and earlier instances is sufficient or insufficient; this is something to be *decided* on the spot. However, an individual judge may be forcibly struck by the resemblance of the present alleged assault and an earlier instance; she may in practice have no doubt about how to decide the case. It may be that she finds her fellow judges in full agreement with her, that they too are struck just as she is struck, and the case can thus immediately be settled. But it may be also that one judge has no doubts one way and another judge has no doubts another way. When this is the case, and when it persists after due discussion, a vote may have to be taken and "what the law really implies" decided by majority. Provisionally decided, that is; for the baby-sitter who smacked the child, or the rugby forward who got her retaliation in first, may always appeal to another panel, perhaps to receive a more favourable verdict from a different majority.[19]

By emphasizing that to follow a norm is to extend an analogy we focus attention on the three theoretically important dimensions of what is involved: the formal, the psychological/behavioural, and the social/collective dimensions. Otherwise, it can be difficult to retain full awareness of what is involved, and in particular the crucial collective dimension may be overlooked. It is this aspect of following rules and norms, after all, that is most frequently absent from everyday understanding of what occurs. Probably this is because, most of the time, people conform to norms and rules without any difficulty or need for reflection, and in doing so find themselves in agreement with the practice of others. It is then easy to forget that analogies are being extended, because the appropriate extensions seem so clear and obvious that they feel externally given – by the meaning of the norm itself as it were. Routine practice may be found "so natural", and agreement in that practice so unproblematic, that no difficulty arises from the belief that it is "the norms themselves" that are responsible. The inadequacy of this view becomes apparent, and the practical need to transcend it becomes pressing, only when we disagree in our practice when following norms and find that a search for the "real meaning" of the norms does not help us.[20]

Conforming to norms is a collective activity. When the members of a collective follow a norm they act in concert to sustain and extend an analogy. Further actions designed to conform to a norm are modelled on existing actions recognized already as conforming to the norm. Existing practice guides future practice. But "guidance" here is not "logical determination". Existing practice *suggests* future practice; that is all. If, as a matter of fact, existing practice moves members alike, if most individuals extend analogies in practical agreement with each other, then the norm in question may persist. In this case the actual manifestly agreed practice may be said to be "what the norm really implies", what counts as following it *correctly*. On the other hand, if existing practice in following a norm suggests a different future practice to different individual members, to the extent that individuals develop analogies in accountably different directions, then "what the norm really implies" ceases to be clear. Either the norm disappears as consensus about its meaning disappears, or else members themselves have to reconstruct a shared understanding of what the norm implies, taking into account their initial disagreements and probably revising some of their initially divergent ways of "following" the norm. Either way, whether the norm continues routinely as a matter of course or by active negotiation, as must often be the case, the norm remains necessarily and irreducibly a *public* entity not a *private* one; it exists as agreement in practice not as an instruction in an individual mind.

We can now return to Parsons better equipped to recognize the difficulty of a theory that privatizes the social through so many separate acts of internalization of norms. Such a theory cannot deal with the following of norms as a coherent public practice. The continuation of such a practice will sometimes be enacted (significantly) differently by different individuals; their immediate, blind, unhesitating moves will not be (accountably) the same; their first spontaneous attempts to follow a norm will create problems in consequence. At such times, if individuals were constrained internally by whatever happened to strike them as "the" implication of a norm, if they each followed the "inner voice" of a "super-ego element", there would be a breakdown of co-ordination and co-operation, a "dysfunctional" clash of individual actions. Parsons does not recognize this because he thinks of norms not as open-ended analogies developed actively by human beings, but as entities with their own inherent properties and powers that take up residence in individual consciences. This image of norms is the provenance of a theory that comes dangerously close to equating social order with a patterned distribution of identical individual hang-ups.[21]

Differences in the initial, blind, matter-of-course responses of individuals only rarely threaten normative order because people are *not* constrained internally by norms and possess the ability actively to adjust their judgements and their actions into closer alignment. Indeed, the continuing existence of a normative order requires that it is *not* internalized, so that continuing active mutual adjustment and development of the actions that exemplify norms may occur. Even the existence of social "equilibrium" or stability is testimony to the public nature of norms. It rests upon the ability of human beings continually to (re)negotiate and (re)establish what norms imply. It is through use of this ability that social stability is maintained, in so far as it is maintained, and given norms and rules continue to be referred to as elements of that stability. Norms and rules are part of the phenomena of order and stability, not part of the explanation of them. They are the outcome of social action, not the cause of it.

This is the key argument against Parsons' conception of the individual, and if it is correct it undermines the entire functionalist account of social integration. On that account, norms operate in opposition to the tendency to rational self-interested behaviour. Therefore it cannot be possible for individuals to escape the pressure to conformity coming from the norms, to decide to have done with inconvenient norms, on rational grounds. For an individual, norms must not be rationally chosen but be *accidentally* acquired.[22] This is why Parsonian functionalism places norms in the super-ego. Here they are internalized in the sense of being implanted. They are a part of the person and not *adaptable* by the acting person. If what norms imply must continually be reconstituted, their applications decided rather than discovered, then the entire structure of normative functionalism collapses.[23]

Normative functionalism mistakenly attributes the power people exercise in deciding what is involved in following norms to the norms themselves. It empowers norms, and represents people as acting under pressure from that power. As we have seen, such a position faces serious formal problems. It has also become more and more difficult to reconcile it with empirical studies.[24] When the relationship of norms and persons is looked at in detail, power proves to lie with the latter not the former. Indeed it is defensible to hold that there are no entities worth calling norms, but only people continuing on the basis of existing practice and speaking of norms and rules as they go on. Certainly if norms are to be referred to in social theory it has to be clear that people do not lack discretion in relation to them. For there to be a coherent public practice, in which it can be said that norms are routinely being followed, it is necessary for people continually to redefine and renegotiate what the following consists in and hence what norms imply. Hence, norms are neither internally fixed and implanted, nor direct sources of reward and punishment, nor in themselves possessed of specific implications for action.

In their life in society, individuals do subjectively feel psychologically constrained by externalities, and do at times experience this constraint as a pressure to conform to or enact a norm. This kind of experience is probably one reason for the considerable credibility that was once enjoyed by the normative functionalist account. But in that account the externalities are wrongly located. They lie not in the individual conscience, but in the social context. As far as the problem of social order is concerned, the externalities are other people – often other people invoking norms; sometimes other people advocating particular highly contestable "implications" of them.

Enough has now been said for the purposes of this particular chapter, but several points none the less remain hanging, and a broad indication of how they would be dealt with in a more extended discussion ought to be given. It might be asked, in particular, whether and in what sense sociological theory should continue to speak of norms and rules. The response must be that norms and rules are the last things that sociological theory should reify. On the other hand, at any particular time there will be practices generally recognized as exemplifying norms and competences that when routinely activated are taken as a matter of course as conforming to them. To that extent, people everywhere tend to know in a sense "what the norms (rules) are". Perhaps theorists should say that genuinely social action occurs not under the internal constraint of norms, but rather in the light of knowledge of what the norms are.

What though is this knowledge about? What are its referents? Knowledge of norms is unusual in being intensely self-referential. To know that a practice exemplifies a norm is to know that most people take the practice to exemplify the norm. For example, to know that driving on the left is a norm is to know that most people do indeed regard it as normative. A collective will make the claim that driving on the left is normative into a true claim by coming to believe it (collectively). Thus, in a perfectly clear and straightforward sense, knowing of norms is knowing what is generally known. And thus knowledge of norms is "about" itself. A normative order exists as a distribution of self-referring and self-validating knowledge. It exists, therefore, just so long as it is (collectively) known to exist. A normative order is a gigantic self-fulfilling prophecy.[25]

3

Interactionism

3.1 A Tudor execution

Social theory needs at all times to keep in touch with the states of affairs it purports to describe or explain. This is not just a matter of checking predictions; it remains essential even if prediction is of no interest to the theorist. It is essential as the means of giving theory meaning: if instances and examples of the use of theoretical concepts are never supplied then it remains unclear, indeed wholly indeterminate, what significance theoretical concepts – and hence theory – might have. Theory without some kind of exemplification is not theory at all. Conceivable, if not necessarily actual, states of affairs must be cited to show what theory and its concepts are referring to. So let us turn to an example of social activity and use it to reflect upon what has been said so far and to prepare the ground for the third form of theory with which we have yet to deal.

Figure 3.1 represents the killing of Mary Queen of Scots in 1587. The contemporary illustration records more than one moment in the whole event, reminding us that it was a drawn-out process involving very many particular actions and utterances. We need not trouble ourselves with the detailed accuracy of the illustration (other depictions appear to contradict parts of it) just so long as we can accept that something along the lines of what is depicted did occur. It will suffice for our present purposes if Mary met her death roughly as contemporary accounts and contemporary illustrations indicate. According to those accounts and illustrations, her death had much of the standard form of a Tudor execution.[1]

The execution, a prolonged sequence of events from one point of view, from another was a single event that needs to be understood in

Figure 3.1 The execution of Mary Queen of Scots. By permission of the British Library. Add. ms 48027. f. 650.

relation to a larger historical context. Queen Elizabeth and her advisers at the English court had evidently concluded that Mary's death was expedient. Local knowledge was no doubt relevant here; of the detailed content of Mary's correspondence for example. But more general and conjectural knowledge would also have been brought to bear, concerning the political situations in the various courts and countries of Europe, the size and seaworthiness of their fleets, and perhaps the opinions of their rulers in relation to matters of religion, sovereignty, marital obligation, and regicide. No doubt the calculations were elaborate. And no doubt the changing political situation constantly modified the results. But it would seem that the advantages of a dead Mary were generally acknowledged some considerable time before the death itself. Why the delay? Many explanations have been given, some involving the peculiar psychology of Elizabeth herself. But perhaps it was also material that agreement on the collective benefits of Mary's death did not resolve the matter of who should pay its costs. Such costs might prove very high, both politically and personally. Good perhaps that Mary should die, but better not to be the one to kill her. An effort was apparently made to make away with Mary unofficially, by methods easily confused with natural causes. Only when the buck proved unpassable did Elizabeth sign and seal the warrant and thereby accept, as sovereign and head of state, responsibility for the act.

This done, the act went ahead with dispatch. Elizabeth pushed the button, activated the routine, and the execution took its course, according to practice and precedent. For there was an accepted form to the execution of those of noble birth in these times, and importance was attached to correct procedure. The Tudor execution was an institution and its enactment was institutionalized activity.

One of the oddities of sociological discussions of institutions is how little attention is paid to their enactment. The Tudor execution was always available, a power in the hands of the state, but its enactment was rare at this time, and few of those qualified were actually awarded it. Could enactment cease yet the institution persist? Is the hanging of traitors currently an institution in the UK? And can the "functions" of an institution be discussed without attention to enactment? "Too many" executions, after all, will secure not the persistence of a social system but rather its disappearance.

We speak of institutions as routines, and tend to imagine them as somehow autonomous and ongoing, actions that produce themselves as it were. But are not routines typically produced at discretion, as needed? And if this is so, is not a problem of user choice associated with every routine, every institution – the problem of why the button is pushed? Is the button-pushing also institutionalized activity, and so similarly the associated judging and deciding? Or is it that some form of non-institutionalized, non-social activity somehow pervades the social order and clusters around every button, every power point? Although individualists may perhaps have difficulties in accounting for the existence and

reproduction of routines such as the one that ended Mary's life, functionalist theorists face difficulties in accounting for their activation and use.
In any event the button was pushed, and the execution was duly performed. The audience arrived and took up position – a complex business: rank and hierarchy had to be respected, etiquette and convention
had to be followed, and a good view had to be secured in the specific
physical environment of the setting. There followed the entrance of the
Queen and her servants (the latter only after protests and entreaties
against their debarment); the reading of the warrant; prayers (a competition, this, between the Latin invocations of Catholic Mary and the English of the assigned Protestant chaplain); the forgiveness of the
executioners; the disrobing (evidently the speech from the scaffold had
been removed from the programme out of anxiety about what Mary
might say, just as the public at large had been excluded from the event in
another departure from best practice); the securing of the executioners'
prerequisites (apparently, on-the-spot negotiations on a cash basis
allowed Mary's crucifix and other ornaments to be retained by her servants); the kneeling at the block; the dispatch, ideally with a single axe-
stroke (but bodged on this occasion we are told); the display of the
severed head. Altogether it was an impressive sequence of performances, especially when most of the actors were first-time participants.

How might an individualist describe activities such as this? What is the
connection between the institutional forms and the wants and preferences
of individual persons? Could every action in the performance, whether
routine or non-routine, institutionalized or not, be connected to some
pre-existing schedule of wants and preferences? And what of Mary herself? Why did she not extemporize a yet longer prayer, a still slower
walk to the scaffold, an expedient faint? It is tempting to talk of Mary's
concern to die with dignity. But how does dignity figure in individualistic
theory: can an independent individual have dignity?

On the face of it, functionalist social theory is better attuned to our
example. The functions of "the execution" in Tudor times, the ways it
contributed to the persistence of the social order, could readily be listed
by proponents of this approach. Social relationships were expressed;
power was made visible as something to be feared; the legitimate order
was strengthened; a threat to that order was eliminated. And, again, the
approach of normative functionalism could be articulated: is it not easier
to understand participants' actions as the following of norms rather than
as the pursuing of individual goals, as flowing from moral obligation

rather than personal preference? And yet the example raises difficulties for functionalism too.

To begin with what, for a functionalist, must be some of the most basic questions: what is the legitimate order that is being stabilized; how is it identified and how is it to be described? Was the Queen of England reinforcing the institution of monarchy by executing a usurper? Or was Elizabeth assassinating the Queen of England with a vast charade designed to uphold institutional proprieties? Or again, was this a case of the institution of Tudor monarchy undermining itself, as a Queen eliminated the legitimate successor to her throne? For here are three viable descriptions of what Mary's death consisted in, all defensible as following from the accepted norms of sovereignty and succession. This, of course, raises particularly serious difficulties for normative functionalism. Far from events automatically following the logical implications of rules of legitimate inheritance, sovereignty, sovereign rights and what was treasonable, the implications of these rules were *decided* in the course of Mary's condemnation and subsequent trial. That she was executed was not a consequence of the implementation of the inherent implications of rules but a symbol of what meanings were being given to those rules at that time, on those occasions.

If the propriety and appropriateness of Mary's death, its legitimacy as an execution, did not follow from the inherent implications of rules or norms, neither did the manner in which it was carried out. Not that it was necessarily anything but a typical Tudor execution, competently accomplished. But all typical actions have their atypical, idiosyncratic features, and Mary's execution was entirely typical in this respect. What was done is best thought of not as the unfolding of the inherent implications of rules or instructions but as a makeshift effort to proceed in analogy with custom and precedent. This makes sense both of the participants' concern to do what was always done, and of their skilled improvisation throughout. The privacy of the setting and the lack of a speech from the scaffold; the attempted debarment of servants, cancelled at the last moment; the bargaining with the executioners; the conflict over appropriate prayer – these were just the more prominent of the improvisations that constituted the execution. They were all on-the-spot innovations, conceived, proposed, negotiated and implemented in the course of the execution, part of what the execution was, precedents for future practice, and yet not derivable from the existing norms of good practice for Tudor executions.

It should be clear from this example that there are problems not just in deciding whether individualism and/or functionalism are correct but also in deciding what they are – what precisely it is that the claims of these theories amount to. At the same time, the example raises the even more profound question of what *social order* amounts to. So far we have tended to assume that this is a clear and simple notion, but it is time to recognize its difficulties and complexities. A hint of the variety of possible ways of understanding "social order" can be conveyed by identifying three separate senses that can be given to the term. First, there is order as peace, harmony or absence of conflict. This is a key concern of Hobbes, and is also assumed by many functionalist writers to be part of what "social order" implies. Secondly, there is order as stability, as the persistence or relatively slow change of a given pattern over time. This is the dominant sense of "social order" in functionalist sociological theory, which indeed perceives its task as the explanation of just such persistence in institutions. Thirdly, there is order as pattern. This is a more general notion often implicit in functionalist theory but rarely explicitly separated out. It is a key theoretical notion none the less: we may well want to explain why social life always appears to be patterned without wanting to claim that any particular pattern is stable or persistent.

Thus the orderly features of Mary's execution can be identified and described in a number of ways and cited to raise very different kinds of theoretical questions. Was the execution an instance of peace or war, strife or co-operation, or both? Was it a continuation of existing patterns or a departure therefrom, or both? Was it in itself an instance of patterned action or of chaos and spontaneity, or both? The answer to these questions is not important here. What matters is that the questions can easily be recognized, in the light of the example, as different – and as substantially independent. We need to be on guard in the social sciences against evaluative modes of thought that lead us, for example, groundlessly to equate stability with harmony, or social change with disorder, or to fail to remember that war is often a paradigm of structured co-operation.

Further reflection on the example of the execution may also help us to recognize a crucial difference between different conceptions of order. Peace, harmony or absence of conflict may or may not appertain in a given context; they are optional extras, as it were, in our social life. So, similarly, is institutional stability or a slow rather than a rapid rate of institutional change. But the existence of pattern in human social life is evidently not an optional extra. Always and everywhere, human beings, in peace and war, co-operation and conflict, relate to each other in systematically patterned ways. Always and everywhere, the relations between human beings are linguistically and cognitively, culturally and practically ordered. Order at this level is deeply sociologically interesting. We should ask what it is that brings it into being and sustains it, knowing that, whatever it is, it is invariably at work, and never absent from any situation wherein human beings are found. And it is worth reflecting also that whatever is the basis for order at this level – at the level of language and culture, cognition and practice – may also be responsible for some amount of order at a more superficial level. That which accounts for the order and pattern universal in human social life may also perhaps be implicated in optional extras like peace, stability, low levels of conflict, and so forth.[2]

Mary's execution was profoundly ordered at the level of language and culture, cognition and practice. Everybody found practically everything that was done meaningful – intelligible in relation to standard patterns and required displays of competence. Let us look at some of its evidently orderly features. For all its idiosyncracy, it would be perverse to deny that something of the standard pattern of a competently performed execution is discernible: an axe swung; a head was severed. The audience would have known this pattern and recognized its manifestation in the actual performance. Also discernible are larger features of an extended institutional order: the Tudor social hierarchy is evident and expressed; the authority of the sovereign is cited. There is pattern too at the level of language and culture, and in the shared knowledge invoked and utilized. But for all that many existing extrinsic sources were drawn upon to bring order, as it were, into the situation, to refer to them by no means exhausts the orderly features evident within it. In describing how institutionalized routines were improvised upon, for example, and how modifications to them were negotiated and accepted, we are identifying a form of orderliness that emerges in the situation itself and is not prefigured in norms or precedents or knowledge or learned routine. Similarly, in considering all the detail of entering and leaving the situation, exchanging courtesies, monitoring appropriate distance and interpersonal spacing, there can be no question of understanding the patterns displayed as manifestations of order that already existed elsewhere and was merely as it were, being automatically replicated or reproduced.

The participants in Mary's execution created order *ab initio*, on the spot. The execution revealed more than pre-existing cultural and institutional order. Perhaps we should say that there was an *interaction order* within the setting of the execution as well as these other kinds of order (Rawls 1987). But it may be that this is a misleading form of description that puts us in danger of underestimating what interaction achieves. It suggests that participants generated order through interaction only in the amount necessary to make up for insufficiencies in a given pre-existing cultural and institutional order, whereas it may be that all the order observable in the situation was the product of interaction. To explore this latter possibility we should consider the idea that the entire event consisted in cultural and institutional *resources* being mobilized and used in the context of the execution, by interacting participants continually negotiating with each other how best to further their various objectives. On this kind of account, cultural and institutional order are not given patterns that enforce themselves upon people but are forms of order that emerge as people interact – forms that people themselves create and re-create. On this account, Mary's execution, in both its routine and its improvisatory aspects, was the outcome of and nothing but participants' goal-oriented use of cultural and institutional resources in ordered interaction with each other.

Looked at in this way, a key active participant in the event was Mary herself, who sought to negotiate a certain kind of death. Truly, she was not only the victim, but one of the executioners. She took her part in the overall performance along with everyone else; it was the lead role and apparently she played it well. It was a peculiarly human achievement.

3.2 Interactionist social theory

The interactionist approach in sociology has sometimes been treated as distinct and separate from sociological theory. And this appears to be consistent with the original self-conceptions of interactionists themselves, who always stressed the virtues of detailed involvement with case studies, and greeted efforts to construct abstract theoretical models with suspicion and reserve. None the less, we should accept that there is an interactionist social theory, and consider whether it is not amongst the most valuable forms of theory currently available in the social sciences.

As a symbol of this approach to interactionism we can gesture toward Emile Durkheim as its fount and origin. Durkheim, prominent amongst the founders of sociology, is often categorized as an exponent of functionalism. But Durkheim denied that social institutions could be explained in terms of their functions and, whenever his accounts and explanations are traced back to their source, that source turns out to be social interaction.[3] Thus, in Durkheim's first book, *The division of labour in society* (1893), both the basic forms of social solidarity and the process of evolution from the mechanical to the organic form are understood by reference to interaction, and the concept of "moral density", more or less a measure of interaction frequency, has a key explanatory role. In his final book, *The elementary forms of the religious life* (1915), solidarity is maintained by the coming-together of the entire community into (ritual and ceremonial) interaction. And throughout his work the recurring theme of the sacredness of the individual prefigures a central topic of later interactionist work.

Durkheim was, of course, a support and inspiration for one of the best-known of all interactionist sociologists, Erving Goffman. But whilst Goffman relied heavily upon Durkheim's ideas he was entirely different in style. Goffman's theoretical insights are developed and expanded entirely in relation to case studies; they are never systematized, ever in the course of change, and very hard to formulate in abstract terms. In these ways Goffman is one of the finest of all social theorists. Like natural scientific theories, Goffman's have to be assimilated by addressing them in use; examples of their application provide the only route of access to them. Thus, to set out an abstract account of Goffman's general theory, as will shortly be done here, is to go against the spirit of his work and even to some extent to misrepresent its content.

There is no misrepresentation, however, in describing Goffman's theory as general, or even fundamental (Burns 1992). Although Goffman presents basic concepts and ideas through cases, he does not present them as relevant only to those cases. Indeed, Goffman is careless to a fault in documenting the time, place and specificity of the situated actions he describes and interprets in his work, precisely because such particulars are not relevant to his interests. His particular cases are invariably illustrative of general kinds of social process: each throws a searchlight into the entire realm of social interaction and illuminates a path for the sociologist to follow.[4]

The first general insight attributable to Goffman as a formal theorist is his characterization of "society" as a series of encounters – occasions wherein two or more human beings come into proximity and act in ways that take account of each other. Goffman's project is to probe particular encounters and express their general characteristics and properties. But it is important to recognize that in proceeding in this way he is also offering a vision of the entire social order quite different from those so far considered. What individualists regard as an array of independently operating units, and functionalists as a system of institutions, may now be reconceptualized as a multitude of ongoing encounters or interactions.

This leads directly to a second, crucial tenet of Goffman's theory: encounters are special. The way in which we orient ourselves to other persons in interaction is quite different from the way in which we orient ourselves to natural objects as resources available for use. This is not merely because other persons have to be acted upon with special care because they can themselves act, and hence react to how they are treated. Nor is it simply because communication with them is possible through signs and signals. Nor is it even that we can guess how others might act by mentally pretending, as it were, to be them, and rehearsing in our own minds the calculations they might make, which we may then take account of. Interactions are not special because other people are objects with very special or unusual properties. Interactions are special because people are not objects at all, and to interact with them is not to act upon them in a purely instrumental sense. So, for example, in the case of a Tudor execution, even at the point of death the individual person remains more than an object, just as the business of effecting death remains irreducible to wholly instrumentally oriented action. These points are sometimes made in the idiom of Durkheim's social theory by referring to the sacredness of the individual in interaction, and to interaction itself as ritual interaction (Collins 1988).

The "individual" of interactionist theories is thus not at all analogous to the individual of rational choice theory. Indeed, it is worth listing the *non-independence* of the individual as the third basic tenet of Goffman's theory. Individuals are susceptible to each other in interaction and it cannot be assumed that an individual will retain given wants, preferences, tastes, inclinations or whatever, heedless of inputs from others. Interactionist theory rejects the claim that autonomous pre-constituted individuals, fixed in properties or nature, combine together strategically to manufacture expedient patterns of interaction. Indeed, some developments of the theory speak instead of the nature of the individual being continually constituted and reconstituted in contexts of interaction.

Clearly, such a rejection of the enduring stability of the individual implies incompatibility not just with individualism but with (normative) functionalism as well. Fixed, internalized norms, independent of interaction context, are no more allowable than fixed wants or preferences. Interaction can never be understood simply as a combination of pre-existing elements that individuals bring into it, whatever these elements may be. This can count as the fourth basic tenet of Goffman's theory: the orderly features of interaction can never be inferred wholly from pre-existing elements, whether of knowledge or competence, preference or desire, commitment or conviction. There is, as Rawls (1987) has put it in her interpretation of Goffman, an interaction order *sui generis*. One of the consequences of this is that wherever interaction is described by reference to a given pre-existing framework of externalities it will manifest an improvisatory quality – as was clearly evident in the case of the Tudor execution. Whether reference is made to costs and benefits and a set of given individual preferences, or to norms and institutions and the commitment to them of a given set of socialized individuals, or to any similar pre-existing fixed framework, orderly features of interaction will remain unaccounted for, features engendered on the spot by agents facing the interactional demands, both general and particular, of the situation in which they find themselves.

In summary, then, if we follow Goffman we will see "society" as a series of encounters or interactions, which have a special and distinctive character. We will recognize the mutual susceptibility of interacting individuals. And we will accept that the orderly features of interaction are not wholly explicable by reference to individual characteristics that precede and remain independent of the situation of interaction itself. But what is special about interaction? And how precisely are individual persons susceptible to each other in the course of it?

Probably the most familiar version of Goffman's answer to these questions is the one that refers to face and face-maintenance (Goffman 1967). On this account, participants in social interaction present themselves as following "lines", and keep face to the extent that their lines are accepted and their performances in following them are recognized as adequate. Participants gauge how successfully they are keeping face by monitoring the responses of others: some responses will signal acceptance, recognition, deference; others a lessening of acceptance, withdrawal of recognition, loss of deference. Many of the relevant responses will be manifest in non-verbal activity with implicit meaning, and some will escape the conscious awareness of respondents. But in any interaction situation each participant will confront a constant stream of such responses and find herself able as a consequence to evaluate her success in face-maintenance at any point of time.

In the course of interaction, loss of face is avoided, whereas the deference and recognition that sustain face are sought after. Accordingly, participants are moved by the responses of others to act in one way rather than another, to act in the face-saving way. What Goffman is describing here is an interactive system of social control. The description has been systematized by Thomas Scheff (1988), who speaks of a deference-emotion system, the existence of which is never explicitly referred to in members' own discourse, but which is none the less always operative during interaction, as is shown by the case studies in Goffman's work.[5] As we monitor the extent of the deference we receive from others, we are moved along a continuum of emotional states stretching from the positive state of pride, which we seek to achieve, to the negative state of shame, which we seek to avoid; hence we are susceptible to the expectations of others, who are able to reinforce these expectations by the withdrawal or intensification of deference. Another way of speaking of all this might be to refer to a socially constructed and sustained state of dignity, which distinguishes interactants from mere objects, and of an association of positive and negative emotions with gain and loss of dignity. In the Tudor pattern of execution (for those of the nobility) the "victim" was allowed and expected to seek what so many individuals in different times and places have regarded as highly desirable, to die with dignity. Accordingly, throughout such an execution everything was likely to remain under control and a recognizably competent performance could be expected.

The face or dignity of a given participant may count as a good for all participants. An inadvertent loss of face rocks the system and disturbs the co-ordinated interaction it sustains. A complete loss of face/dignity/sacredness means that the participant becomes immune to withdrawal of deference and to that extent dangerously out of control: if she is to be threatened with loss, she must have something to lose. Goffman recognizes the great importance of this point and documents it at length. We routinely combine together to sustain each other's dignity. Keeping everyone in face is a crucial part of the maintenance of an ongoing interaction order. Thus we have the unheard fart, the rush to remedy the spilled glass of water, the speedy supply of anodyne interpretations for tactless remarks. And of course in Goffman's early paper "On cooling the mark out" (1952) we have a wonderful insight into the limitless possibilities for professionalizing this kind of activity.

Participants in a situation conspire to keep each other in face so that a stable interaction order persists wherein the actions of one may be subtly modulated by signals from others. But how do participants seek to modulate the actions of others? What use do they typically make of the system of influence or control? In Goffman's case studies participants refer to rules and norms and press them upon each other. But where are the rules and norms drawn from, and why are they invoked and recommended? For the most part, Goffman seems to take norms as given, and remain content to believe whatever it was that Durkheim believed about norms. And indeed it is even possible to give an account of Goffman on norms that is consistent with Parsons' theory. One can agree with Scheff, for example, that Goffman describes a deference-emotion system for the enforcement of conformity to norms, and combine this with the view that participants use the system to enforce those norms that they have internalized. Parsons will explain which norms will be sanctioned and why, and Goffman will tell us how the sanctioning gets done.

But the substance of Goffman's case studies is not consistent with this account. In these studies, norms and rules are "there" right enough; their importance as given elements of encounters is recognized as much by Goffman as by Parsons. But norms are given for use rather than given constraints. All the images and metaphors employed by Goffman stress the manipulability of norms, and their existence as features of situations rather than fixed internalized imperatives in individual minds. The metaphor of dramatic performance and part-playing implies distancing from norms. So does the metaphor of front room–back room social organization, where conformity in the former emerges from calculative preparation and indifference to conformity in the latter. The image of the encounter as a game has similar implications. Indeed, Goffman has some difficulty conveying *authenticity* in the relationship between individuals and the norms they recommend. He is more at home recording the way that the interpretation of norms, the choice of different interpretations, the choice of conformity or deviance, or even of accepting or challenging the status of a norm, may be matters for expedient calculation. All this is a thousand miles from Parsons. Goffman is documenting the availability of norms for our examination and manipulation, an approach later to be followed systematically and with full awareness in the invaluable studies of the ethnomethodologists.

In the last analysis, however, norms and rules remain problematic in Goffman. He has no clear theoretical account of them. And his case studies, wonderful as they are for revealing deficiences in other accounts of norms and rules, provide no positive account. To that extent his theory remains a partial theory, insufficient itself to provide a sociological understanding of social order. He is clear enough that we make norms and that they do not make us. He is even clear that we make norms interactively. But on the making he is silent. The interactionist approach itself, however, can be and has been taken beyond this point. Interactionist studies have shown how rules and norms may be continually produced and reproduced by interaction itself.

To understand how norms and rules may exist as the products rather than the determinants of social interaction it is necessary only to discard the misleading Parsonian image of a norm as an instruction embedded in an individual mind. Following the argument in section 2.4 above, this image must be replaced by one where norms exist only in the public domain, and where "what a norm really means" must be collectively decided, not discovered, by individuals whose initial private convictions on the issue will be liable to vary. How such decisions are made will be a contingent and variable matter. It may involve negotiation and persuasion; it may involve coercion – whether by a majority or a powerful minority. But however decisions regarding "what the norm means" are made, they are likely to be made in the course of social interaction as the norm is invoked and applied.

If this is indeed the case then norms will stabilize only in contexts of social interaction, not in the minds of particular individuals. There is indeed good evidence that just this is the case, not least in the case studies of another seminal figure in the interactionist tradition, Howard Becker (1970). Many of Becker's case studies look at individuals who move from one situation to another. This enables him to judge how well norms travel, whether they remain secure, stable and well protected in the skull of the mobile individual, or whether they fade away as the situation that defines and sustains them is left behind. The clear conclusion is that stable norms are features of situations, not of individual minds. When individuals move into new situations they rapidly adjust to the normative patterns encountered in those situations: a process of *situational adjustment* occurs as the individual learns to "make out" in the new situation and to avoid falling foul of the demands and expectations of others in that situation. Thus, for example, Becker documents how medical students very rapidly modify both their technical standards of appropriate medical treatment and their more generally and abstractly formulated values and ideals when they enter the world of work and come face to face with "the realities" of the work situation. The powerful "socializing" norms of the medical school are revealed by Becker's method as not intrinsically powerful at all. The people "behind" the norms are the source of the power that is attributed to "the norms themselves", and this becomes inescapably apparent once interaction with them ceases on departure from the medical school (Becker et al. 1961).

This insight is the product of comparative method, and requires observation from a distance. For a single involved individual, norms may still be experienced as having a fixed meaning beyond her own discretion and as pressing upon her judgement like an external force. This is just one of many instances of the fact that what is created and controlled collectively may be experienced as given and coercing individually, and what is actually the power of many other people may be experienced individually as a power external to people altogether (see also p. 117). This has surely been an important source of support for the credibility of Parsons' theory of norms.

If we cease to confuse the power of people with the power of their norms, we need then have no problem in understanding that norms do not take us along but rather we take them along. Norms can then be understood as produced and reproduced in interaction. Note, however, that there is a crucial difference between this treatment of norms and Parsons' treatment. In Parsons, norms are used to explain; in an interactionist account, norms are in need of explanation, or at least they are provided with none. If, formally speaking, a norm can imply any number of things, then the one thing that it is as a matter of fact taken to imply on a given occasion of use still needs to be accounted for. Where before we had a general explanation of social order, now we have a vast array of particular actions once more unexplained.

Is there anything interesting to be said about the particular pathways we take norms along as we interact? Does anything distinguish the paths we select from those we ignore? Two points are worth making here, although they amount to far less than an adequate explanation of what is occurring. First of all, the concern of individuals to sustain interaction itself will be material to how they take norms on. Imagine interaction beginning on the basis of commonly known and understood norms, norms evident in existing matter-of-course practice. Participants will be perfectly well able to question or reconstruct anything in this existing practice, or to take it on in any number of diverse ways. But only a certain (small) amount of questioning, reconstruction and diversification will be possible at any one time if interaction itself is to persist and the communication it facilitates is to continue. Agreement on what most norms "really mean" must necessarily be accomplished on the basis that what is automatically being done is being done correctly (see section 2.4). Blind, unhesitating rule-following, wherein most participants find themselves acting unproblematically in agreement with each other, and where all agree in accounting their actions as following the same given rule or norm, must be taken most of the time as the *prominent solution* to the problem of what counts as *correct* rule following (see also section 1.2). What is done automatically is the necessary basis for the accomplishment of a sense of what is done rightly. Even in Goffman's studies of the active manipulation of norms this basis is required, and present.[6]

None the less, and this is the second point, the need to maintain a coherent interaction order does not preclude continuing pragmatic, expedient adjustments over time, which will allow norms continually to be realigned as changing objectives require. Because norms are the products of interaction, not its determinants, they must be seen as manipulable to further the ends and interests of those who create and sustain them. These, however, will not in general be individual ends or interests; rather they will be ends and interests identified, agreed and sustained collectively. Norms are collective goods, and to ask if interaction can generate and sustain them is to ask if the problem of collective action is soluble by an interactionist theory.

3.3 The problem of collective action revisited

So far we have looked at two unsuccessful attempts to solve the problem of collective action. The beautiful simplicity of the problem made it ideal for use as a probe with which to identify the strengths and weaknesses of a theory, and it did indeed allow us to identify the crucial defects of both individualism and normative functionalism. These theories fail to account for collective action because, in the last analysis, they refuse to acknowledge the *essential* role of the connections between persons in accounting for how they act. In individualistic theory the refusal takes the obvious form of the independence postulate: the independent individual has no cause to be concerned with the collective good and will not act to further it. In functionalism, the refusal is implicit in the conception of internalized norms separately present in each individual: the Parsonian actor is in the last analysis no more concerned with the collective and its good than is the independent rational individual. Once action needed for the collective good varies from the action enjoined by internalized norms, the Parsonian actor can no longer supply it: to put the point modestly, she is liable to find herself furthering last year's collective good rather than this year's.[7]

The rational, calculative, informed, active agents of individualistic social theory are incapable of identifying, creating and enforcing norms of action that redound to the good of the whole collective, because they operate separately and calculate separately. The agents of an interactionist social theory are similar in their calculative capabilities and in being actively oriented to norms, but they are not independent of each other. Interactionism stresses the lack of independence of individual persons, their essential connectedness, their mutual susceptibility. All this is just what is required of individuals if they are to act together, as members of a collective, in the furtherance of its good. Precisely how collective action may emerge from the interaction of mutually susceptible "individuals" is, however, something that remains to be shown.

Why might interacting, mutually susceptible individuals act collectively where separate, independent individuals would not? Presumably mutually susceptible individuals can affect each other's understanding so that a shared definition of their situation is sustained; they can identify (collectively) beneficial courses of action in that situation and give them recognition as norms; and they can press each other toward enacting such norms through symbolic communication that threatens or enhances "face" or "dignity". The last point is perhaps the one to stress for the moment. The mutually susceptible individuals of interactionist theory are able to press each other toward collective action through communications that, although wholly symbolic, none the less operate as (positive or negative) sanctions; unlike ER individuals, they may hope to generate collective action through mutual symbolic sanctioning.[8]

On the face of it, this interactionist account of the generation of collective action is very plausible. First of all, the power and ubiquity of symbolic sanctions and social pressure are generally recognized; human beings everywhere are evidently deeply susceptible to them. Secondly, the overall empirical incidence of collective action is better understood in these terms than in terms of alternative theories. For individualistic theory there is too much collective action in existence: any genuine collective action at all is a problem, and there is no doubt that there is lots of it about. For functionalism, on the other hand, there seems to be far too little collective action and far too much free-riding. But if mutual sanctioning is the incentive to act collectively and the prophylactic against free-riding, then perhaps there is just as much collective action as we should expect. For mutual sanctioning may be easy or difficult to implement, strong or weak, frequent or infrequent, avoidable or unavoidable. Only where sanctions find their mark will collective action be a possibility, and only when they are sufficiently strong will a given form of collective action with its particular level of costs come into play. And, finally, there are specific empirical examples that fit with the argument. In strikes, for example, solidarity is maintained through sanctioning, often purely symbolic in form but none the less effective for that: strategies of peaceful picketing or sending to Coventry may be extremely effective in preventing free-riding and sustaining solidarity.

Given all this, many sociologists routinely look to mutual sanctioning and social pressure as the explanation of collective solidarity and collective action, and the eventual conclusion of the argument here will be that they are right to do so. But this position is rarely advanced in the context of systematic social theory, because, as both functionalists (p. 51) and individualists emphasize, sanctioning is itself action that needs to be accounted for, and as such can be only a second-order, rather than a fundamental, factor in explanations. It is particularly interesting here to consider how individualist theorists have treated symbolic sanctioning and social pressures. It offers insight into the limitations of individualism and identifies the precise point at which this approach to human behaviour encounters intractable formal difficulties.

First of all, individualist social theorists do recognize the existence of symbolic sanctioning and social pressure and accept that human beings generally appear to be susceptible to them. Mancur Olson, for example, acknowledges this in *The logic of collective action* (1965: 61). But whereas other theorists would see this as implying the malleability of individual wants and preferences, their variability from one social context to another, and hence the invalidity of the independence postulate, individualists draw no such conclusion. They simply add social incentives and freedom from unpleasant social pressures to the preference schedules of individuals; they are simply another kind of individual want. "Social incentives", Olson tells us, "must be analysed in much the same way as monetary incentives" (1965: 61). From the perspective of this "economic approach to human behaviour", our susceptibility to other people is no different from our susceptibility to heat and cold, or to all manner of other environmental factors. It is just another condition of existence that we have to try and cope with as independent rational individuals. We calculatively exploit its existence in other people. We take account of its existence in ourselves. Our orientation to it is *instrumental*. In so far as it is an externality, it is there to be manipulated; in so far as it is internal, it is a condition of the nervous system that we are stuck with and have to make the best of.

Given that people are moved by social pressures and incentives, these sanctions can be applied to induce people to act as they otherwise would not. Why then should they not be used to induce collective action? The individualist approach responds to the question by considering the economics of sanctioning. Sanctioning itself is a form of action, and must itself be accounted for. ER individuals will sanction each other only if it is "rational" to do so. And sanctioning for the collective good, in general, is not rational. It generates indivisible benefits for the collective, not private benefits for the individual, and is thus itself a form of collective action. To attempt to account for collective action by reference to sanctioning is evidently circular. Collective action remains highly problematic from an individualistic perspective even if our manifest susceptibility to social pressures and social incentives is recognized.

An interesting attempt to bridge the gap between theory and observation here has been made by Coleman (1988, 1990) and by Heckathorn (1989). Coleman's approach relies upon the idea that, although all collective action is costly, some forms of it are very much less costly than others. To sanction for the collective good may be very much cheaper than to act for it directly, and hence it may be very much easier to produce collective action indirectly, as it were, via sanctioning, than directly as so many independent individual actions. In particular, symbolic sanctions such as encouragement (Coleman's own favoured example), approval or honour, or, conversely, contempt or disdain, are extraordinarily *cheap* to produce, yet very strong in their effects. This means that even miniscule individual gains of increased collective action might suffice to make symbolic forms of sanctioning profitable to the individual.

Heckathorn offers a systematic treatment of this claim, using the familiar result that the individual benefit of a given "collective" action

79

declines rapidly as the size of the collective increases. Only in extremely small groups is direct collective action "rational", i.e. individually beneficial. In somewhat larger groups such action is "irrational", but it may none the less still be "rational" to sanction other people into collective action, given that the "costs" of doing so are extremely small. Eventually, with increased group size, even sanctioning of the collective good becomes irrational and unprofitable and no collective action can be sustained. The basic problem of collective action in large groups remains unsolved. But the analysis suggests that much of the collective action observed in small groups may be understood as the product of mutual sanctioning rather than direct independent decision. As Heckathorn (1989: 80) puts it, in an interesting terminological revelation of the attitude of rational choice theory to these issues, most collective action may be the product of "hypocritical co-operation" in the business of sanctioning others to act. Thus, what might better be identified as a fundamental foundation of moral action is characterized from the perspective of rational choice theory as hypocrisy.

To reiterate: even assuming general susceptibility to pressures and sanctions and the extreme "cheapness" of these "commodities", the free-rider problem in large groups of ER individuals remains insoluble. Large-scale strikes remain unintelligible, for example, as genuine collective actions. Mutual encouragement and discouragement, and similar forms of mutual symbolic sanctioning, remain irrational in the context of collectives above a very modest size. According to the logic of the Coleman–Heckathorn approach, the larger the crowd at the football match, the less rational it is to cheer. Even so, the approach is of great theoretical interest.

Precisely because they are so persistent and systematic in their efforts to deal with its difficulties, Coleman and Heckathorn reinforce the conviction that the rational choice theory must be fundamentally unsatisfactory. But their approach also hints at why this might be so. They identify encouragement, honour, approval, etc. as *special* kinds of activity, although the insight is expressed in the all-pervasive language of cost–benefit analysis: symbolic sanctions of this kind are extraordinarily cheap to produce, yet much desired (or feared) by others and potent in their effects in consequence. There is something odd about this "economic" perspective on symbolically communicated sanctions. They are extremely cheap to produce, and they can be supplied by millions of independent producers. How is it, then, that they have any significant value or power at all? If "encouragement", "approval", "honour" and so forth are merely desired commodities, then a plentiful supply should be obtainable through exchange, and there should be no need to act in any seriously costly way in order to obtain a sufficiency. We should all find it easy to exist upon pinnacles of self-esteem, as members of mutual adoration societies, satiated with approval "paid for" with reciprocated approval. But we do not. For honour or approval offered out of expediency in this way, as goods in a trade, are by that very fact drained of value; indeed, they are no longer honour and approval at all, but mere counterfeits thereof.

Honour and approval and other forms of symbolic sanctioning simply cannot be treated as commodities or instrumentalities. They are indeed special, as Coleman realizes, but special in that they resist assimilation to his cost–benefit, rational choice framework. It is this that provides the key to understanding how symbolic sanctioning operates, and this that individualist theorists have been unable to acknowledge. In fairness it must be said that the point is often overlooked by theorists in other traditions. Even Goffman fails to give an unequivocal emphasis to the point. In Goffman, those who put forth evaluations of respect, honour, approval, etc. often appear to be concerned entirely with their effect upon recipients: the "cooler-out" (see p. 89) is the example *par excellence*. However, although this kind of account is doubtless appropriate in very many particular cases, it cannot serve as a sufficient basis for a general understanding of the communication of evaluations and symbolic sanctions. It is no accident that the cooler-out is also a deceiver. When evaluations are generated merely to manipulate the recipient they are being produced *inauthentically* and, if the lack of authenticity is recognized, the status of the evaluations is undermined. The presumption of the authenticity of evaluations is necessary to their standing as evaluations. Although it is true that Goffman gives us case after case of individuals willing to supply counterfeit honour and approval, and remarkably few instances wherein they are accorded authentically, it must none the less be kept in mind that, just as in the case of forged banknotes, the corresponding demand is solely for the genuine articles. Perhaps Goffman found it otiose and laboured continually to make such an obvious point and often left it to be inferred by his readers. Or perhaps, in a culture where there was a taboo on acknowledging mutual susceptibility and the constant operation of the deference-emotion system (Scheff 1988), it was actually easier to make its inauthentic use credible than to establish its full role in the context of interaction.[9]

Mutual symbolic sanctioning must be recognized as an entirely different form of activity from sanctioning by coercion or by provision of financial reward. These last kinds of sanctions are straightforwardly costly. It is not unreasonable to include the costs of the prison service or a trade embargo in a cost–benefit analysis. But this cannot be done with the "encouragement" incorrectly described by Coleman as costing but little, or with approval and disapproval, or honour and dishonour, or respect and contempt. What needs to be recognized here is not that production costs are low but that the very notion of production cost is obscure, problematic and indeed inapplicable. The sanctions here are streams of symbols, verbal and non-verbal. It is wholly unconvincing to hold that their production involves a costly diversion of symbol-generating competences away from some prior significant task: what is this prior task, and what evidence is there that it comes remotely close to demanding the full output of our symbol-generating systems? It is just as unconvincing to speak of absolute production costs, as if every output of symbols somehow entails a consumption of scarce resources, a loss to the economy of the human body. This would suggest that the preferred state of the individual is something close to a coma, which is nonsense (Barnes 1988, 1990).

There is no sensible way of costing outputs of symbols (see also pp. 35–6). Symbolic manipulation and symbolic communication cannot be treated in this way, as mere instrumentalities. Indeed, any attempt to treat them in this way immediately encounters not just technical problems but general logical difficulties. The exercise merely reveals the fundamental limitations of individualist social theory. The independent individuals of this theory are rational calculators with given preferences. If these individuals are to realize their preferences they must calculate appropriate ways and means in the light of what they know. But such calculations are manipulations of symbols. And the knowledge incorporated into such calculations is transmitted and received, exchanged and evaluated, stored and recalled, through the manipulation of symbols. If symbolic communications are costly then rational calculation is itself costly, and to make such a calculation is to incur a cost before one knows what the cost is – and to modify the cost every time one attempts to identify it and quantify it. If symbolic manipulations have costs then the rational calculator is faced with the impossible task of allowing for the costs of her own calculations, even as she makes them. Any theory that attempts to describe all human activities without exception as rational, calculative and goal oriented self-destructs at this point. Communication, calculation, cognition, representation and so forth must be set outside the scheme. These symbolic activities actually constitute the context and framework within which possible "rational" actions can be appraised and those of them that are indeed "rational" enacted.

The normal mode in which we communicate our ideas and evaluations, and in which we transmit symbolic sanctions to others, is not that of expedient calculation. Rather, we do it as part of life, as it were: it is normal and natural to us to exist, not in a coma but in a state of communicative engagement with others. We live psychically in an atmosphere of symbolic communication, transmitting and receiving messages as a matter of course, just as we live physically in a material atmosphere, breathing it in and out as a matter of course.[10] Just as our susceptibility to the evaluations of others is everywhere taken as given by social theorists, so too must be our disposition to put forth such evaluations. So, for example, if we are to speak, following Scheff, of a deference-emotion system that allows us to exercise influence on each other, we must recognize that the system is not just a reception system. It is a system that binds us together as both receivers and transmitters of evaluations, and in neither of these communicative roles can what we do be understood wholly in terms of instrumental orientations.

Encouragement and discouragement, approval and disapproval, honour and contempt, the whole range of symbolic sanctions that allow us to press each other into collective action, are not cheap to produce, as Coleman suggests, but are givens associated with no costs at all. No extrinsic individual benefits are necessary to elicit these things: individual pay-off is irrelevant to their production. Accordingly, we must think not of ER individuals able profitably to sanction the collective good of groups up to a certain small size, but rather of social agents interacting and communicating in a system that is wholly unintelligible in terms of the postulates of individualism.

It is true, of course, that agents capable of eliciting collective action will not necessarily do so, and that the basic argument above needs to be supplemented with some account of the circumstances in which collective action is successfully elicited and those in which it is not. When will those capable of exerting "social pressure" or offering "encouragement" for collective action actually choose to do so, and for what good?

This question raises crucial issues that will continue to be salient throughout the remainder of this book, and it is essential to understand just what it amounts to. It is actually a question about the incidence of co-ordinated cognition and shared understanding. Where there is agreement on what the collective good comprises, that good *ipso facto* is going to be encouraged. Imagine an interacting group that does succeed in recognizing its collective good. Suppose that it identifies and formulates for itself that it would be good to build a bridge, or drain a marsh, or form a cartel. Then what it is crucial to recognize is that, *in thereby being formulated, the good is also by that very fact sanctioned and encouraged*. To recognize a collective good is at the same time to imply honour for those, if any, already involved in it and discouragement for those acting or arguing against it. Symbolic sanctions and evaluations are not specialized messages; they are communications that perform descriptive and evaluative tasks simultaneously. It barely makes sense to say: "That was a fine thing you did; remind me to praise you for it when I have time." We do not first identify and then formulate and then evaluate and then encourage collective action. We do all these things together. The ongoing communicative activity that establishes a collective good in the collective understanding at the same time sanctions it and encourages its realization. Thus, when we ask whether a collective is capable of sanctioning the collective good we are actually enquiring about its collective *cognitive* capabilities, about its ability to *think the collective good*. If the good is *thought* in the collective, if it is consistently evident in speech and communication, then it is *sanctioned* in the collective. And of course, although interesting theoretical problems of explanation remain here, the ability of members of collectives to think their good in this sense is not in doubt empirically.

There remains the crucial difference between conceiving and sanctioning the collective good and actually enacting it. Action in the latter sense can meaningfully be said to be costly. Sanctioning the collective good may or may not effect its enactment, depending upon the individual sacrifice required and the power and the coherence of the sanctioning. Think of a community settled by a river facing rich lands on the other side. The value of a bridge will everywhere be recognized. Perhaps collective co-operation will build one, or perhaps not. It may be that the wider and deeper the river, the less probable the building of the bridge. It may be that with just one narrow place a bridge would be built, but with two narrow places discord between those living near the one and those near the other would derail the project. All kinds of contingency may prevent the translation of shared understanding into collective action. But, where there is agreement in understanding, the possibility of agreement in action always exists.

The case for interactionism is now made. It can account for collective action in a way that individualism cannot, and the manifest empirical incidence of collective action suggests that the interactionist view, emphasizing the profound interdependence of individual persons, should accordingly be preferred to the individualist view. However, since the argument is both crucial and difficult it may be worthwhile to summarize it once more. Its starting point lies in networks of interaction between mutually susceptible individuals. Continuing communication in the course of interaction both requires and engenders agreement in cognition and understanding, evident in some degree of shared knowledge, shared culture, shared competence. Constant interaction, with message transmission and reception ongoing as a matter of course between persons, is essential for cognition at the collective level, just as constant interaction with message transmission and reception between neurones is essential for cognition at the individual level. And to put a price on the operation of the system is as inappropriate as putting a price on the operation of a single brain, for example as it thinks its way through a cost–benefit analysis. To identify a collective good within this system of collective cognition is no more costly than identifying an individual good by taking thought as an independent person. Thought is free, as it were, in both cases. But to identify a collective good in the shared cognition of the collective *just is* to sanction the action implied by that cognition. Thinking the collective good as a collective is sanctioning it, in the sense of encouraging its enactment by individual members.

3.4 Knowledge, interaction and the micro–macro problem

There are few critical evaluations of interactionism from the outside, as there are of individualism and functionalism. Interactionists have long criticized each other in their search for the most satisfactory version of the approach, but external criticism has been scant and largely confined to a single issue: rather than looking for empirical failings or internal inconsistencies it charges interactionism with irrelevance. Interactionism is micro sociology and as such is not applicable to the central problems of social theory, which are macro problems. So many macro theorists have said, and their micro colleagues have rarely disagreed;

which is strange, for counterarguments are easy to find. Individualism is a respected micro theory readily linked to macro phenomena. If macro phenomena can be understood to some extent as arrays of individuals, then why not as arrays of encounters or situations? The truth is probably that the original American interactionist theorists had no taste for macro theory and that there was a culture clash between micro and macro sociologists in the USA (Rock 1978), with both sides conniving at the maintenance of separate spheres of operation. Thankfully, however, the finest theorists are now at last able to move easily to and fro across the supposed divide: Randall Collins (1981, 1988), for example, makes exemplary use of Goffman in his macro theory, and Jürgen Habermas (1984, 1987) develops his *Theory of communicative action* through reflection on the work of George Herbert Mead, Goffman, Harold Garfinkel and other micro theorists.[11]

Not that the micro–macro problem, as it has become known, is spurious. There is an evident gap between micro and macro phenomena, between a suicide, for example, and a suicide rate. Famously, Durkheim spoke of groups and societies manifesting irreducible emergent properties that had to be studied in their own right by an autonomous academic discipline, sociology. For Durkheim, as generally interpreted, micro and macro phenomena were distinct. Many of his critics argued the opposite: that emergent properties and macro phenomena had to be accounted for as composites or aggregates of micro phenomena, that sociology (and economics) merely studied aggregates of individual behaviour and to that extent were "reducible" to psychology.

It is sometimes assumed that emergent properties and the consequent problem of the relationship of micro and macro phenomena are difficulties encountered only in the social sciences, but this is incorrect. Think of a traditional egg-timer. Sand runs from the glass chamber at the top, through a narrow neck, to the chamber below, giving the egg about four minutes to boil. The four minutes is an emergent property of the system: induction from experience indicates that each pass of the sand takes roughly four clock minutes. The egg-timer is a mechanical system of rare symmetry and simplicity, encapsulated in an extremely stable, closed-off environment. Yet there is no way in which the time of passage of the sand may be calculated from "micro" theory. It is not just that a fundamental particle physicist would fail. Even a sand-particle physicist would fail; she would fail even if all the sand grains were identical spheres, so many identical atomic individuals. The classical mechanics of rigid objects has difficulty treating five particles rigorously, let alone fifty thousand. Most of us retain a touching faith that the particles of sand in an egg-timer are obeying the laws of mechanics, but what is really going on in there God only knows. Whatever else, references to the motion of "the sand" in this context will continue to be scientifically reputable and pragmatically sensible, and claims that "the sand is really its particles" ontologically ungrounded and pragmatically pointless.

If by "reduction" is meant the replacement without loss of a "macro" account by a "micro" account, with the elimination of references to "emergent properties", then reduction is not going to occur. Sociology will not "reduce" to psychology, any more than psychology will "reduce" to biology or biology to chemistry. Those who share Durkheim's concern for the continuation of sociology as an independent discipline may rest easy on this point. But it is not the case, as Durkheim occasionally implies, that macro and micro phenomena are wholly separate and independent of each other. When the egg-timer is used, the motion of "the sand" and the motions of the particles of sand are not separate and independent. References to "the sand" and to "the particles" are the basis of alternative descriptions of one and the same state of affairs. And, because of this, accounts of sand particles and accounts of sand must fit coherently together. If, for example, particles of sand were spontaneously explosive, then it is hard to see how sand itself could be other than spontaneously explosive.

In the social sciences, accounts of micro phenomena and accounts of macro phenomena often refer to the same states of affairs. Where they do so, the accounts must be *consistent* with each other, which means that they will have implications for each other and ought to be of value to each other. The persistent sin of macro sociological theory has not been to combat reductionism, as Durkheim rightly did, but to take little heed of micro studies and assume that their findings could not be related to macro states of affairs.

A significant obstacle to the development of social theory across the micro/macro divide is the widespread assumption that, for any given state of affairs, there exists just one correct description. The thought behind the assumption tends to be: everything has been mentioned; take away what has been referred to and there is nothing left; therefore there is nothing more to be said. It is crucial to recognize the flaw in this argument, the reason that its "therefore" cannot stand. Consider the human body. If we say that the body is so many molecules, we make reference to everything that makes up the body: if we remove all the molecules nothing is left over. But in *referring* to everything, we have not *described* everything worth describing. We could equally describe the body as so many cells, or as so many functional units – limbs, internal organs, bones, etc. Each description adds to what has gone before. Each is consistent with what has gone before. No such additional description, however, identifies new constituents of the body. The molecules of the first description are the cells of the second are the functioning units of the third. Each description identifies patterns and relations absent from the others but no new material not already referred to by the others. To refer to everything that makes up an entity or object or state of affairs is quite different from describing everything of interest about it.

Micro social theory is comprehensive in the way that a cellular theory of the human body is comprehensive. If we identify a "society" and then subtract from it all the encounters or interaction situations, nothing remains. And it can indeed be useful to appreciate that, for all our routine talk of nations, governments, organizations and so forth, there is no substantial reality to those things outside of persons and the encounters and interactions between them. But this does not mean that all sociology needs is micro theory. For this amounts to the claim that there are no other patterns discernible in what micro theory describes, and no underlying patterns that might usefully be postulated in an additional macro-theoretical account of the same states of affairs. Such a sweeping claim cannot be justified: macro-theoretical accounts have to be taken as they come, judged on their specific merits. The impressive achievements of interactionist social theory in no way restrict the scope or significance of any macro-level theory and may actually be of service in the development of such a theory.

What follows precisely attempts to connect the general approach of interactionism into the context of macro social theory. First, it will be claimed that crucially important extended patterns and connections are apparent in the vast array of encounters and interactions that constitute social life, that these patterns are routinely referred to in interactionist studies themselves, and that their importance is made clearly evident in those studies. Secondly, it will be shown how the existence of these patterns allows situated social interaction to engender extended collective action and a situation-transcending normative order. The patterns being referred to here are those constituted by members' shared knowledge.

Contributions to micro sociology generally take the form of an analysis of a form of encounter or localized interaction. Goffman's very early paper "On cooling the mark out" (1952) is typical in this respect. It reminds us of a standard form of fraud. A team of "operators" move in on their "mark" (the potential victim of their "racket") and through, for example, an invitation to gamble, relieve her of her cash. Sometimes, in such situations, one of the operators, who has remained unidentified in the background, stays behind to "cool out the mark", reconcile her to her loss, dissuade her from making trouble, reconstruct her shattered sense of dignity.

Stories of this kind have a peculiar fascination, and focus our attention wholly upon the appalling details of encounters themselves. But we should direct attention also to how the relevant encounters are made out as part of a larger scheme of things. The operators – skilled through their involvement in previous encounters – smoothly engage with the mark and disengage with her cash. The mark's "economic" knowledge allows, perhaps forces, her to recognize the loss that disarranges her dignity. The operators' "sociological" knowledge, derived from previous encounters, tells them that marks with disarranged dignity are "bad for business", and accordingly they invest in a "cooler-out", a free counselling service that calms down the mark and forestalls any inconvenient "squawking". Mark and cooler together are able to review past mistakes and future opportunities, to recognize that life goes on, that tomorrow is another day with other encounters, that not everybody knows what has just happened and that where ignorance persists dignity exists. Looking to past knowledge and future expectation in this way brings consolation and dissipates inconvenient anger.

In summary, the encounter Goffman describes is that encounter only because it follows earlier remembered encounters and precedes later expected ones. What connects such encounters together is members' knowledge and inferential skills, which are, to a degree, situation transcendent and portable.

Should we speak then of persisting situations wherein linked sequences of encounters or interactions take place, and analyze "social systems" into so many separate co-existing situations? As we saw in section 3.2 above, Howard Becker takes just this approach: a stable social order is so many stable situations between which individuals move. The mobile individuals themselves, being concerned to "cope" or "make out", generally adjust to each particular situation, enact its routines and verbally rationalize them by invoking the appropriate local norms. But

Becker recognizes also that the situations between which individuals move are not independent of each other, precisely because of individual mobility between them. And because of this an individual will sometimes stand out against situated social pressure, and pursue courses of action in no way advantageous in terms of the immediate goal of "coping" or "making-out". Becker attributes "commitment" of this kind not to internalized personal convictions but to the fact that individuals have to operate in many different situations and will not necessarily take the most expedient course in one situation if they know that it entails the risk of loss in another. The perceived "self-interest" of the individual in a given situation may thus be an indirect expression of social or collective interests enjoined on her in other situations of which she remains all the time aware and knowledgeable. Playing the game of making-out in any one situation is always complicated by the "side-bets" the mobile individual has in other situations. Eventually, in balancing off the various demands of different situations, the individual may find that highly routinized ways of acting are essential if she is to make out optimally, and that few variations will be compatible with all the diverse demands she must meet. This offers a theory of the stable individual personality as one constrained by the pressures of interlocking social situations, but it is also *ipso facto* an interesting general theory of social order.

If he had ever sought to set out explicitly a general theory of social order, Becker's would have been different from both individualism and functionalism. Contrary to individualism, norms and routines that relate to collective rather than individual interests are interactively stabilized in given situations. Contrary to functionalism, individuals orient to such norms and routines calculatively, as participants in many situations with continuing knowledge of all of them. The routines are enacted sufficiently often, and the norms thereby reconstituted, because such enactment is frequently the optimal solution to the problem of co-ordination constituted by all the diverse situated pressures and demands that individuals face. From the weft of situations and the warp of individual life-courses the fabric of a tolerably persistent social order is thereby woven.

In Becker's work, as in Goffman's, encounters and situations are described in ways that entail their being connected into a larger whole. And, again as with Goffman, the connection is made by reference to participants' situation-transcendent knowledge. Nor is this true just of Goffman and Becker; it is true of the entire interactionist tradition. What goes on in a situation is invariably understood in terms of mutual susceptibilities within the situation and shared knowledge of what lies beyond it. In the background of all studies within the tradition, however narrowly focused, the shadow of an entire social order is invariably present. Thus, the description of interactionism set out so far has been unduly narrow. Interactionism does not in practice confine itself to what occurs within encounters or situations: it routinely points beyond situations in the course of understanding what goes on within them. It speaks of human beings who are mutually susceptible and interactively constrained within situations, but knowledgeable and interested beyond them.

Individual lives transcend particular situations and interacting individuals accordingly evolve and carry a stock of knowledge that includes a mapping of many situations and their relationship to each other. Indeed the stock of knowledge will typically evolve so that it extends beyond not just any given situation, but all; it will come to include items that are wholly abstracted from context and available for use in any situation at all. Just as a shared conception of the nature of the entire physical universe may evolve from a shared awareness of what, relatively speaking, are but a few scraps of experience, so similarly a shared conception of "the social order" may grow. The stock of knowledge will come to offer representations of "nature" and of "society" far surpassing the situated experience of any individual or even all the individuals in the interacting collective. And of course, in both cases, as situation-transcending knowledge is acted upon it will engender situation-transcending patterns in the action thereby produced, which patterns will in turn become known about and taken account of in the shared stock of knowledge.[12]

Thus, human beings will typically interact with each other on the basis of a commonly known natural and social order. Much of sociological significance flows from this. It has, for example, considerable significance for the problem of collective action. In section 3.3 we left the problem, having noted that if a collective could think its good then it could sanction it, and hence might possibly enact it. But knowledge is what we think with. Since interacting human beings possess situation-transcending knowledge, we can now understand how they might sanction action for a situation-transcending good.

If interacting human beings recognize some action as good for all and each of them then they will *ipso facto* encourage it by symbolic sanctioning. But whatever benefits a category of which all know themselves to be members will indeed benefit all and each of them, even if it also benefits others beyond the interaction situation as well. Thus, a specific interacting group of women may sanction action for the collective good of women in general, or a large number of women including themselves. And so similarly with interacting groups of trade unionists or medical practitioners or poll-tax payers. The macro phenomenon of action for the good of very large groups can at last be given a theoretical rationale, and, perversely, it proves to be compatible only with the variety of social theory that long resolutely avoided discussion of macro phenomena.

It is important to recall at this point that the "individuals" of an interactionist theory are not ER individuals, for whom sanctioning of collective action very rapidly becomes unprofitable as group size increases. Interacting individuals recognize, and thereby automatically encourage, collective goods as part of the normal and natural operation of cognition. Whatever redounds to their good they may encourage and hence perhaps engender, whether or not it benefits large numbers of others as well. The basic process that encourages the collective good is so constituted that any "we" in which interacting human beings know themselves to be included may possibly have its good encouraged. A given individual may recognize her membership of a category, think the good of that category – i.e. think of the relevant "we" and of "our" good, instead of "I" and "my" good – and *ipso facto* sanction and encourage that good. In this way the manifest existence of collective action for the good of large, extended but networky groups can be made intelligible, and the move from micro to macro problems effected.

An encouragingly similar approach to collective action can be found in social psychology in the guise of *self-categorization theory* (Turner et al. 1987). This theory begins with the claim that a person's conception of self is built out of the categorizations of self available in the shared stock of knowledge. Each categorization groups the self as the same as some persons and different from others. The category of the distinct unique individual is just one of those available. Sometimes a person thinks as an "I", different from all others, sometimes as part of a "we", the same as the others in that "we". The person is neither fundamentally an individual who sometimes lapses into group thinking, nor intrinsically a part of a collective that sometimes individuates itself. Rather, both collective and individual representations are part of the set of categories a person is able to draw upon in the course of cognition. Turner et al. (1987) cite extensive empirical evidence that individual persons do frequently think as part of a "we" and that such thinking is capable of being translated into action. Moreover, they insist that membership of a given social category may be cognitively salient irrespective of any prospect of individual gain or relationship of interdependence with others in the same category.[13]

By documenting how extended, situation-transcending membership categories are drawn upon in the course of cognition, self-categorization theorists reinforce the present claim that action for the good of large extended collectives may be interactively sustained. If goods can be thought, so it has been argued, then they may possibly be furthered. Self-categorization theory implies that the relevant goods can indeed be thought.

Of course, possibility is not the same as actuality. Collective action for the good of large numbers does not just get thought into existence. Possible courses of action must be *available*, and there must be agreement on which possibilities are indeed beneficial and which of those should have priority, since to act in one direction precludes simultaneous action in another. The need for agreement in cognition here implies that large-scale collective action, although possible, may none the less often be much harder to achieve and less intensely pursued than action based in smaller, localized interacting groups and oriented to their good alone. For, the larger the collective the greater the range of outside interests and commitments that members are likely to have, and the larger the number of different "we"s in which they are also members. And hence the fewer the courses of action that will not clash with the external interests of some members. Large group size implies a tendency to weak collective action and an increased difficulty in sustaining group solidarity, but not the absence of any collective action predicted by individualistic social theory.

4

Knowledge

4.1 Knowledge and social order

Individualism and functionalism are both unable to offer a satisfactory account of social order, and the reason is much the same in both cases. Neither individual desires nor the promptings of norms fixed into individual consciences will remain in continuing alignment with changing collective requirements – requirements that are met notwithstanding, in all societies, by co-ordinated social action. With an interactionist theory, however, presuming not independently moved individuals but mutually susceptible individuals, this problem is soluble. And, as we have just seen, with an appropriately extended system of shared knowledge such individuals may sustain a correspondingly extended social order.

It remains for this chapter briefly to consider the nature of the knowledge itself, and to make clear why this is of importance in the context of macro social theory.[1] In most traditions of social theory, with the partial exception of Marxism, knowledge has not been treated as problematic. Individualist theorists have routinely taken for granted the existence of shared knowledge, which they have conceived of as shared information. Unsurprisingly, they have favoured an individualistic theory of knowledge in which units of information are products of individual observation, and correspond item by item with elements of the environment. Talcott Parsons also took for granted the existence of shared knowledge, which his actors needed in order both to follow self-interest and to conform to norms. And Parsons too accepted an individualistic account of knowledge: any individual could check its validity through her own independent actions and observations. Ironically, of the varieties of social theory considered here, the only one that cannot readily be reconciled with a standard individualistic account of shared knowledge is the one in which the existence of shared knowledge promises to solve so many difficult problems: interactionism is incompatible with the individualistic account of knowledge, because it has no room for the concept of the independent individual.

Interactionism does, however, fit nicely with an alternative, sociological view of shared knowledge, and indeed perhaps just such a view should be attributed to interactionist social theory. Goffman, after all, looked to Durkheim as the theorist of situation-transcending categories and rules, and Durkheim (1915) provided a sociological view of knowledge in which categories are socially constructed and rules socially sustained and interpreted. Indeed, Durkheim was seminal to the sociology of knowledge just as he was to interactionist theory; he ran the two together. In *The elementary forms of the religious life*, for example, the categories of experience emerge from interaction, and are sustained and reinforced through repeated interactions.

Durkheim's concern was precisely to understand the shared character of knowledge and cognition, to show why, in a world where concepts and beliefs vary enormously between different human beings, they none the less manifest a high degree of uniformity among the members of particular collectives. His contrast between the fluidity and diversity of individual perceptions and the relative unity and stability of shared representations is designed to emphasize the status of the latter as collective accomplishments:

a certain intuition of the resemblances and differences presented by things has played an important part in the genesis of . . . classifications. . . . But feeling the resemblances is one thing and the idea of class is another. The class is the external framework of which objects perceived to be similar form, in part, the contents. Now the contents cannot furnish the frame into which they fit. They are made up of *vague and fluctuating images* . . . ; the framework, on the contrary, is a *definite form*, with fixed outlines, but which may be applied to an *undetermined number of things*, perceived or not, actual or possible. In fact, every class has possibilities of extension which go far beyond the circle of objects which we know, either from direct experience or from resemblance . . . The idea of class is an instrument of thought which has obviously been constructed by men. ([1915]: 146–7)

What individualism takes to be a happy coincidence of individual experiences Durkheim takes to be "constructed by men". He refuses to let the world itself account for the unity of belief about it in a given collective, aware that the world itself is also accessible to other collectives with very different beliefs. His account reminds us that shared knowledge is a basic condition for social interaction and social order as we know them, something whose unity and coherence are going to be sustained whatever the world is like, and however it is perceived. Perception is one thing; knowledge is another. The long- and the short-sighted, the astigmatic and the colour blind, those with the finest aberration-free spectacles and those with cheap and nasty ones, those who use no optical artefacts at all, all feed in their many and various reports of experience; and all draw upon the one shared account of what there is, which continues to be sustained notwithstanding. That is to say, they all draw upon the body of knowledge that is being sustained in and as the local culture; for, in the tribe across the river, or the laboratory down the road, or the other social science department along the corridor, a different body of collectively sustained knowledge may be drawn upon by individuals with similarly various eyeballs assisted by equally diverse artefacts.

Many aspects of the account of knowledge provided in *The elementary forms* have been taken up and developed in the social sciences. Crucially, the claim that the world does not classify itself, that it must actively be ordered and organized and the particulars encountered in it actively grouped together, is accepted. This leads to the thought that many different ways of ordering particulars exist, that all are acceptable to "the world itself", and that different ways may be found in different contexts, adapted to different pragmatic concerns. Furthermore, since different classifications are "equally good" as far as the world is concerned, it is plausible to cite the authority of the collective to explain why its members typically proceed on the basis of just one classification, one cosmology. It is indeed a central theme of *The elementary forms* that shared knowledge always enjoys, directly or indirectly, the support of authority, which authority often tends to sacralize it. It is this authority, of course, sustaining a particular shared body of knowledge and classification over time as well as space, that makes the knowledge easy to acquire as a coherent practical resource from the ancestors, and to pass on to descendants. Not, however, that we should think that it is authority *rather than* the world that allows the transmission of knowledge in this way; for Durkheim does not deny the importance of the resemblances we "feel" or the "images" of experience we perceive. The Durkheimian picture is not a wholly idealist one in which the world is dispensable; it is a picture wherein knowledge and classification rest upon the natural and the social in symbiosis, wherein what merits recognition as the truth is at one and the same time an empirical and a moral issue (Shapin 1994). Current sociological work on knowledge is, of course, no simple continuation of the thought of *The elementary forms*, which is in any case, like all seminal texts, full of flaws. Indeed, present-day theorists systematically differ from the Durkheimian approach in being much less concerned with the stability of knowledge and classification and much more with the endlessly problematic nature of classifying and with the application of knowledge as an ongoing activity. None the less, practically every social science field that has addressed itself to the detailed study of knowledge and cognition has come to accept in some interpretation Durkheim's claim that classifications and cosmologies are "constructed by men".[2] In the field of the sociology of knowledge, and particularly in the part of it that is concerned with natural-scientific knowledge, constructivist theories are now paradigmatic. They are widely employed in social anthropology. Ethnomethodology offers outstandingly interesting insights into knowledge as a collective accomplishment. And in all these fields theory is well exemplified through case studies and has been checked, refined and improved over a considerable period in relation to such studies. Constructivist approaches can now readily be evaluated in studies of scientists and professional experts. Their role is well known in relation to the application of medical knowledge and the attribution of physical and mental illness. Constructivist accounts of suicide rates and suicides now have something of a classic status in sociology and are recognized as of great methodological significance. Ethnomethodologists have produced impressive studies of the use of both "lay" and "sociological" knowledge of social context.[3]

Unfortunately, however, the acceptance of constructivism turns shared knowledge back into a problem for social theory. It is no longer possible to take knowledge for granted in understanding social order, to assume that the world unifies knowledge and cognition for us, as it were, and that we can help ourselves to the result. If knowledge is a collective accomplishment, then an account of how it is accomplished is needed. The social order problem has not been solved but merely reformulated as a problem of cognitive order. Such a reformulation does none the less represent a worthwhile advance. For the problem of social order, as generally understood, implies the need to eliminate or confine conflicts, to overcome forces, to induce people to act as "of themselves" they would not, whereas the achievement of cognitive order implies none of these things. The acceptance of shared knowledge, the learning of language, the co-ordination of inference, the mastery of communicative conventions, and similar cognitive activities require no special inducements. It needs neither material reward nor the prompting of conscience to bring them about. The threat of deviance in relation to them is not alarming. To that extent, it is unsurprising that cognitive order is everywhere, and to present social order as the expression of cognitive order does indeed throw light on why there is social order, always and everywhere.

It could be said that the acquisition of shared knowledge and the co-ordination of cognition and understanding are in every individual's interest. But this, although perhaps true, puts us in danger of forgetting that the individual human beings being spoken of here are not ER individuals, and do not operate on the basis of cost–benefit analysis. Cognitive order is not sustained because calculation indicates its expediency; cognitive order is what makes calculation possible. Should we not consider then what kinds of human being do sustain cognitive order, and what native skills and proclivities it is necessary to impute to them? This is a perfectly reasonable suggestion, even though interactionists themselves are often suspicious of its implication that there may be universal situation-independent human characteristics. Formally speaking, there is no contradiction between the endless variety of individual persons as revealed in interactionist studies and the existence of universal powers and proclivities residing in "the interactive individual".

We have already noted in section 3.2 how Goffman's case studies are taken by Thomas Scheff as revelatory of universal human characteristics. The deference-emotion system whose elucidation Scheff credits to Goffman is not just given and universal; according to Scheff it is biologically based. Scheff cites Goffman, along with psychologists and even the naturalist–biologist Charles Darwin, in his account of the system, before describing it as "a *biosocial* system that functions silently, continuously, and virtually invisibly, occurring *within* and *between* members of a society" (Scheff 1988: 405). Scheff is unequivocal that the basic form of the "deference-emotion system" is not culturally transmitted: it is not taught but present prior to what is taught, and hence available when we come to ask how teaching or "socialization" is itself possible.

Scheff offers a nativist account of mutual susceptibility, which presumes that a "social" component is built into human nature itself. He describes human beings as social animals rather than independent utility maximizers (see also Molotch 1990: 305). At one time, when "human nature" arguments were routinely (mis)used to bolster every kind of reactionary nonsense, and before work such as that of Chomsky had encouraged better and more widespread understanding of their flexibility and lack of any specific normative significance, sociologists tended to look askance at nativism. But the need for anxiety in this area is past, and indeed the question now can be not whether or not nativism is allowable, but how far it might be pressed. The work of Mead has interesting nativist implications and is often made use of as a way of understanding the basis of social interaction. But there are alternatives to Mead in present-day empirically oriented social psychology. One is represented by the work of Colwyn Trevarthen, which sets out one of the most strongly and uncompromisingly nativist accounts currently available of the interactive capacities of human beings.

Trevarthen (1988, 1989, Trevarthen & Logotheti 1987, 1989) reviews both his own empirical research and an extensive supporting literature in order to argue that every human being is natively endowed with the equipment and the motivation necessary for her ready development into a knowledgeable participant in an interacting collective. He begins with biology. The anatomy of the mouth, he points out, is elaborately adapted less for biting and eating than for complex modulation of the voice, the production of elaborate signals, vocal communication. Over 90 adaptations of the skeleton and musculature of the mouth and jaw are intelligible only as adaptations evolved for speech. The brain and sensory apparatus are likewise specially adapted to the detection of speech. From before birth, babies are selectively attentive to speech above other sounds, and become selectively attentive to the speech of their mother over other speech. From birth, babies will look in the direction of a voice and focus upon an identified face as the source. Trevarthen concludes that "A baby is not vacuous 'biological' material waiting to be socialized, but a being adapted, in the course of evolution, to function intersubjectively in communication" (Trevarthen & Logotheti 1989: 51).

Nor is it that the child arrives in the world "a born communicator", in possession of the requisite communicative competences, and awaits a teacher to impart particular meanings and significances and to reward signs that they have been correctly grasped. Even prior to any

99

socialization, the child is a complexly motivated active agent who in the earliest stages of infancy produces "potent control behaviours . . . that stimulate a particular diet or syllabus of supportive and instructive behaviour from caretakers' (Trevarthen 1988: 37). Further study of behaviour as infancy progresses confirms this identification of the child as innately a meaning-seeker, pre-formed as a potential communicator with a self–other scheme available from the very start as the basis for communication. The child actively seeks communication and actively co-ordinates her use of symbols with their use by others in the course of communication. Indeed, the child has an "*enthusiasm* for communicating with symbols" (Trevarthen & Logotheti 1989: 51, my italics) and for co-operating in practices in which her use of symbols can be co-operatively developed in conjunction with that of others and co-ordinated with theirs.

As with symbols and meanings so with knowledge. Existing knowledge is not a standardised version of the world that new members simply absorb, into which they are indoctrinated or passively socialized. The child has from the start a "primary motivation to gain an evaluation of experience that has inter-personal and communal validity" (Trevarthen & Logotheti 1987: 77). She is born with an "inherent readiness to link her subjective evaluations of experience with those of other persons" (Trevarthen 1988: 37), and with a "self-regulating strategy for getting knowledge by negotiation and co-operative action" (p. 39). Thus, the child connives in the transmission, evaluation and application of the knowledge teachers make available. She does not merely assimilate. It is existing knowledge which the child acquires and perpetuates, not because the child is passive and the teacher active, but because, for the relevant problems of co-ordination in cognition, existing knowledge is the prominent solution. The transmission of knowledge is the joint accomplishment of two active agents.

Trevarthen identifies a particularly interesting stage of infant development that occurs toward the end of the first year. At about this time, the child begins to seek out and engage in person–person–object interaction. Rather than being oriented to direct communication with another person (primary intersubjectivity), the child becomes attentive to the other person in action upon the world (secondary intersubjectivity). The child orients to how the other person does things, how the other person might serve as a model or instructor in doing things, how things can be done with the other person – all this before, if only just before, the advent of speech. From this point, the child's learning about the physical world is also at one and the same time the development of cultural competence and the generation of a shared awareness of the environment through communication with others. And increasingly, of course, the communication is symbolic communication, so that the significance of symbols is recognized through their application in person–person–object interactions:

> . . . the . . . function of symbols is to be found first in communication, not in the thinking of one head. We think and remember symbolically because we communicate symbolically. *Intra*subjective processes of reflective thought, solving problems, remembering causal relationships and planning strategies of action appear to grow out of *inter*subjective exchange, in which motives for consciousness and action in different individuals are linked up and mutually adjusted. It follows that a general and complete definition of "symbol" must specify how motives are articulated, perceived and interrelated between subjects. (1989: 738)

Both the general account of secondary intersubjectivity given by Trevarthen and his specific descriptions and exemplifications are wonderfully rich and suggestive. Indeed, the basic image of person–person–object interaction has value in itself as a memorable symbol. It displays the learner, the teacher and the physical environment all taking a role in what we conventionally refer to as socialization. It reminds us that nature and culture are not distinct entities that we address separately. And it rightly represents learning as doing, and doing collectively. All this represents a valuable corrective to images of learning in which the individual being taught or socialized is the receiving vessel for separate inputs of sensory information from the world and verbal information from a teacher.[4]

Actual descriptions of person–person–object interaction reveal the child actively seeking opportunities to monitor how others act upon objects and to get involved in that activity. The child seeks to master the techniques and competences involved in that action and then to become involved herself in the interaction, in co-ordination or co-operation with the other. All, this, moreover is done for its own sake, for the pleasure of competence and mastery, as it were, not for extrinsic ends; for what is observed here is "only play" and not "genuine" instrumentally oriented action. Nor is there any sign in this activity that the skills and competences involved, although clearly they are internalized in a certain sense, pass beyond the discretion of the child so that their enactment or their use in a specific way or on a specific occasion becomes a moral imperative or a matter of moral obligation. On the contrary, the descriptions are full of instances of the deliberate misuse of skills, of innovation and experimentation, of playful opposition to the "teacher", of the accomplishment of a practice to an accompaniment of joking and laughter and its reproduction in a manner suggesting power, autonomy, distance and control.

In summary, what Trevarthen is describing, both here and elsewhere in his work, is the cognitive and cultural development of a child natively motivated and equipped for social interaction, interpersonal communication, and the development of shared knowledge and collective skills. Whether what is described is correctly described is, of course, an open question that cannot be resolved here. But it is worth noting that Trevarthen's individuals, with their essentially social human nature, are capable of enacting a social order in a way that neither ER individuals nor normatively committed individuals can. In Trevarthen's individual – it scarcely matters whether it is as scientific description or as memorable reification – lie incarnate the fundamentals of an interactionist social theory. The native endowments of Trevarthen's individual make possible her self-transformation, in a given context of interaction, into a *competent member*.

Child development on Trevarthen's account is a process of becoming a competent member, or a participant in a form of life. Harold Garfinkel's useful term and Ludwig Wittgenstein's earlier notion are not identical, but may be taken as near enough equivalent for present purposes. Garfinkel and Wittgenstein relate the individual to the social context in a way that is not just different from but quite transcends the conceptual frameworks of individualism and of normative functionalism. It scarcely makes sense to ask whether a competent member utilizes culture rationally or irrationally, egoistically or altruistically, because the very notions of altruism and irrationality lack grip in the contexts being considered: paradigm examples of altruistic or irrational activity stand in no clear and evident analogy to instances of cognitive and communicative activity. Similarly, the readiness of the individual to align her cognition with that of others and co-ordinate her activity with theirs will be misconstrued if it is described as conformity – whether conformity to norms or rules or instructions or routines. References to the innately co-operative orientation of the child do not imply that she is in any sense a latent assembly-line worker, waiting her placement in some ongoing system of complex co-ordinated activity. Rather, the child possesses competences that permit rapid co-ordination of cognition and co-operative interaction. In practising and perfecting these competences, the child is enthusiastically developing powers that lie under her own active control. In putting these powers to use in relations with others, the child is not subordinating herself to, but rather constituting, social relationships. Innate propensities are not the constraints that bind the child into a given social order; they are the resources that facilitate her participation in a form of life.

The child has become a competent member when she is able to participate as well as existing members in an ongoing form of life. She is then a part of a membership that finds itself in a kind of continuing agreement. At one level this is agreement in cognition, a very general form of agreement in understanding that is essential to agreement – or disagreement – in the more specific matter of opinion. But it is also agreement in practice, in ways of doing things, for without agreement of this kind we cannot say that people agree at the level of understanding: it is by taking note of agreement in practice that we attribute agreement in cognition.

Agreement in practice is achieved by human beings everywhere. All human beings exist in cultures or collectives identifiable precisely by the existence of such agreement and the order it implies. It must be emphasized, however, that where there is order of this kind there may remain any amount of disagreement, disputed opinion and even overt conflict. Indeed, in a context of agreement in practice, conflict may be the more intense as co-ordinated action puts power in the hands of factions and increases their ability to destroy. It is crucial not to romanticize the kind of social order characterized as agreement in practice – the kind of social order that everywhere exists. It is no paradigm of love and harmony, no moral ideal. Within it, all that is moral and all that is immoral have their being; it is the condition of good and evil, not a manifestation of either. Indeed, the need to emphasize this point is one reason that the discussion of knowledgeable interaction began in the previous chapter with the case of a Tudor execution.

4.2 Knowledge and authority

Let us consider now the possible significance of constructivism for macro social theory. Until recently it has been neglected in this context, which is odd, given that it derives from Durkheim, one of the greatest and most influential of social theorists. The neglect seems even odder when the importance of Durkheim's contributions to the sociology of knowledge and to social anthropology is noted, and the way that sociological, constructivist theories have been developed in both those contexts with some considerable success. Conceivably, over a long period when their cognitive authority has been suspect to say the least, and during much of which they none the less aspired to recognition as "social scientists", sociologists reacted adversely to a theory that permitted a degree of scepticism about knowledge and acknowledged its "invented" rather than just its "discovered" aspect. But, if this is so, the question remains why they should have seen a difficulty where Durkheim saw none, and indeed where natural scientists have seen none. For instrumentalist, pragmatist and fictionalist philosophies, all of which are closely analogous to constructivism, have never lacked adherents in the natural sciences, wherein it is sometimes held that scepticism is an essential component of a properly scientific approach. Nor has any better approach been available for those who have sought to understand why our accounts of the physical environment should differ from those of the ancestors, of alien cultures, and of professional experts in our midst – and why those accounts are themselves constantly being revised and reformulated. We need to accept Durkheim's edict that classifications of nature are "constructed by men" – which edict can of course be interpreted and developed in many different ways – if we are to understand this variability.[5]

Durkheim himself of course mainly considered variations of cosmology between rather than within societies. The problem in the present-day world is often slightly different owing to continued differentiation and what is now a very highly developed division of technical and intellectual labour. Knowledge and competence today within any industrial society are carried by many distinct bodies of experts and specialists, who put different constructions on experience and amongst whom conflict and controversy are endemic. In these conditions the problem of what to believe becomes increasingly transformed into a problem of which of the available competing sources of expertise to trust, and in which context.

Even here, however, in this familiar terrain of the modern sociologist of knowledge, the continuing importance of basic themes deriving from Durkheim is apparent.

"When the scientist has a very serious message to convey he faces a problem of disbelief. How to be credible, this perennial problem of religious creed, is now a worry for ecology. Roughly the same conditions that affect belief in a denominational god affect belief in any particular environment." Thus Mary Douglas (1970: 230), in a brilliant lecture on the problem of credibility, asks us to reflect on our own conceptions of the physical environment. Accounts of the environment are provided by recognized sources of knowledge, but which sources do we credit, and with respect to what? Douglas makes us see the generality of the problem: "We are far from being the first civilization to realize that our environment is at risk. Most tribal environments are held to be in danger in much the same way as ours . . . Always and everywhere it is human folly, hate and greed which put the human environment at risk" (1970: 230).

Initially stimulated perhaps by the great debates on impending environmental catastrophe that ran through the 1960s, Douglas uses a Durkheimian, constructivist conception of knowledge to develop conjectures about the different physical environments people regard themselves as inhabiting. She offers a comparative sociology of cosmologies and their credibility, which relates shared knowledge to the contingencies of the circumstances in which it is accepted, and its pragmatic utility to the active human beings who sustain it. As people use their classifications of nature, so they will modify them better to suit their needs and concerns. Because these concerns vary, so too will general conceptions of the environment, of the threats to it and dangers within it, and of the authorities who can be trusted to give reliable accounts of these things. One widespread pragmatic concern is to defend a way of living against behaviour perceived as a threat or a challenge to it. Often the physical environment is invoked for this purpose. That which is socially threatening is made out as physically threatening. Those who pose the threat are condemned for putting the whole environment in danger. This is why it is those allegedly guilty of "folly, hate and greed" who are so often seen as the instigators of disasters or sources of environmental pollution, and why the cosmos is constructed to allow the appropriate connections to be made. Thus, for example, Douglas would not find it difficult to understand the emergence of the various conflicting folk-theories of the origin of AIDS, and their different credibility in different social locations.

Douglas's approach is a completely general one. She addresses the credibility of all versions of the cosmos, including our own, indifferently, in the same framework, in accord with Cassandra's law that truth and belief are independent. Trust in scientific knowledge and the authority of scientists will vary from one social location to another, and is likely to be stronger at the centre than at the periphery of the main institutional systems, reflecting different pragmatic concerns in these locations (Douglas & Wildavsky 1982, Douglas 1992). And, within science itself, trust will be differentially accorded, with audiences again looking to those particular groups of specialists whose claims have the greatest pragmatic utility. The implications of this are important in the very highly differentiated context of modern science where institutionalized disagreement between different bodies of scientific expertise is ubiquitous, and frequently expressed in the context of practical decision-making. Dorothy Nelkin (1979) has studied a considerable number of technical controversies in rich detail and finds that in all cases controversy is marked by divided expertise and conflicting technical expert advice. Moreover, the effect of introducing scientific expertise into such controversies is actually to broaden and intensify them, not to resolve them, as opponents support those scientific authorities who suit their cause and the authorities themselves add their own technical differences of opinion to the existing issues in dispute.

What Douglas does not do is tell us which competing cosmologies to accept and with which authorities to place our trust. And perhaps this is as it should be; perhaps sociologists should be content to make known their conclusions on the basis of belief, and to leave their audiences to consider for themselves, taking sociological studies into account if they will, where to place their trust. Certainly, this avoids having to consider on what authority social theory can run the rule over other bodies of knowledge and decide which are fit for human consumption and which are not. There are, however, other conceptions of social theory, which lay less stress on disinterest and detachment and more on commitment, and nothing makes a constructivist account of knowledge intrinsically incompatible with them. Like any other account of knowledge, constructivism can be used normatively and as a weapon in the defence of particular perceptions and policies. Indeed, it has been ingeniously used in just this way by Ulrich Beck in his *Risk society* (1988).

To understand Beck's interest in theories of knowledge it is necessary to make brief mention of his general social theory. Beck is a macro theorist concerned with the general characteristics of present-day European (mainly German) society, and how it is likely to evolve. His point of departure is the familiar observation that the productive forces in industrial societies are continuing to grow at a formidable rate and have transformed the quality of life for most members of these societies. But Beck looks at this development from the point of view of a committed environmentalist. The productive forces, he says, have always produced private goods, to meet individual wants and needs, and public harms, in the form of environmental dangers and pollutions, as "side-effects" of their operation. Recently, however, the production of goods has so effectively satisfied needs that the whole "logic" of production has undergone a sea-change: it is now the "side-effects" that have become central to debates concerning the development of the productive process. This sea-change got under way in Germany some time in the 1970s and is likely to occur in other European countries in short order. It leads to the "risk society".

In the risk society, concern with risk replaces concern with need, although this by no means weakens the pressure for increased production. On the contrary, whereas human needs are limited, risks are liable to expand endlessly so that production generates its own motor at the level of demand and productive activity grows and markets itself precisely as a means of risk reduction. Moreover, the demand for risk reduction is effective demand, since risk, unlike poverty, affects rich and less rich alike, the powerful and the impotent indifferently; "poverty is hierarchic, smog is democratic" (1988: 36). Given the remarkable human capacity for remaining miserable even in the most unhelpful conditions, risk generates a society afflicted by fear instead of hunger, a culture dominated by anxiety rather than need. And the anxiety is intense and likely to become even more so; for the risks associated with current production are global, ubiquitous, ever-increasing threats to the survival of the planet, while the traditional institutions of industrial society – the family, the status order – are ever-weakening sources of personal protection and security, less and less able to intervene between the individual and the threatened and hence threatening environment. The risk society represents a transformation in perceptions so profound that it is bound eventually to lead to a transformation of institutions and far-reaching forms of social change.

Beck's contrast of our present "culture of anxiety" with what preceded it raises endless questions. Did not members even of the legendary "traditional society" also face intangible yet potentially catastrophic threats? Were there not rumours of spreading plague or marauding armies, and did not itinerant priests occasionally drop by to proclaim the end of the world? Fortunately, however, how far Beck's overall vision is valid does not matter here, where it is relevant only as a background that makes intelligible his treatment of knowledge and expertise. It is because Beck sees our current state through the eyes of a committed environmentalist that he is led to give theoretical prominence to the problem of knowledge and to take a constructivist point of view.[6]

Beck is concerned about the increasing globally consequential risks linked to nuclear power and chemical pollution. He believes that these pollutions already cause significant harm, and, worse, that just a small increase from their present incidences will suffice to bring on an ecological disaster. But he faces a problem of evidence here, a shortage of material signs and auguries. At the beginning of the Great War, Moltke, the German Chief of Staff, was confronted with one version after another of the triumph of his armies during the rapid advance into France. But Moltke trusted none of all these many and various verbal accounts. "Where are the bodies?" he is said to have asked. Significant military success, on any account, implied prisoners, in vast numbers; their absence told Moltke of the failure of the Schlieffen Plan. For Beck, there is this same problem of a lack of bodies, of enough deaths or pathologies plausibly attributable to poisons and pollutions, although Beck's problem, unlike Moltke's, is to convince not himself but his audience.

At the present time, Beck acknowledges, the major risks are invisible. They exist only at the level of knowledge, not as tangible referents of knowledge. We are aware of them largely because scientific expertise has identified them and attempted to estimate their future significance. If our future depends upon present judgements of the significance of risks, then it depends upon present evaluations of the natural sciences and their knowledge claims. Typically these evaluations are very positive, and this in turn finds expression in the way we speak of scientific evidence. Scientists and their specialized instruments, it may be said, have accumulated information about a variety of pollutions and dangers to the environment, information that offers a reliable account of how things stand at present and a reasonable basis from which to project future trends. But it must not be forgotten that some people distrust science: they are more likely to speak of biased estimates and fabrications, constructed to serve producer interests perhaps, or to save the bacon of hard-pressed politicians or senior bureaucrats. For it is a convention of our rhetoric to relate knowledge that we trust to a reality in correspondence with it, and knowledge-claims that we distrust to the machinations of their originators.

Where does Beck himself stand on the matter of the trustworthiness of the natural sciences? His position is an awkward one. On the one hand, he is intensely distrustful of science. It encompasses a range of conflicting views, and sells appropriate opinions to any willing purchaser. It abets the downplaying of risk by vested interests. It thrives on the invention of palliatives that merely perpetuate and intensify risks in the long term. In all these ways it is a potent weapon in the hands of those who would undermine the environmentalist challenge. On the other hand, Beck is dependent upon science to give standing to his own warnings of risk and would undermine his own environmentalist position were he to denounce science as "ideology". There would be no credible message for him to deliver without science and its authority: every serious threat currently faced by the environment has been given its initial visibility through scientific research. Characteristically, Beck is only too well aware of this predicament, and that it is faced by every environmentalist movement: "It is precisely the awareness of its dependence on the object of its protests that produces so much bitterness and irrationality in the anti-science attitude" (1988: 163).[7]

Thus, although most of Beck's specific references to risks treat them as authentic phenomena, and denials of their existence are dismissed as mistakes or else deceptions, his explicit account of knowledge is a constructivist one. The contrast of "science" and "ideology", formerly employed by radical critics of the social order, is avoided. Beck does not denounce scientific assessments of risk but neither does he treat them as in correspondence with reality. To acknowledge that the risks that are held to threaten the future of the risk society are "really there" would be to admit that the scientific accounts of these risks – the only basis for recognizing their existence – have a special standing. But to treat these same risks as fictions would deny Beck's own environmentalist account any standing at all. Beck wants to keep questions of risk open and contestable, to deny a monopoly to scientific expertise on the matter, to give a chance to the processed versions of the "scientific evidence", with their enhanced estimates of risk, that are offered by environmentalists. Hence his presentation of "scientific" and "environmentalist" versions of risk as alternative social constructions; of readily available epistemologies, constructivism meets his pragmatic needs particularly well.[8]

It is worth recalling, at this point, that there are many versions of constructivism, many ways of interpreting Durkheim's injunction to treat classifications of nature as "constructed by men". Beck's version is evident in his specific formulation of the relationship between risk and our knowledge of it: "because risks are risks in *knowledge*, perceptions of risks and risks are not different things, but one and the same" (1988: 55). This is an *idealist* form of constructivism, one that denies the existence of an independent external world. It does not, on the face of it, serve Beck's purposes particularly well: even if people were to continue to be alarmed by "risks" when the "risks" were equated with perceptions and their independent existence was denied, this would merely strengthen the position of the scientists and technical experts who are market leaders in the provision of perceptions of risk. Moreover, to take literally the equivalence of perception and actuality asserted by Beck suggests the possibility of some radically new approaches to improving the environment of which he would be unlikely to approve. If getting the lead out of drinking water is expensive, why not stick some valium in the water instead? If the educated middle classes are increasingly suffering from acute anxiety about ecological uncertainties, how about free psychotherapy for everybody entering higher education? The banal answer is that people are not referring to their own perceptions, or other people's, when they speak of risks and pollutions. They are trying to put a construction on the nature of external reality. This is why manipulation of subjective states is routinely (and rightly) rejected as irrelevant to problems of risk.

It is arguable that Beck's fear of realism as a doctrine that will unduly bolster expert authority is misconceived. Even in rampantly scientistic societies, the robust common-sense realism of everyday life continues to provide some degree of protection against the overblown pretensions of expertise, while at the same time allowing good use to be made of that same expertise. Those who would resist overweening expertise would do well to defend everyday realism, wherein on the one hand there is an external reality independent of our perceptions, and on the other hand there is talk about it, claims to know it as this or that. Such a realism leaves all verbal formulations, whatever their provenance, open to potential criticism as "inconsistent with experience", "not what you find when you look", etc. The sense of difference between talk and reality sustains endless possibilities for the criticism of knowledge, and allows the articulation of scepticism in relation to any body of expertise or set of knowledge claims (Barnes 1993). Provided only that no particular body of knowledge or knowledge-claims is taken as definitive of "the world itself" or "external reality", expertise may then routinely be called into question. Provided only that none of the socially constructed accounts of risks currently available is confused with the actual state of reality itself or presumed to be "in correspondence with it", both Beck and the scientists may have their due. Accounts of risk may compete. Awareness of the constructed character of all accounts, and of the difference between accounts and actual states of affairs in the world, will help to prevent any given account, however institutionally powerful, from turning into holy writ. In a nutshell, Beck's needs would have been better catered for by a realist version of constructivism – by Moltke constructivism let us say – than by the idealist version advocated in his own work.

4.3 Tradition

Social theorists are now paying increasing attention to knowledge and the social distribution of its credibility, if not always for the right reasons. It is sometimes said that we are living in an increasingly knowledge-based society, which is a profoundly misleading way of describing the proliferation of technical knowledge, the extraordinary division of mental labour and the ever-growing dependence on specialized expertise, all of which are undoubtedly in evidence. Be that as it may, social theorists are now aware that they can no longer afford to ignore problems of knowledge and credibility or to get by with cursory use of formulaic accounts of them, and it is likely that the relevant sociological literatures will eventually be taken properly into account in this context. There is also likely to be much more work that follows, for example, Douglas and Beck in recognizing the "invented" character of knowledge by use of some version of constructivism. And in due course the relative merits of the many different possible versions of constructivism will surely become a matter of central importance, just as it is already in the context of the sociology of knowledge.

It is not possible to make a properly detailed comparison of the different forms of constructivism here, or to offer an evaluation of their strengths and weaknesses. It is possible, however, to convey some sense of what most of them have in common, and a good way of doing this is to consider what they imply for an understanding of *tradition*. Let us treat tradition here simply as inherited knowledge.[9] And let us assume that knowledge is everywhere constituted into traditions and transmitted as such – a view neither distinctive to constructivism nor, any longer, at all controversial. We can now proceed to state what is interesting about the constructivist position, which is what it implies for the relationship between human beings and tradition. For all that human beings often appear as the recipients or even the receptacles of tradition, it is none the less they who have created (constructed, invented) it. How then can they be regarded as controlled by it or subservient to it? Is it not wholly implausible to imagine that the human beings who collectively construct a body of shared knowledge should then somehow switch out of active mode and subsequently operate in ways determined by what they have made? If constructivism is accepted, then the presumption must surely be that tradition is the *continuing* collective accomplishment of human beings, that it is lacking in any power of its own, and that it exists through the continually exercised powers of human beings themselves.

The thought that tradition does not carry us along but rather that we carry it along is perhaps most difficult to accept when tradition is conceived of as knowledge. Admittedly there are different bodies of knowledge, incarnate in different traditions, and perhaps there is a sense in which all are equally good, but surely, once we are oriented to one given body of knowledge, we must acknowledge its implications and be guided by them. In fact, however, received knowledge does not force implications on us in this way, by its own inherent power as it were. We have actually already been through the argument that establishes that it cannot do so. Recall the discussion of following norms in section 2.4, and recall how norms were identified in passing as items of knowledge. This earlier discussion highlighted the lack of power in a norm by thinking of its application as the extension of an analogy. The application of empirical knowledge generally can be understood in just that way.

Let us take the earlier arguments about norms (p. 53ff), and restate them as arguments about knowledge. The simpler the example, the better for this purpose, so consider our knowledge of dogs. To recognize the next dog as of a given kind it must be identified as relevantly analogous to previous cases or examples of that kind. Following the previous argument, first of all there is no logical or formal determination here. Secondly, there may none the less be a strong psychological inclination to recognize a given dog as definitely of one kind, to respond to a query on the matter without hesitation, as a matter of course. Thirdly, this psychological response may or may not be counted the correct response, depending on how it relates to the responses made by other members. Sometimes all the immediate individual responses in a collective will be in harmony and all will feel that they just know, somehow, what kind of dog that particular dog is. But at other times immediate responses will vary, and some will have to be discounted. Active intervention will be necessary to modify routines and automatic responses, at the individual psychological level, in order to keep tradition constituted and allow the routine implications of traditional knowledge to unfold at the collective level. It may be that minority deviance has to be overruled here, or that majority opinion defers to expertise and/or to power, or some other route to consensus may be negotiated. In any event, however consensus is established, and whether easily or with difficulty, the outcome will be a revisable judgement. It will be collectively decided that the dog is of a given kind, rather as a court may decide that an action is, say, an assault, and make a revisable judgement to that effect. Indeed, the example here can be fleshed out by recalling that, since 1991, courts in Britain have been deciding which dogs are and which are not pit-bull terriers. And some of the decisions on this life-or-death matter have gone to appeal, and occasionally have been reversed.

In summary, the applications of knowledge and the extensions of classifications are like the implications of norms in being open-ended and indeterminate beforehand. How knowledge will relate to the next case will be decided not by the knowledge "itself" but by the carriers of the tradition in which it is incarnate. In so far as an agreed application to the next case is made, it will be the collective accomplishment of those carriers.

These conclusions, which are of great generality and importance, amount to what is sometimes described as a *finitist* account of knowledge, culture and tradition. It is an account that emphasizes the nature of these things as flexible resources in the hands of their carriers, and it can be seen being put to work in this way in the constructivist literature of the sociology of knowledge and in ethnomethodology.[10] Finitism, of course, is far from being uncontroversial, and any extended evaluation of it would have to review a considerable critical literature. But many of the reservations relating to finitism in the social sciences derive not from technicalities so much as from its counterintuitive character and its strange "feel" on initial acquaintance.

More than anything else, this strangeness derives from the way that the routine and repeated activities of a collective are made problematic on the finitist account and in need of the active monitoring of the collective if they are to remain routine and repeated activities. Macro social theory has traditionally focused on the problems and difficulties of change, often against the presumed background of an altogether unproblematic status quo: to change is difficult, whereas to stay the same is effortless. Finitism, in contrast makes a problem of the very distinction between stability and change, and emphasizes the difficulties involved in going on in the same way. Because it is liable to condition responses to finitism, it is important to emphasize that this is not a mere philosophical conceit, but is rather a thoroughly practical point that has usefully informed a good deal of careful sociological work. This is strikingly illustrated by studies in the sociology of natural science, which have made the investigation of repetition and replication one of their central concerns. These studies suggest that what a collective is willing to regard as a repetition or replication is one of its most sociologically interesting features and that controversies between collectives often concern precisely what should be counted as a repetition of what. In work such as this, to take for granted the meaning of "going on in the same way", and to presume that cases of sameness and difference, tradition and innovation, routine and deviation are identifiable by their intrinsic characteristics, is to overlook precisely what sociologically are the most interesting and important features of collective interaction (Shapin 1994, Collins 1985, Shapin & Schaffer 1985).

A finitist account of "going on in the same way" may be most strikingly illustrated in the context of natural science because of the importance of the notion of replication in idealized accounts of scientific method, although examples are no less easy to find elsewhere. It is interesting to focus on the form of language used in such examples to account things or practices as "the same as" or "different from" each other. Everywhere, this proves to involve some version of the language of realism, of reality and appearances. Use of this language signifies whether "mere" appearances are to be accepted as reliable indications of "what is really there" or dismissed as erroneous or misleading. These alternatives are available in some form in all cultures, and to that extent the realist mode of speech is a cultural universal. Examples of its use are legion, both in everyday life and in the specialized context of natural science. In science, results may be counted as signs of what is really there, in the cloud chamber, or the sectioned tissue or the liquid in the test-tube, but they may also be discounted as artefactual or as attributable to instrument failure; in the latter case it will be said that the relevant experiment has failed, and, should it be a repeat experiment, that it is not really a replication of what has gone before.

The articulation of existing knowledge in a realist mode of speech makes its future use entirely open-ended, because the underlying "reality" referred to is invisible and inaccessible and cannot itself govern what is said about it. By employing a *realist strategy*, a body of knowledge may be kept in being as an all-embracing, irrefutable sense-making system, capable of making out any and all future events or observations as routine and unsurprising. Alternatively, a realist strategy may be used to question existing knowledge and weaken its authority by denying that it gets to grips with reality at all. The ubiquitous availability of realist strategies puts knowledge at the disposal of its users, as it were, and exemplifies their power over that which they use.

What is referred to here as the realist mode of speech has been studied and analyzed by Harold Garfinkel (1967) as "the documentary method of interpretation". Following the sociologist of knowledge Karl Mannheim (1952), Garfinkel characterizes documentary method as assuming the existence of "an identical homologous pattern underlying a vast variety of totally different realizations of meaning". The pattern "itself", however, is not directly accessible. Documentary method has to take "actual appearance as 'the document of', as 'pointing to', as 'standing on behalf of' a presupposed underlying pattern. Not only is the underlying pattern derived from its individual documentary evidences, [they] . . . in their turn are interpreted on the basis of 'what is known' about the underlying pattern. Each is used to elaborate the other" (Garfinkel 1967: 78).

Many insightful studies of the use of documentary method have been made by Garfinkel and other ethnomethodologists. Among the examples used by Garfinkel himself is his famous study of Agnes, a person seeking to live routinely as a female while in possession of a complete and fully developed set of male genitalia. For many years Agnes sought recognition for her own self-definition as "really a female" in the context of relationships with family, boyfriend, everyday acquaintances and the experts she was endeavouring to persuade to employ surgery to correct her anomalous anatomy. Agnes employed the realist mode of speech with skill and ingenuity to sustain a particular sex–gender status in unusually adverse circumstances, thereby highlighting the strategies in routine use to sustain such statuses in "normal" circumstances. All the sociologically interesting features of the use of knowledge can be identified in the context of the case study. The open-endedness of the future application of knowledge is exemplified by the alternative accounts proposed for Agnes's condition. Agnes described herself as "really a female" with a pathology, but she was painfully aware of an alternative method of accounting according to which she was "really a male" with a fantasy. The frequent uniformity in the routine, matter-of-course application of knowledge is evident in the initial general tendency to document her as a male, even though such a designation was not indefeasibly superior to her own. The tendency for majority and deviant designations to acquire the status of correct and incorrect respectively is symbolized by the fact that Agnes's male status had a privileged position expressed by her birth certificate and the sex indicated by the designation thereon. And the revisability of that initial judgement of Agnes's real and correct status is evidenced by the surgery eventually enacted upon Agnes's body and the rationalizations created to establish its legality and desirability.

Ethnomethodology and sociology of knowledge, and indeed social anthropology and other fields concerned with the detailed study of knowledge and culture, all point toward the same view of the nature of tradition. First of all, tradition is ubiquitous and essential. In all cultures and subcultures, knowledge is inherited from the ancestors, extended and modified in the course of life, and passed on to descendants. In all societies, learning is a matter of extending, adapting and at times pruning the inherited knowledge. The world is never apprehended directly: experience and tradition (nature and culture as is often said) acting together, symbiotically, inseparably, define the conditions in which perception and cognition proceed. But, notwithstanding this, tradition itself is unconstraining. Tradition is models, classifications, images, techniques, procedures, practices, all available for use in the future, to facilitate not to restrict what we do. In using such resources we take tradition forward; it doesn't take us forward. In so far as it stays the same, it is because we keep it as it is; in so far as it changes, we change it.

It is important to recognize the full significance of these last points. If tradition lacks power then it is not that it is reduced to an inert mass, as it were, that people are free to use or not use, change or leave unchanged.

The implication is a more profound one: that tradition lacks the power to persist, and hence to exist at all, of itself. The active intervention of people, *their power*, is necessary even to keep tradition in existence as "what it has always been" and to define the routine application of the knowledge incarnate in it. The work of Garfinkel is of especial value for the emphasis that it gives to this point, and for its exemplification of the way that routine itself continues only as a creative collective accomplishment. Garfinkel shows through examples how accounts involving the use of shared knowledge are themselves actively monitored, reflected upon and made the objects or referents of further accounts, as part of the routine business of everyday life; he notes that this "reflexivity" in accounting is an *essential* reflexivity (1967: 7).

The notion of tradition as constituted in use and lacking in inherent power is actually a very widely accepted one, both in sociology and more generally; but it is accepted and employed only in particular narrowly defined contexts. In considering artistic and literary traditions, for example, "tradition" is understood in this way, and sociological studies in these areas offer some of the best and theoretically most salient accounts of the evolution of traditions.[11] However, neither in sociology nor in everyday life is this conception of tradition the dominant one, and there is an ever-present tendency to sideline it or even to forget it altogether. In speaking of many of the familiar received components of social life – ideas, laws, norms, knowledge, and especially perhaps religious doctrines – the tendency is to empower tradition and regard it as a source of constraint.

To some extent, it may be that a misinterpretation of individual experience lies at the root of this: participation in a tradition can be experienced by particular individuals as highly constraining, even though the collective carrying the tradition is not at all constrained by it. When the "we" that is carrying a tradition forward seeks to move in very close concert, very strong social pressures may come into play between individual members, and what is collectively allowed to count as a valid continuation of tradition will indeed then be individually experienced as constraint. The collective will operate in the name of the tradition and collective powers will flow through communications that forcefully and uniformly indicate what the tradition "really implies". The power of human beings acting in this way may then be conceptualized as the power of tradition itself. Similarly, where dominant groups in a collective seek to move the collective as a whole one way, while other groups seek to go another, it may be that the conflict becomes formulated as one between "tradition" and "change", whichever way round, and again "tradition" becomes treated as empowered.

It would be extremely strange, however, if major trends in sociological theory derived from nothing more than a misinterpretation of the experience of specific individuals considered out of proper context. And the empowerment of tradition is a most important tendency in sociological thought. Indeed, such empowerment is extended to reified conceptions of any and all of the elements of tradition: ideas and ideology, norms, laws and legitimations, knowledge and doctrine, even "technology", may be perceived as inherently constraining in this way. Many important debates in sociology revolve around the question of whether or not empowerments of this kind are valid and such arguments occur in all the important traditions of social theory. Thus, not even Marx's own materialist analysis of "ideology" could prevent the subsequent empowerment of ideas in later Marxian theory, and their use as ways of explaining why people were not behaving as they "ought" to have been behaving. Perhaps there is a clue here to why tradition is so commonly presented as separate from people and possessed of power over them. It is a strategy that allows excuse for present actions in the guise of disempowerment and hope for future actions in the guise of re-empowerment. Consolations of this kind are not so readily available on a finitist view.

Coda: myth and reason

Having offered an analysis of tradition and its relationship to those who carry it, the discussion in this final section represents a major shift of emphasis. The role of myths and stereotypes of tradition in discursive social theory will now be considered, and the significance of such theory as myth will be touched upon. These are issues that lie to the side of the main flow of the argument, although they will be taken up again in the second coda, at the end of Part II of this book.

It is a truism that the historical backdrop to the growth of sociology in Europe was the perceived need to understand the transition from "traditional" to "industrial" society. This originally gave sociological theory an ambivalent position, partly belonging to but partly reacting against a more broadly based stream of thought concerned to understand and justify social change as "progress". As theory developed, however, it became more and more assimilated into that broadly based stream. To be sure, it remained at all times a source of critical perspectives on modern capitalist societies. But it none the less became increasingly suffused with progressive, evolutionary and teleological conceptions of history, and increasingly inclined to take for granted the special status of the present as the most "advanced" form of society, set at the very tip of time's arrow. The central role of Marxism in the discursive macro sociology of the post-war period, a role only seriously called into question quite recently, was just one manifestation of this.

The broad stream of thought of which Marxism is generally reckoned to constitute a part is often described as "Enlightenment thought" or "the project of the Enlightenment".[12] It is a source of widely diffused stereotypes of "tradition" and "traditional society". The original, unreconstructed orientation to tradition in Enlightenment thought has been nicely described by Jürgen Habermas:

> In the tradition of the Enlightenment, enlightened thinking has been understood as an opposition and counterforce to myth. As *opposition*, because it opposes the unforced force of the better argument to the authoritarian normativity of a tradition interlinked with the chain of the generations; as *counterforce*, because by insights gained individually and transformed into motives, it is supposed to break the spell of collective powers. Enlightenment contradicts myth and thereby escapes its violence. (Habermas 1987: 107)

Enlightenment thought originally contrasted belief crystallized in tradition, dependent on the overriding of reason by authority and collective pressure, with belief consistent with reason and able to sustain its credibility directly in the face of the rational scrutiny of a questioning individual. In its most uncompromising formulations it treated history as a progressive movement from the one basis of belief to the other. And it saw contemporary societies as themselves positioned along a continuum from "traditional" to "modern" that recapitulated history itself. In its most shamelessly teleological forms it treated the movement from tradition to reason as the consequence of "progress" itself, acting as a kind of force, immanent in history.

This particular kind of "enlightened" approach is of course long gone, and one has to look back many years to find examples of it. Tradition, it is now accepted, is everywhere. The received knowledge that constitutes it is used, and hence trusted, in "modern" societies as in others. And reason too is everywhere. That the basic cognitive skills that constitute "rationality" exist in even the simplest societies is now generally accepted, even if sometimes only with reserve: "Adult members of primitive tribal societies can acquire basically the same formal operations as the members of modern societies, even though the higher-level competences appear less frequently and more selectively in them" (Habermas 1984: 44–5).

The idea of progress as a swing from tradition to reason cannot be sustained: the old-fashioned "enlightened" approach must be discarded. But it is worth reflecting upon it for a moment before passing on. Suppose we ourselves were to take on its characteristic faith in the superiority of the present, and suppose with this attitude we were to look back, perhaps as far as the nineteenth century, picking out whatever were to strike us as its worst excesses. Probably we should point to a Whiggish history that ordered, interpreted and evaluated the past simply as a route to the present. There would be a sociology and psychology inclined to speak of irrationality, prejudice and credulity where we now might talk of difference. We should find examples of an atrocious anthropology that documented the unreason of "savages" blinkered by tradition, and made out their relationship with "civilized" colonial power as a fortunate one.[13] And it could be that we would be critical of orientations to modern science not based on due honour and simple respect but redolent of the way that the "savages" in the just-mentioned anthropology allegedly addressed their totem poles. All in all, an "enlightened" evaluation of this "enlightened" thought would probably condemn it as unreflective and prejudiced ethnocentrism.

Of course, the social sciences have abandoned this way of understanding the inferences and beliefs of other people in favour of far more careful, sympathetic and self-aware approaches. We should now want to ask whether even this worst of the older literature might not possibly have had some validity in its context. We would consider using interpretative and hermeneutic methods to reveal the "rationality" and "internal consistency" of even the most unpromising materials. We should now recognize how "enlightened" thinkers of the nineteenth century had to work on the basis of received classifications and received knowledge, and how widely accepted stereotypes of race, sex, religion and so forth would have been difficult for them immediately to transcend. Perhaps, too, we would have some sympathy for writers seeking to satisfy the enormous market demand for ethnocentric forms of "enlightened" thinking, a demand that they catered for with encyclopaedias, histories, natural histories and other works of learning, which sold on a considerable scale. Perhaps we should even acknowledge that these treatises compare favourably in many respects with the gobbets in which social theory and social thought are increasingly served up as "educational" fare today, gobbets that tend more and more to the written equivalent of the sound-bite.

Not even the most sympathetic understanding of this literature, however, is likely wholly to subdue the thought that overweening ethnocentrism generates appalling social theory, and that ethnocentric perspectives are in general problematic in the context of such theory. Yet all cultures are ethnocentric and differentially sensitive to their own immediate position and the problems specifically associated with it. Should, then, social theory frame its concerns to reflect those of the wider culture, and seek to refine and improve existing patterns of understanding, possibly at the cost of reinforcing their more suspect basic assumptions? Or should the task of theory be more radical, a matter of standing against the self-images of the age and seeking to emphasize precisely those important themes that are most often ignored or filtered out of everyday social thought?

Whatever the answer, it will be relevant in what is now a radically changed context. Old-fashioned "enlightened" thinking is behind us. No longer is it assumed that, where tradition is, there reason is not. Now the question concerns how these two ever-present entities are related. In current social theory, a reformulated Enlightenment dualism now contrasts traditions that restrict and traditions that encourage the operation of reason, and retains a sense of progress as movement from the former to the latter. And one of the ways in which this position is opposed is by a monism that understands all traditions indifferently as rational human beings using, developing and passing on their particular form of life. Central to the dualist approach has been the work of two critical-rationalist philosophers, Jürgen Habermas and Karl Popper. Popper's view of natural science as tradition disciplined, pruned and filtered by the critical questioning of rational, sceptical individuals, and his conviction that the value of science lies in its critical method and not in the stock of knowledge and competence it carries, in its reason as it were and not its tradition, have of course been immensely influential, particularly in the English-speaking world.[14] But the very closely related ideas of Habermas are even more apposite to the needs of the discussion here, since they remain widely used by social theorists and constitute an explicit defence of the continuing relevance of "the Enlightenment project".

In his *Theory of communicative action* (1984, 1987), Habermas expresses his dualist position through the contrast of "myth" and "science". Both are traditions carried by individually rational or logically competent human beings. Both are transmitted from generation to generation as received knowledge. Both are taken up by individuals because they are traditions and carry the authority of tradition. But Habermas contrasts the closed character of myth with the openness to criticism characteristic, in his view, of science as a tradition, and goes on to label the latter a "rational worldview" in a sense that the former is not. Habermas feels able to characterize worldviews themselves as rational or irrational in so far as they facilitate or prevent a critical orientation to action by those who accept them, which critical orientation represents a superior form of rationality, a more satisfactory expression of "reason".

Habermas's detailed treatment of "the mythical worldview" is in effect a catalogue of characteristics that stifle rational criticism. Myth is totalizing, in that it has a pre-ordained place for everything within a grand overall scheme that connects everything to everything else; it is concrete and shallow; it is undifferentiated and confused, at least by modern standards, in that it fails to distinguish between the natural, the social–cultural, and the individual; and it is reified, particularly because it fails to distinguish language from the referents of language and thereby to allow the former to be criticized by recourse to the latter:

> . . . in a mythical worldview, the burden of interpretation is removed from the individual member, as well as the chance for him to bring about an agreement open to criticism. To the extent that the world-view remains sociocentric in Piaget's sense, it does not permit differentiation between the world of existing states of affairs, valid norms and expressible subjective experiences. The linguistic worldview is reified as the world order and cannot be seen as an interpretative scheme open to criticism. (Habermas 1984: 71)

So much for "the mythical worldview". In contrast, Habermas then specifies what is required of a cultural tradition if it is to sustain a critical orientation amongst those who participate in it. Such a tradition must be "stripped of dogmatism" and allow reflective awareness of itself and revision of its elements in the light of criticism. And it must be differentiated. The objective, social and subjective worlds must be clearly distinguished and separately addressed in its knowledge and culture. Specialized cultural subsystems must exist as bases of permanent criticism, and the means for feedback between these differentiated subsystems and the mainstream tradition must exist. And, finally, instrumental, success-oriented activity must be differentiated from activity of other kinds, so that instrumental rationality can be given its most effective expression within its proper and appropriate domain (1984: 71–2).

Habermas's conditions for rational conduct correspond in detail to life today in the "advanced" societies. Even the differentiation of a sphere of wholly instrumentally oriented action, the kind of action denounced by Marx as lying at the core of the tragedy represented by alienated labour, becomes not merely tolerable in Habermas but necessary.[15] Marx's account of alienation is questioned, and Marx himself is criticized for failing to recognize the "*intrinsic* evolutionary *value*" that fully differentiated systems of purposive rational action possess (Habermas 1987: 339). There is no mention here of any need for meaningful and intrinsically satisfying work as part of the essential nature of a good society.[16] Indeed, throughout the entire account, Habermas's recognized standing as a penetrating critical analyst of capitalism is overshadowed by his efforts on its behalf. Even though he goes on to recognize that instrumental rationality is liable to get out of hand, and that certain forms of unfortunate reification are endemic under capitalism, his work still amounts to an unequivocal statement of the (rational) superiority of modern capitalist societies and their unique position at the end of a line of progressive change.

All this, however, is by way of digression. Central to the discussion here is not Habermas's questionable evaluation of modern capitalism but his conceptualization of tradition in modern and pre-modern societies. Habermas's contrast of closed myth-bearing traditions and open reason-sustaining ones precisely permits the old dichotomy between "traditional" and "modern" society to continue, little changed, under a different nomenclature, along with its crucial implication that present-day societies represent by and large the "highest" and "most evolved" forms.

Let us look at how tradition is conceptualized within this account. We are asked to think of a movement from traditions that constrain to traditions that permit. Constraining traditions include those that embody "the mythical worldview". In myth, "the concept of the world is dogmatically invested with a specific content that is withdrawn from rational discussion and thus from criticism" (1984: 51). Evidently myth is empowered; myth itself prevents its own contents being oriented to and put to use in particular ways. Certainly something prevents this. In cultures where the tradition is that of myth there is a "lack of reflexivity in worldviews that cannot be identified as worldviews, as cultural traditions. Mythical worldviews are not understood by members as interpretive systems that are attached to cultural traditions, constituted by internal interrelations of meaning, symbolically related to reality, and connected with validity claims – and thus exposed to criticism and open to revision" (1984: 52–3).

Within the Enlightenment project – and this is also the dominant common-sense view in "modern" societies – "tradition" has always been used to refer to constraint and limitation and to confer negative evaluations. Whereas the old view of reason replacing tradition has been abandoned, and the need to awaken from the "nightmare of all the dead generations" is no longer so strongly felt, tradition remains something to be resisted and kept in bounds, not to be cherished and appreciated. The sense of superiority always implicit in "enlightened" thinking remains linked with the supposed ability of the modern to deal successfully with tradition as adversary. And Habermas's analysis of the superior reflexivity of modern society has indeed become the most recent means of giving expression to this sense, and has been extensively employed for that purpose.

On the face of it, if the argument of this book is correct, then Habermas's argument is not. His reference to a "lack of reflexivity in worldviews" clashes with the claim that reflexivity is all the time necessary in the continuation of tradition, even to keep the tradition constituted and achieve a sense of its being stable and unchanging. There is a conflict between, for example, Garfinkel's analysis of the *essential* reflexivity of accounts and Habermas's references to the different amounts of that property present in different traditions. One "solution" that has been adopted here involves the reflexive reconstruction of Garfinkel. He is understood as the humble ethnographer of unusual cognitive convolutions in 1960s' California, the herald of a reflexivity that just happened along some time recently, the sensitive observer of a distinctively modern affliction. But this is grossly to underestimate Garfinkel.

Another possible solution here would be to recognize that the work of Garfinkel has a universal interest and applicability, and rather to suggest a reformulation of Habermas. Perhaps the reflexivity that is crucial for him is not "reflexivity in worldviews", but rather institutional reflexivity, in the sense of feedback interactions between differentiated institutions, or between the mainstream of culture and specialized cultural traditions (Habermas 1984: 71–2). But if this is the case then reflexivity must have a stabilizing more than a "critical" role: feedback interaction now becomes that which is necessary to keep the differentiated system stably constituted. Where a system differentiates, and yet remains one system, the parts must interact. This has been a familiar theme of sociological theory, at least since Durkheim.

Yet another way of dealing with the difficulty here has been proposed by Anthony Giddens (1990). Giddens follows Habermas in his dualism, his belief in the superior reflexivity of the modern, and his stereotypical understanding of tradition. Yet he acknowledges that there is a "sense in which reflexivity is a defining characteristic of all human action". He attempts to reconcile these things by claiming that: "in pre-modern civilisations reflexivity is still largely limited to the reinterpretation and clarification of tradition" (p. 37). In contrast, "What is characteristic of modernity is . . . the presumption of a wholesale reflexivity" (p. 39). "The reflexivity of modern social life consists in the fact that social practices are constantly examined and reformed in the light of incoming information about these very practices" (p. 38).

Why, though, should changed or "reformed" practice be evidence of "wholesale" reflexivity, and the continuation of tradition be evidence of "limited" reflexivity? Does not this confuse reflexivity and change? The possibility that thoroughgoing "wholesale" reflexivity might continually reconstitute the status quo of a "traditional" society is never considered here at all. The argument is systematically biased in a way that associates the highly valued process of "reflexivity" with the highly valued social state of "modernity".[17]

The argument, moreover, relies upon the Enlightenment stereotype of "traditional society" as static and relatively resistant to change. This stereotype, together with that of the closed "mythical worldview", needs to be called into question. It is perfectly possible to delve into historical and anthropological case studies without finding anything reminiscent of them, so it is reasonable to ask what the evidence for them is considered to be.[18] Certainly, Habermas recognizes the relevance of empirical studies here, but his work fails to provide what is needed. His discussion of anthropological debates in *The theory of communicative action* is too far removed from ethnographic materials to be illuminating. And his fascinating study of "the public sphere" (1989) is unfortunately almost entirely concerned with the history of "modern" societies. It is hard to know what examples to cite when considering his account of "the mythical worldview".

Should we perhaps consider the "mythical worldview" of classical Greece? Was Greek thought confused, reified and relatively undifferentiated, or was it marvellously innovative, penetrating, profound and self-aware? Perhaps the answer is that it was both. But Greece is often considered an anomaly, a fragment that has snapped off from the great tectonic plate of modernity and somehow slid back through time for a couple of millennia or so. It is probably against the rules to refer to the Greeks. Perhaps Christian theology would be a more appropriate focus. Was not this a paradigm of "traditional thought" in the "premodern" era? If it was, it is worth remembering that it can also be seen as a vast motley of heresies and innovations, an endless theatre of debate and conflict, a showcase of human cognitive skill and ingenuity. And if we are ready to ask whether orthodoxy over the ages has not simply been the heresy that happened to win at the time, this would nicely raise the question of whether "closure" should ever be attributed to "worldviews" or "traditions" rather than to the ferocity of other people.

Needless to say, none of this amounts to an argument. It is merely a pointer to the need for an argument, one that is linked in proper detail to historical or anthropological materials. Because there has been insufficient argument of this kind, "tradition" and "traditional society" exist in the literature of "enlightened" discursive social theory as no more than foils to what continue to be, in the last analysis, self-congratulatory accounts of "modernity". Perhaps nothing more is needed if what we want is to be glad we are alpha-reflexives, but it will not do if we seek an authentic understanding of our own past, and still less if we recognize that the past is all there is, the sole basis for reflection on past, present or future.

A society like our own rightly retains a sense of being notably different from those of recent history, and even perhaps of existing in a state of relatively rapid social change. One way of thinking of sociology and especially sociological theory is as a repository of ideas about the nature of this difference, and indeed its literature is full of theoretical descriptions of scientific and technological change, the growth of productive forces, industrialization, urbanization and increased organization. We have, too, stemming from Durkheim once more, accounts of continuing institutional differentiation and its consequences – including its cognitive consequences – as well as the sobering reflection, available also of course in Marx, that the powers, capabilities, dynamism, versatility and flexibility of differentiated societies and their systems of institutions are not at all the same as, and may indeed form an ironic contrast with, the corresponding properties of their constituent individuals. But sociological theory must be more than a mere repository of specialized ideas on difference. As part of what can still be glossed as its concern with the truth it needs to consider similarities, affinities, continuities, the extent to which social order and social life everywhere are variations on a theme, if it is to keep open the possibility of genuinely learning from ancestors, aliens and deviants as well as from experts. And it is even arguable that it should stress similarities and affinities, precisely as those valid relationships that are the most likely to be overlooked in common-sense thought.

It is, of course, important here to keep in mind the banal point that all societies tend to tell themselves stories of "tradition" and "history" as a part of their own self-understanding, and that such stories need to be understood in terms of their immediate utility and not the extent of their correspondence with past states of affairs. There is great variation in attitudes to and rationalizations of received knowledge and culture, even in tribal societies. Religious texts record accounts of tradition that vary from those that regard it as a repository of the divine to those that see it as the crucial obstacle to be overcome in gaining access thereto – whether through trance and spiritual ecstasy or through meditation, contemplation and the calm of reason. At this same level of narrative, "crises" in tradition, whether vaguely threatening, or immediate, or in the recent past, are among the most familiar of social constructions, as are accounts of the rediscovery of precious remnants of tradition, which often feature as part of the activity of their invention. Cycles of decay and renewal, deconstruction and reconstruction, defilement and sacralization, are typical of the course of development of a cultural tradition, and different accounts of the nature of "tradition itself" are to be expected as such cycles proceed. Considered from this kind of perspective, the myth of the Enlightenment is as old as the hills, even if, in the period of the Absolute Monarchies and since, it has been given a greatly expanded amount of work to do.

Part II

Social formations and social processes

The following chapters look at accounts of some of the social formations that have interested sociological theorists working at the macro level. They allow the illustration, evaluation and elaboration of the theoretical ideas developed in Part I, using materials that are, if not unproblematically empirical, then not wholly abstract and hypothetical either. Let it be clear that theoretical conjecture is no substitute for direct investigation, and that reliable knowledge of social formations is to be looked for in the work of those who study them, on the ground as it were. These chapters reflect a reluctance to accept that theoretical ideas in sociology have the right to float free of substantive materials. It may be, however, that they also point to the genuine utility of theory as a basis for the recognition of analogies and similarities between states of affairs that might otherwise be considered, to our loss, wholly distinct and separate.

5

Status groups

5.1 Status groups and economic action

A social group can be defined as a set of individuals within a larger collective who are generally categorized as different from others but the same as each other in some respect. Such a categorization may be based on a recognized physical characteristic or on evident features of behaviour or ability, or it may be applied to a disparate set of persons who have been selected for treatment in some special way and are distinctive only in that respect. Among such collectively recognized groups or categories of individuals there will be some whose members emphasize their own distinctiveness and claim a special standing for themselves on the basis of it, an entitlement to recognition and treatment as possessors of a specific social status. Members of a social group of this kind will typically act to maintain recognition of their status and the distinctive treatment associated with it. Max Weber, the seminal theorist in this context, defines such a *status group* as "a plurality of persons who, within a larger group, successfully claim . . . a special social esteem" (Weber 1968: 306).

A status group is a group that is particularly easy to identify and demarcate, since it is clearly defined by the collective itself, both linguistically and in terms of practical action. As such, it makes a suitable starting point for a theoretical discussion of social formations. Let us begin by asking about the social processes associated with the emergence of a status group. Why might a subsection of the membership of an existing collective seek to constitute itself as a status group? No doubt there may be many reasons, but it is clear empirically that economic considerations are very often the stimuli for such a development. "For all practical purposes, stratification by status goes hand in hand with a monopolization of ideal or material goods or opportunities" (Weber 1968: 935).

The simple structure of the status group, which in effect divides the collective into insiders and outsiders, members and non-members, facilitates processes of monopolization and exclusion. Members may seek to enrich themselves not by an increase of production but by a concentration and confinement of the existing product into fewer hands. If the group can confine enjoyment of specific goods or opportunities to insiders and deny them to outsiders, it will advantage its members at the expense of others. Profit will be achieved not from any productive action but from the (notional) redistribution of goods across the group boundary. And, because the profit is achieved entirely through "redistribution", the boundary itself may be arbitrary in its basis. Weber nicely encapsulates these points in what amounts to an origin myth for a status group:

Usually one group of competitors takes some externally identifiable characteristic of another group of (actual or potential) competitors – race, language, religion, local or social origin, descent, residence, etc. – as a pretext for attempting their exclusion. It does not matter which characteristic is chosen in the individual case: whatever suggests itself most easily is seized upon . . . In spite of their continued competition against one another, the jointly acting competitors now form an "interest group" towards outsiders; there is a growing tendency to set up some kind of association with rational regulations; if the monopolistic interests persist, the time comes when the competitors, or another group whom they can influence (for example, a political community), establish a legal order that limits competition through formal monopolies; from then on, certain persons are available as "organs" to protect the monopolistic practices, if need be, with force. (Weber 1968: 341–2)

This is a passage that not only conveys the theoretical simplicity of the monopolization process, but also indicates something of its very great practical significance. And Weber further reinforces this last point with an extended survey of historical examples of the monopolization of economic opportunities: guilds and occupational associations of all kinds are cited and the practice of reserving offices to specific estates; slavery is treated as an exclusionary device; marriage rules and conventions are identified as means of monopolizing women as property; even property itself is seen as the outcome of an initial act of collective appropriation of land and resources and an associated exclusion of outsiders from the benefits of their use. Indeed Weber's overall account of the history of economic activity and organization until the advent of market capitalism reads very much as an account of a long series of monopolizations and exclusions by status groups.

Nor does the importance of exclusion and monopoly diminish as we move into the context of modern industrial market societies.[1] Weber's analysis continues to be crucial to our self-understanding today, as Randall Collins in particular has shown in his invaluable study of *Weberian sociological theory* (1986). Collins is not content merely to show that exclusivity based on factors such as race, ethnicity, language, religion, descent and so forth still exists, and that it constitutes a source of potential particularistic divisiveness that should not be underestimated. He presses the more controversial claim that mundane economic activity in modern societies remains ordered as an array of monopolies, partial monopolies and efforts to monopolize. Workers in organizations seek to monopolize access to senior posts therein, and to gain privileged access to new and junior posts for their dependants or allies. So successful are exclusionary practices of the latter kind that recruitment into US industrial organizations has been found to proceed more frequently on the basis of who knows whom than on strictly meritocratic lines (Granovetter 1974, 1985). High up in these same organizations, officials and administrators engage in the games of bureaucratic politics. Besides the traditional game of empire-building, they seek to sustain a range of cushy-number posts for their exclusive occupancy, a "sinecure sector" in which the easy life may be enjoyed by a fortunate circle of eligibles. And more generally, throughout the economy as a whole, an entrenched system of *credentialism* operates, wherein paper certificates serve to restrict access to privileged positions rather than to guarantee appropriate training and technical competence as they purport to do. Credentialism is a highly flexible system of monopolization based on adjustable criteria of exclusion that create forms of "pseudo-ethnicity" (Collins 1979).

What is being described here is not the intrusion of anomalies into a labour market properly described by the standard individualistic economic theory. It is not that the free flow of labour, normally a stream of independent individual units, is occasionally restricted by a certain lumpiness. Rather, lumpiness is the normal condition of labour: monopolization processes are endemic to economic activity. "Status groups should be conceived of not as non-economic phenomena but as an example of the kind of process that is central to the economy. . . . Status-group organization . . . is the natural form in which economic interests can act socially" (Collins 1986: 129). This is a complete theoretical reformulation of the nature of a modern economy, a sociological account systematically different from the accepted general theory of economics.

Indeed this is just the beginning of Collins' challenge to standard economic theory. Having documented monopolistic practices and the presence of status groups in the context of labour, he goes on to identify the same phenomena amongst capitalists and entrepreneurs. And he treats the existence of these phenomena, their normality and ubiquity, as the solution to what has long been recognized as a fundamental difficulty for traditional economic theory. Where does profit come from? In a stable system of circulating goods and services it is hard to see from where it can be drawn. Adam Smith was clear that any genuine profit that did exist in such a system would attract in competition until it was eliminated: in the long run, profit would be zero and everyone would get from exchange the equivalent of what they put in. Karl Marx accepted Smith's argument and invented his ingenious labour theory of value to account for profit as the result not of fair exchange but of exploitation; even so Marx believed that, as labour was replaced by machinery, so that there was relatively less labour to exploit, the rate of profit would fall. Thus, rightly or wrongly, Smith and Marx agreed that profit would tend in the long term to zero under competitive capitalism.

There need be no problem, however, if, as Collins believes, capitalist producers are not genuinely competitive but rather organized as a series of monopolies, because monopoly profit is then available as a normal feature of the operation of the system. Collins invokes a series of authors and arguments to substantiate this version of capitalism, beginning with the economist Joseph Schumpeter (Schumpeter 1911). Schumpeter accepts the argument that there is no source of profit in a stable system of production and exchange with free competition. Profit exists in actuality, he says, only because the system is never stable. Entrepreneurs are constantly reconstituting the productive forces through adaptation, recombination and innovation, and in the last analysis it is from this innovation that profit flows. Were innovation to cease and the system to stabilize, profit would disappear; hence the strong systemic incentive to innovation and change characteristic of capitalist productive systems. But why is genuine profit associated with innovation? Because, for a time, the innovator has the market to herself. Until the competition catches up she is a monopolist and enjoys monopoly profits. While the competition is catching up the profits can be invested in further innovation, preparing the ground for another burst of monopoly profit. Should this profit not suffice to keep the cycle going, a helpful state power willing to legislate patent protection will be useful to lengthen the period of monopoly.

Clearly, if Schumpeter's basic argument is accepted it can readily be extended and developed. Innovation in the normal sense is by no means the only way of securing a temporary monopoly. Careful product advertising to establish a brand-name creates an effective monopoly – given a state willing to assist with copyright and trademark legislation. Thus, Guinness would probably retain its market share and its value even if a rival were to poach its chief taster and blender; and Kit-Kat did retain market share and value (evident in its purchase for close to £1 billion sterling) even when the competition had found out how to make chocolate wafer biscuits. Another, related, strategy to avoid competition is that of subtle product differentiation: a firm can always arrange to be the sole producer of precisely that particular product, the only trainer with that spongy sole, the only sunglasses with that particular shape, whereupon monopoly profit may ensue. Collins cites the work of Harrison White (1981) as evidence that "niche marketing" of this kind is characteristic of US suppliers of consumer goods, and that in consequence they are interested in monitoring the activities of their fellow producers to avoid overlap rather than the preferences of consumers.

It is beyond the scope of a theoretical discussion to evaluate how far Collins' vision of modern economies is empirically correct, but we should consider what follows if it is. Let us suppose that economic life is indeed predominantly constituted of competing status groups seeking to appropriate goods and opportunities for their exclusive use. What is the theoretical significance of this? Is the message that the individual benefits of exclusionary forms of strategic behaviour have been overlooked in analyses of modern economies? Has attention focused too much on processes of wealth production and too little on actions designed to maximize shares in consumption? Has the investigation of economic activity been unduly influenced by moral and evaluative notions of fair and free competition when it should have been more involved in extended calculations of the individual costs and benefits of exclusionary action against others. Might this perhaps have afforded a better picture not just of, say, the Japanese and Italian economies, but of the economies of industrial societies generally?

Certainly, there is value in calculating the costs and benefits of exclusionary strategies. To exclude takes work; it is necessary to take organized action to overcome resistance. And the more powerful are those who are excluded, the more work is required to exclude them. Moreover, to exclude is to forgo opportunities: a group could be producing instead of excluding, and could be profitably and productively allied to the excluded group instead of having to expend resources upon controlling it. And again, the more powerful the excluded group the more is forgone by refusing co-operation with it. The creation and maintenance of a status group will benefit its members only when the returns of exclusion and monopolization exceed the costs of practising exclusion and the opportunity costs of forgoing alternative productive and co-operative activities.

Should we infer then that status groups will tend to arise only in certain circumstances, and that individuals will participate in the creation of such groups only when it is in their individual interests to do so? Might we conclude that exclusionary groups will proliferate when opportunities for increased production are exhausted, and that it will be the weak and powerless who are predominantly excluded, on grounds of cost? The answer is that, although these last conclusions may possibly be correct, the inferences by which they are arrived at are fallacious. Rational self-interest will not lead an independent individual to help to implement an exclusionary strategy, or even to sustain the group boundary that is the necessary prerequisite of any such strategy. It needs to be emphasized as a matter of fundamental theoretical importance that the exclusionary strategies of status groups, and indeed the very existence of such groups, whether or not they are involved in strategies of exclusionary closure, are unintelligible on the basis of the standard assumptions of individualism.

Exclusionary and monopolistic strategies may indeed yield considerable gains for the members of a status group, gains that greatly exceed any costs incurred in implementing the strategies themselves. The strategies may be collectively expedient. But the overall gains and overall costs that may imply a profit for the group are not the gains and costs that will feature in the calculations of group members if they are ER individuals. The standard problem of collective action arises in this context. The gains of exclusion accrue to members simply by virtue of membership, by virtue of their being appropriately coloured or sexed or anointed or qualified or whatever. They are collective goods. But the costs of exclusion are for the most part individually paid. Specific individuals must refuse outsiders employment even though they are short of labour, lose opportunities for trade, reject attractive offers of dowry, deny themselves access to valuable skill and wisdom, suffer hostility and specific acts of retaliation from slighted outsiders. ER individuals in these circumstances, aware that they will not be denied the benefits of their status however they act, will leave others to pay the costs of sustaining the flow of those benefits. They will fail to act to support their monopoly privileges. They will fail to act to sustain the status to which those privileges attach. Everyone will free-ride on the collective action of others. Thus, there will be no collective action, no exclusion, no group boundary, no group.[2]

In his seminal discussions of status groups, Weber himself strongly hints at their incompatibility with individualism without ever quite formulating the general point explicitly. He frequently contrasts the "irrationality" associated with status with the "rationality of the market", and sees the former as a frequent source of distortion and disruption in the latter. And, more significantly, he recognizes that monopolies must be sustained by "joint action" and that monopolized resources remain monopolized only so long as they remain under the control of the group and not the individual. Once an individual obtains freedom in the disposal of "her" portion of a monopolized resource, she is able to sell it on the market and erode the monopoly. Indeed, Weber considers this to be a process of great historical importance, not least in the origin of the private property whose exchange constitutes a market:

> If the appropriated monopolistic opportunities are released for exchange outside the group, thus becoming completely "free" property, the old monopolistic association is doomed. Its remnants are the appropriated powers of disposition which appear on the market as "acquired rights" of individuals. For all property in natural resources developed historically out of the gradual appropriation of the monopolistic shares of group members. (Weber 1968: 343)

Thus Weber's account of status groups, both in its initial formulation and yet more clearly when its implications are more systematically teased out, is formally incompatible with individualistic forms of social theory. According to the standard individualist approach, status groups should not exist. That they exist is a problem for the theory. That they are ubiquitous is very close to being a decisive refutation of the theory. Individualists sometimes recognize collective action as a minor aberration, indicative of the existence of small amounts of irrationality and/or altruism, but as no real challenge to the hegemony of their basic conception of society (Hardin 1982). Were they to recognize the true incidence and importance of collective action – that it is invariably involved in the instrumental activities of status groups, which groups are the ubiquitous vehicles for the furthering of economic interests – they would surely acknowledge that what we have here is no aberration. What we do have is a major anomaly for individualism, and a powerful argument for preferring any alternative theory that can account for the collective economic action at issue.

5.2 Collective action by status groups

Weber's account of status groups is no easier to assimilate to a normative functionalist perspective than it is to reconcile with individualism. Functionalists often take status groups as given features of "the social system" and take their existence for granted as part of a "functioning status quo" that needs no particular explanation. It is presumed that the status group plays an important part in a larger system and that the actions that sustain it are enacted as a consequence of an internalized commitment to social norms. But, although the monopolistic activities of status groups are incompatible with individual rationality, they remain clearly oriented to economic gain, and it is distinctly odd to attribute them to a non-rational commitment to norms rather than to an awareness that they are, when collectively produced, individually beneficial. Indeed, these actions cut right across the standard contrast between rational, expedient, calculative, instrumental, profane, "economic" actions and the non-rational, intrinsically valuable, moral, sacred kinds of actions commonly held to need "sociological" explanation. In this regard, they are actions of the utmost theoretical interest and importance.[3]

It is clear that the monopolistic activities of status groups are calculated to achieve particular objectives, and continue to be performed only so long as a probability of achieving these objectives persists. Members are constantly at work sustaining exclusivity, monopoly, privilege and enhanced esteem, and constantly monitor what they are doing in relation to those ends. Collective action is liable to be adjusted or even abandoned to the extent that it is reckoned expedient to do so. Thus, in the context of the economy, status groups appear as the temporary crystallized products of an ongoing stream of goal-oriented activity. The particular status groups come and go; the monopolization process itself continues, forever seeking out opportunities.

> This process [of monopolization] is dynamic, carried along by struggle. . . . Weber's picture seems congruent with Schumpeter's emphasis on both sides of the monopolization process: both its ubiquity (at Schumpeter's innovation stage) and its transitoriness (as the competition for money and its pressure on prices throughout the economy forces monopolists who are no longer growing to sell their holdings). (Collins 1986: 128–9)

In a nutshell, the collective action of status groups is shown unequivocally by Weber, Schumpeter and Collins to have the character of calculative action. Perhaps we should characterize it as collectively calculated action. Be that as it may, such action is unintelligible as the consequence of the operation of internalized norms.

We are left with interactionism as our third theoretical resource. From this perspective, collective action is the result of shared conceptions of the collective good emerging and being mutually sanctioned in the course of interaction (see Ch. 3). Ongoing symbolic communication, of a kind normal and natural to us as human beings, provides a context in which we collectively think and encourage the collective good; given our susceptibility to such encouragement – to honour, praise, approval, esteem, and of course their opposites – it is liable to engender the enactment of that good.

What are the conditions for successful collective action implied by this account? First of all, above all else, there must be interaction, which means that the collective must be a *network*, or at least have networky characteristics; a corollary of this is that the collective must share language and culture so that interaction in the fullest sense is possible, interaction that exchanges information and mutual evaluations. And, secondly, the interaction in the collective must not be wholly bound up

with and fixed upon immediate instrumental necessities and the requirements of self-interest. There must be sufficient freedom and variability
in interaction for the collective good to be imagined, thought upon,
debated, agreed and enjoined; collective instrumental action will emerge
only if there is a context or a dimension of interaction that is not primarily instrumental at all.

What now of collective action in the particular context of status
groups? What has to be remembered here is that status group members
are also members of a wider collective and, in seeking to agree and enjoin their distinctive collective good, may well be agreeing and enjoining
a bad for outsiders. This implies an amendment to the two conditions set
out above. What is now required is a *separate* interaction network, with
the corollary of a *distinctive* shared form of culture, including possibly a
separate language or dialect. In particular, the context of communicative
interaction in which the collective good is thought into being must be
separate and distinct, inaccessible to non-members and the conflicting,
or at least confusing, conceptions of appropriate collective action they
would proffer. Moreover, because members may leave a status group
for the larger collective of which they are also a part, there must be
inducements for their remaining in the distinctive interaction context.
There must be significant exit costs, or else members must find participation in the distinctive context of interaction intrinsically rewarding, a
pleasure in itself as it were. Finally, because the collective good is sanctioned by honouring and shaming and similar processes, and because
outsiders may have quite different conceptions of that good from insiders, it is often necessary to reject the good opinion of outsiders as a
legitimate source of honour. A special sense of honour is required, associated with the good opinion of members only. Where these conditions
appertain, a status group might be expected to be able to act collectively.
But collective action is necessary for such a group to persist and hence to
exist. The above, therefore, stand as postulated *essential* characteristics
of a status group, essential conditions of its existence according to an
interactionist analysis.

As it happens, these characteristics are very close indeed to those identified by Max Weber when he turns from the economic role of status
groups to a discussion of their general characteristics (Weber 1968:
932–8). When Weber identifies a distinctive lifestyle, restricted social
intercourse with outsiders, and a sense of their own special honour as the
most noteworthy features of status groups, he is precisely identifying

groups with the capacity to act for their own specific collective good. Weber's account of what is manifest in status groups corresponds with an interactionist analysis of what is essential to them. In discussing the nature of status groups as empirical phenomena, Weber, perhaps inadvertently, provides both a solution to the problem of collective action they present and powerful support for an interactionist theory of their operation.

According to Weber, status groups must possess a common and distinctive style of life. This entails a shared language as the basis for communicative interaction, and often a distinctive language or variant of language (Latin, French amongst German and Russian nobilities, "high" Arabic, etc.) which in itself tends to confine areas of interaction to group members. Moreover, particular attention is paid to the non-instrumental aspects of lifestyle. Economic considerations may contribute to the way a group lives: those monopolizing an occupation, for example, may find much in how they act being common and distinctive simply by virtue of what they need to do. But the codes of status groups themselves give more attention to other matters: for example, to religion and ritual or, what is perhaps the same thing, to clubs and sport. And they may attach great importance to the arbitrary and non-instrumental dimensions of dress and diet. Indeed, concern with these matters may be extreme, as is evident in the strict sumptuary laws that such groups have often sought to impose, or in the complex dietary regulations of caste societies. Here is the expected concern of the status group to sustain a shared form of culture and a distinctive form.

That a distinctive lifestyle is essential to a status group does not mean that participation in it cannot be a source of positive pleasure and satisfaction. On the contrary, if Durkheim is correct to claim that we are drawn to those we resemble and "love the company of those who feel and think as we do" (Durkheim [1893] 1964: 102), then the status group member, constituted in feeling and thought by participation in the distinctive lifestyle, becomes peculiarly dependent upon social intercourse with fellow members and hence upon their acceptance and recognition. Withdrawal from group interaction thus automatically entails high exit costs.

Sociologists often treat the lifestyles of status groups as distinctive patterns of *consumption* and regard such groups as components of consumption-based systems of social stratification. This is perfectly legitimate, and of course it was recommended by Weber himself. But, if the present arguments are correct, any analysis of status groups that confines itself to this framework will be narrow and impoverished. In terms of theoretical significance, distinctiveness of lifestyle must be primary, and extent of consumption secondary. A distinctive lifestyle is not an accidental consequence of how members are able to live, given their position in a hierarchy of consumption privileges. It is nearer the mark to think of a collective need for exclusivity and distinctiveness that has to be met through consumption. Where groups are unable or unwilling to use coercion or legal strategies, their only means of ensuring that their lifestyle cannot be emulated may be to make such emulation beyond the means of outsiders.

A second feature of status groups, according to Weber, is the restrictions they place upon social intercourse with outsiders. Members may be required to live in proximity to other members and distant from outsiders; to marry within the group and to marry off any progeny under their control similarly within the group; to spend their leisure time in the company of the group. All of this may be read as an extension of the basic emphasis on the distinctive lifestyle essential to the group: the restrictions increase the extent of interaction within the group, and minimize its extent and significance where outsiders are concerned. Again it is interesting how much stress Weber lays upon non-economic interaction in his discussion. Indeed, "social intercourse" is explicitly and uncompromisingly defined as intercourse of no instrumental significance: "intercourse which is not subservient to economic or any other purposes" (Weber 1968: 932).

Finally, Weber mentions the "special honour" of the status group, which is both claimed by members as a general entitlement and mutually accorded in their interactions. If honouring and dishonouring are what engender collective action generally, then accord or denial of special honour will engender action specifically for the collective good of the status group. Such honour is the honour of membership itself, and its allocation lies in the hands of those who determine membership – members themselves. An individual attuned to such special honour and moved to collective action thereby is responding only to the messages of fellow members, and hence only to a clear and consistent message enjoining the good of the group. The special honour of the group serves as a currency of symbolic reward distributed among the membership and inalienable from them: action related to such honour is autonomous group-oriented action, decoupled from the influence of outsiders. The effectiveness, potency, sensitivity and potential for elaboration of systems of within-group control based on special honour in this way are evident empirically in the operation of groups as diverse as military officers and professional natural scientists, where the former may serve as a paradigm of strong control and the latter as one of its complexity and sophistication. In both cases, the ability of the membership to withdraw recognition from recalcitrant individuals and to nullify their special honour, either through physical expulsion from the group setting or by symbolic degradation, is the final sanction of the collective good, and, as the evidence clearly indicates, a more than adequate one.[4]

Max Weber is by no stretch of the imagination an interactionist social theorist, yet his work on status groups deserves recognition as an important contribution to that theoretical perspective. Weber regards status groups predominantly as monopolizing and excluding groups oriented to economic and instrumental objectives. Yet his description of the groups concentrates on their constitution as interacting networks and their concern with apparently "non-economic" activities. Whether because of his extensive study of historical materials, or otherwise, Weber is aware that the instrumental dimension of action is secondary in so far as the explanation of the operation of status groups is concerned. This awareness is most vividly apparent in his assertion of the importance of restricted social intercourse, which, as we have just seen, is defined as "intercourse which is not subservient to economic or any other purposes". From an interactionist perspective, the crucial importance of a social intercourse not immediately bound to extrinsic instrumental considerations is that it can be varied and modulated freely for other ends. As such it can serve as the context in which the collective good is conceived, agreed and enjoined. And the restriction of that context to members only ensures that precisely the collective good of members will be the good enjoined.

In the activity of the status group, that which is subservient to no purpose is at the same time the most purposeful activity, and that which is most tenuously connected to the pressures of expediency is actually the most expedient of all. It is because it is a network of interaction that a status group has a potential for collective instrumentally oriented action. The non-instrumental dimension is prior to the instrumental.

In this way an interactionist approach can account for the existence and operation of status groups, and thereby show how "economic interests can act socially". But before passing on we should take note of what the account implies about "economic interests" and their basis. First, we must clarify what interests are. It is confusing in this context to equate

interests with the wants or desires of isolated individuals.[5] They are better thought of as routes and pathways that lead to whatever fulfils wants.
A state of affairs, or a change in an existing state of affairs, is in the
interests of an individual if it facilitates the fulfilment of her wants or
desires. Great numbers of individuals with diverse and varied wants may
all see the same states of affairs as conducive to satisfying them and in
that sense have common interests. This of course is a familiar experience
in societies in which the institution of money is pervasive and access to
a source of monetary reward is access to all the diverse and varied want-
fulfilling goods and services that money can buy.

Members of a status group act to defend shared interests in exclusivity
and monopolization. They share these interests because monopoly profits are the route to the fulfilment of all the diverse individual wants and
desires of the members of the group. But these interests did not exist
prior to the existence of the status group itself. Prior to the emergence of
the group there would have been so many individuals with innumerable
possibilities for association and group creation, each conceivably profitable, each a potential source of monopoly profit if actually implemented.
Even in a very small collective (say of 49 individual members) there are
an enormous number of ways for members to combine in small numbers
(6, for example), to define a subgroup, co-ordinate and organize, and
thereby engender the power to exclude others and monopolize resources.
Where a project or possible course of action benefits an individual, that
individual may be said to have an interest in it, but in an unorganized
collective there are thousands of possible projects that may be in the
interests of an individual, namely all the different possible ways of
organizing with and against fellow individuals. Indeed, it is scarcely
worth referring to the interests of such individuals. Only as groups and
group boundaries crystallize will the shared interests of individuals as
members become visible and defined, and as group organization in the
collective proceeds and changes so the interests of any given group
therein will change. Yet often in the social sciences we assume that it is
the given, pre-existing interests of individuals that explain how they
come together, organize and act.

Status group interests become defined as a group boundary comes into
being. Formally speaking, any boundary is as "good" as any other, as
Weber takes pains to emphasize. Whichever set of individuals it is that
comes together, organizes and engenders the power to exclude non-members, it creates the opportunity for monopoly profits. In practice, how-

ever, monopolizing status groups emerge from individuals who are already together, whether interacting in a distinct context of social intercourse or in a condition easily transformed in that direction. It is not that independent individuals have prior interests that induce them to combine in particular ways and act together. Rather it is that individuals living and interacting together are able, on the basis of their knowledge of their situation, to evoke conceptions of shared interests and to enjoin action to further them. What comes first, as it were, is being together, proximity, social relationships, social intercourse, ready opportunity to intensify and organize interaction. Then comes shared interest; and then comes action.

Thus, the Weberian analysis implies a general scheme for the explanation of collective action in which it is interaction patterns and not interests that take priority.

$$
\begin{array}{ccccc}
\text{organized} \\
\text{interaction}
\end{array}
\rightarrow
\begin{array}{c}
\text{shared} \\
\text{interests} \\
\text{formulated}
\end{array}
\rightarrow
\begin{array}{c}
\text{collective} \\
\text{action} \\
\text{enjoined}
\end{array}
\rightarrow
\quad \text{enactment}
$$

Only as a network of interaction begins to be established and a membership defined do agreed formulations of shared interests begin to emerge out of a great diversity of particular conceptions, some compatible, some conflicting. Only when there is a network can members review available opportunities for action in a given physical and social environment, formulate those beneficial to the members as a whole, and enjoin collective action in pursuit of them.

5.3 Status groups in context

The discussion so far has concentrated wholly upon the internal operation of status groups, where there was a point of crucial theoretical importance to be made. But how effective such groups actually are in their monopolistic activities can be understood only by reference to context, and here too theoretical problems are encountered, which, if less profound, are none the less far from devoid of interest.[6] Given that a status group is generally involved in the exclusion of outsiders from goods and opportunities, external opposition to it can be assumed to be normal, even if not inevitable. Hence the combating of such opposition will also be normal. Which strategies are used here will depend upon circumstances. Faced with power comparable to or superior to its own, a status group may well modify its exclusionary practices and extend access to its privileges in order to placate hostility and buy alliance and co-operation. Faced with relative weakness, the group may prefer to confront opposition, or to respond with nothing more than an offering of bland legitimations. Thus, we might expect to find monopolizing status groups servicing powers high in a social hierarchy, and exploiting groups situated lower down. And widespread use of the same general strategy – placate strength, exploit weakness – must often lead to layered hierarchies of status groups and patterns of repeated and multiple exclusion, visiting intense relative deprivation upon those at the bottom of the system (Parkin 1979).

Status groups will not merely seek to placate and mollify external powers by rendering them service; they are likely to look to them for protection and for help in solving any problems of collective action that they face. The relationship of status groups with the state can serve well here as a model of the form of their relationship with external powers generally. Max Weber rightly stressed the historical role of the state in providing support for status groups. The state might grant monopolies and legalize their operation; it might redistribute them, or extend the membership with access to them, or even turn against them and seek to eliminate them through legislation. The state might even deliberately create status groups *ab initio*, or else deliberately import them, to balance the power of an overweening existing group perhaps, or to create a constituency of reliable supporters, or to fill a gap in the supply of labour. Thus it is unsurprising that, as a matter of history, status groups have sought to influence the state in their favour, or even to capture it and place it in the hands of their nominees. Once the power of the state is available to buttress a group monopoly, the amount of internally generated collective action that must be directed to that task is greatly reduced.

When a state apparatus exists, the relationship of status groups to it may take a number of forms. It is useful to identify two contrasting extreme forms of this relationship. Where the territory controlled by the state encompasses a number of spatially separated status groups with little dependence upon each other, then it may be that the state is captured by one of the groups and used to its advantage without undue concern to reconcile those excluded and exploited. This is a familiar pattern in territories with distinct and separate ethnic groups. Apartheid South Africa provided a good example, albeit dominated by two allied status groups. Ex-colonial "plural societies" also fall into this pattern (Furnival 1948, Kuper 1974, 1977). And even in democratic polities the state may be dominated by and oriented predominantly to the interests of just one of several status groups.[7]

In a territory where status groups are highly interdependent and/or are characterized by cross-cutting memberships, as is the case in many highly industrialized countries, links with the state tend to be systematically different, just as the operation of the state itself is different, being relatively more concerned with overall co-ordination and the achievement of a *modus vivendi* between groups. In a plural society, members of a single subgroup, usually an ethnic group, may monopolize the resources for violence and coercion through control of the state and use them comprehensively to dominate a territory and the rest of its inhabitants. What Weber (1968: 901) refers to as the "political community" is in that case drawn from or constituted by a single status group. But in practically every highly industrialized society the political community has become progressively broadened through successive extensions of the franchise so that access to membership is no longer monopolized by any given subgroup or groups. No doubt this reflects widespread recognition across groups that, in the prevailing conditions in these societies, co-ordination and co-operation in production are collectively more expedient than costly exercises in rigid and unrelenting exclusion.

In order to get a theoretical grasp on this alternative extreme case, it is worth considering an idealized picture of the state in a modern industrialized democracy as the organized dimension of a giant status group constituted by the entire citizenry.[8] To the extent that this picture is appropriate, the citizens may then be considered as an excluding group acting collectively to monopolize the resources of a territory and the material and institutional infrastructures that rise upon it. This represents a major extension of the theory from subgroups to social wholes, but it is a shift that presents no fundamental problems. In just the way that a status group distinguishes member and non-member, so can a distinction be drawn between citizen and foreigner, or even between human and non-human. (A truly creative social theorist might even seek to treat contraception as a form of exclusion.) Nor is there any reason why an entire citizenry should be unable to generate collective action to secure its monopolies, even if it is extremely large and/or riven with divisions and conflicts.

As far as sheer size is concerned, the previous discussion has already shown that this is of no fundamental importance in accounting for collective action. On an interactionist account, sanctioning the collective good is not primarily a form of instrumental action: it does not decline as it becomes less individually profitable, because it is not engaged in for profit in the first place. On an interactionist account, the football crowd continues to cheer however large it grows.[9] Analogously, there is no limit of size or number that would prevent extension of the account even to an entire citizenry or "nation". Nor does internal differentiation, or division and conflict within a citizenry, in itself constitute a problem. In his origin myth, Weber envisages a status group being formed by *competitors* who continue to compete (1968: 342). He could equally well have spoken of enemies who continue in conflict. Neither in Weber nor in the extension of his account here is there anything to imply that harmony amongst status group members is more than an optional extra.

But a status group, whatever else, must surely be a network of interaction, and will not an entire citizenry be too large to exist as such a network? In fact the question can be addressed to most significant status groups – ethnic groups, religious groups, castes, professions and others – and the answer must be the same in all cases. No such large group can exist as a network in which every individual is connected to every other, but it may exist as a networky structure that allows sufficient appropriate interaction to sustain mutual sanctioning of the collective good of the group. A system of interaction situations connected by mobile individuals, perhaps by individuals who as "representatives" are specifically concerned with securing an alignment of cognition throughout the group, may count as such a networky structure and may be created in a group of any size. Admittedly, such structure may be less potent and less resistant to fragmentation than an everywhere-connected network, but this need cause no theoretical concern: status groups, including "nations" vary in their internal stability, and on occasion they do fragment.

However it is accomplished, the membership of any viable nation-state must be able to encourage and engender nationally oriented collective action.[10] And, on the account of collective action proposed here, this implies the existence of appropriate conditions of interaction. Hence it is reassuring from a theoretical point of view to find that those characteristic features of status groups identified by Max Weber, the features discussed in section 5.2 above, are strikingly similar to the conditions that nationalist leaders and movements strive to encourage and secure when their concern is to increase and intensify collective action. Familiar concerns to establish a single shared "national culture", inventing if necessary a "nation" as its carrier and a "national" history, stand in close analogy with the requirement for a shared distinctive lifestyle. Efforts to exclude minorities link with the concern for a restricted social intercourse. References to "national" honour exemplify the importance of the special honour of membership of the status group.

History would suggest – and this was certainly the view of Max Weber – that members of "nations" or nation-states are capable of generating high levels of "nationally oriented" collective action.[11] It is equally the case, however, that in democratic industrialized nation-states this capacity is rarely fully exploited, and that collective efforts are often devoted to preventing its exploitation. Such states typically run on a relatively low level of "national" consciousness, with small outputs of associated collective action. "Strong nationalism" is actually more commonly associated with movements that seek to fragment and dismember the nation-state to which they belong. Often these are movements of minorities conscious of linguistic and/or cultural discrimination and aware of the benefits which might accrue from a separate polity with a separate bureaucratic administration monopolized by persons of their language and their culture. Such minorities may be significant political powers when their membership is heavily regionally concentrated – as in Scotland, for example, or Quebec – which again may stand as testimony to the relevance of interaction conditions (cf., however, Hechter 1987).

There are, of course, many reasons why political communities in industrialized democracies would eschew strong nationalism, not least those deriving from the interdependence of their economies and the importance of "foreign" trade. But it is interesting to note that the "ideal" conditions for strong nationalism and intense collective action are next to impossible to maintain in a "successful" nation-state. Should it happen that a "nation" was created as a giant, culturally homogeneous status group, then its effective operation would tend to erode its homogeneity: military success implies territorial expansion and the incorporation of new groups; economic success attracts immigrants. The idea of "the nation" as a gigantic, culturally homogeneous status group including all the inhabitants of a territory, or all its full citizens, has been and remains important in practical political thought, but cultural diversity is going to remain the actuality among the memberships of modern nation-states. Any advantage deriving from the imposition of restrictive conceptions of a "national culture" will inevitably be offset accordingly by disaffection amongst minorities – disaffection that may be extremely costly in economies with high division of labour and dependent on elaborate co-ordination, trust and interdependence. Better, it may be thought, weakly to unite all the different groupings in "the nation" than strongly to unite just a part of it and alienate the rest.

Having said this, it is necessary immediately to go on to recognize striking examples in recent history of industrial nation-states, even industrial democracies, where the completely opposite view has been implemented: better strongly to unite a part, and gas the rest. It is important, in the face of tendencies to forget these events, or to associate them with an "earlier stage" of economic and institutional development, or to believe the reams of reassurance since produced to the effect that "this could never happen again", to recognize that there exist at present no good theoretical reasons why similar events should not recur, even in the context of the most "advanced" political and economic systems, which was, of course, precisely where they occurred before.

It is none the less the case currently that, in the most highly industrialized democratic nation-states, the strongest political support is for strategies that secure maximum inclusiveness. Consequently, in these states only minimalist conceptions of national culture are upheld in the public realm and the value of mutually coexisting cultural traditions is emphasized. In states of this kind the claims to special honour made by all the many status groups in their midst present for politicians and bureaucrats a problem of management. Claims to monopoly rights, or even special honour, based upon religion, ethnicity, descent or similar particularisms, are especially problematic because of their potential for dividing the membership generally, and any "official" recognition of such claims will be correspondingly rare and exceptional. Thus the forms of status differentiation and stratification that have hitherto been central to the structuring of complex societies in every period of history will no longer be "officially" recognized as the basis of hierarchies of social esteem. Just two forms of status claim will remain generally acceptable. Claims based on special skill, knowledge and experience may still hope for overt state support, because the relevant groups may be made out to be serving the "national" good and membership of them to be equally accessible to all. And the claims of nationality itself will persist, being the basis of exclusionary and monopolistic practices in which everyone shares, and of a definition of equality by which everyone is encompassed.

Equality of this kind is, of course, substantially the same as that disparagingly referred to as "bourgeois equality" within Marxism: it consists in formal equality of honour, of political and legal citizenship rights, of "opportunity" in the occupational system, but not of wealth or income or control of economic resources. It is worth asking how far this form of equality is sustained primarily out of "national" expediency, and not "class" expediency as Marxists have long tended to assume. Certainly, it is striking how often claims to equality of all kinds are advanced in a way that implies their relevance only within the context of a given polity, in a way, that is, that takes for granted that the claims of nationals are being put forward, not those of human beings in general. This appears to be the case with "class"-based claims to economic equality just as much as with claims of other kinds (Vogler 1985).

To the extent that processes of monopolization and exclusion are found reprehensible, the identification of the membership of a nation-state as a status group may be especially depressing. For many who are repelled by exclusion on the basis of colour or creed are happy to exclude on the basis of nationality; it has a widespread legitimacy in every sense of the word. That any general principled condemnation of exclusion and monopoly must inevitably include a condemnation of exclusion based upon nationality makes the general case so much less credible; while attacks upon exclusion by race, religion and so forth that are accompanied by special pleading on behalf of nationality will be recognizable on detailed scrutiny as *ad hoc* and less than disinterested, even if they do carry credibility. Moreover, if nationality is a form of status exclusivity, then Collins' account of economic activity as a long series of monopolizations extends itself into the political realm. The result is a view of the future that offers no assurance of an end to political exclusion and the exploitation associated with it, a view at variance with those visions of change as necessarily progressive which have long served in so many contexts to inspire optimism and rationalize political involvement. On the other hand, for those to whom this is a loss, some comfort may perhaps be taken from the general argument of this chapter. Status groups, including "national" groups, take work to sustain. Collective action must continually be expended to ensure their persistence, and will be so expended only in so far as it is collectively expedient. When it ceases to be expedient, a few minutes are enough for change. This version of history may offer no rosy vision of the future, but neither does it impute any "natural" stability to the status quo. Monopoly is not always the best policy.

6

Social movements

6.1 Resource mobilization theory

There is no generally agreed account of what constitutes a social movement. To say that it is a collective actively involved in promoting or resisting social change is a widely accepted way of beginning, but it is insufficient. Social movements are conventionally distinguished from political parties and from pressure groups; unlike the latter they operate, not primarily through the channels of insider politics, but by the direct mobilization of opposition to what goes on within those channels. And yet the distinction between movements, parties and lobbying organizations is often hard to draw, as is the distinction between social and religious movements, and between movements and clubs or associations.

It is even questionable how far a social movement should be described as "a collective". Rather than thinking of a unified entity it may be better to characterize a movement as constituted by loose connections between "a plurality of groups, individuals and organizations" (Diani 1992), wherein individuals may or may not conceive of themselves as alike in being "movement members". It is even arguable that those activities that move us to refer to movements thereby engender a fantasy entity, that while the activities are real "the movements themselves" are imaginary. It is true that, despite these definitional and ontological problems, paradigm examples of social movements are generally recognized – the green movement, the women's movement, the civil rights movement – but it is less than fully clear what is being referred to by any of these designations. And there are many problematic cases that may or may not deserve to be treated as social movements and resemble the paradigm examples to a greater or lesser extent: the Provisional IRA; Neighbourhood Watch; hunt saboteurs; Hezbollah. It is as well to bear in mind the diversity of such cases, and the different forms they can apparently take in different social and cultural settings, because most theories of these movements relate, even if they do not always say so, to only a narrow selection, drawn from specific contexts at specific times. At least some of the differences of opinion amongst theorists of social movements derive from the fact that they are talking about different phenomena.[1]

Social movements in modern industrial democracies have long been highly favoured sites for sociological research, and their study has always had an intimate connection with the great fundamental issues of sociological theory. They have had a particular significance for functionalists. From the point of view of much functionalist theory, social movements have implied incomplete system integration and the presence of some degree of dislocation in the institutional structure. For normative functionalists they have also implied a lack of social integration: individual members of movements have apparently failed both to internalize the norms and values that would integrate their activities harmoniously into the existing order and to develop the institutional affiliations that would co-opt them as recognized and satisfied participants in the status quo.

In the USA by the end of the 1950s normative functionalism had become established as the dominant form of general sociological theory, largely due to the efforts of Talcott Parsons, and when it was applied to social movements, as in Smelser's *Theory of collective behavior* (1962), it did indeed treat them as symptoms of institutional dislocation and the activities of their individual members as a product of lack of social integration. Moreover, the conservative cast of normative functionalism at this particular time and its tendency to treat the status quo as the natural "healthy" state of the social order, led it to a correspondingly negative evaluation of movements and their members. Movement participants were often characterized as irrational and suggestible, and their actions as emotionally inspired. Similar points were made by the "mass society" theorists, who at much the same time were attempting to produce general explanations of political extremism (Kornhauser 1959). Mass society theory accounted for Nazism and similar political movements as the result of atomized, isolated individuals becoming available to manipulative, populist elites, who could incite them to irrational forms of action. Atomized individuals, and hence extremist movements, would proliferate only in societies deficient in the intermediate groups, associations and communities characteristic of stable pluralist democracies. Extremism was the product of individual irrationality going unchecked because of a lack of social affiliations and hence of social control.

The prominence of analyses of this kind gave the detailed case studies of social movements undertaken in the USA in the 1960s and 1970s an immense theoretical significance. These studies made it clear that social movements were ubiquitous in stable modern democracies, part of the routine institutionalized activities thereof; that individual movement members, far from being atomized individuals, were more likely than others to be members of groups and organizations in the "mainstream of society"; and that activity in movements was notable for its calculative rationality, not to mention its cognitive sophistication and reflective awareness. No doubt the findings of these studies helped to encourage scepticism about the particular inherited form of functionalist theory, but they also had a positive theoretical significance. They served as the context and inspiration for original theoretical thinking, the outcome of which – the resource mobilization theory of social movements – is in itself of considerable interest and importance.[2]

Resource mobilization theory dismisses the idea that social movement activity is in any way abnormal or pathological or indicative of institutional or ideological breakdown. On the contrary, such activity is normal, ubiquitous and collectively rational. To be sure, it articulates grievances and perceived injustices, but these are everywhere around us, part of the normal state of things. Grievances, therefore, even if they are necessary for the emergence of movements, do not account for that emergence; for grievances are always to hand, yet movements arise in response to but a few of them. To understand where movements do arise, the emphasis must shift away from grievances themselves to the opportunities and resources that allow their articulation and action directed to their remedy. What needs to be asked is how participants are recruited, and whence the money comes; for movement activity, according to resource mobilization theory, is *costly*, and to account for it is above all to show how its costs are borne and what induces its supporters and benefactors to pay them.

In a nutshell, with the advent of resource mobilization theory, what had been conceived of as an emotional response to perceived injustice was reconceptualized as rational action reflecting a calculative appraisal of a balance of costs and opportunities. The consequence has been a series of impressively detailed case studies, continuing over many years, offering invaluable insights into how movements operate and where. Thus, studies of movement mobilization have again and again revealed the importance of block recruitment, of involving and incorporating existing organizations and associations, and of entrepreneurial activity. They have shown that movement members are likely already to be incorporated as active participants in the institutional order and well integrated into communal life; often they are members of existing movements. Conversely, detached individuals stand revealed as underrepresented in movements, and it is evident that social isolation and atomization encourage not movement participation but apathy and depoliticization.

Many of the conclusions of these studies are, of course, theoretical in only a narrow sense. And because they relate to movements largely drawn from one particular social and cultural context, how far they should be generalized is an open question. But the literature of resource mobilization theory has also been permeated, right from the start, by ideas and theories of a fundamental kind. Most, although not all, of these derive from the individualist tradition in social theory, as one would expect given the "economic" orientation of the resource mobilization approach. Perhaps the most spectacular expression of this orientation is to be found in the work of Zald & McCarthy (1987c), who speak of the various "social movement industries" that make up the "social movement sector" of the economy. Zald & McCarthy show how macroeconomic models can be brought to bear upon the understanding of social movements: for example, if disposable incomes rise, more services will be purchased from the social movement sector and movement activity will increase; as a provider of luxury items the sector will grow more rapidly in these conditions than sectors that provide staples and necessities.

As well as its inherent charm and its value as a memorable symbol of the basic posture of resource mobilization theory, the central metaphor being deployed here can be defended as a source of substantive insights. Arguably, in the USA in particular, many "movements" are indeed quasi-industries, and work on industrial organizations should be redeployed to make sense of them. We take it as a matter of course, for example, that the products of an industry may be purchased for any number of reasons, relating to the innumerable possible motivations of individual purchasers. There is no one motivation or rationale for buying a car or having a haircut. Transposed into the context of social movements this warns us against the assumption that movement participants and supporters all act on the same basis, with the same motivations, seeking the same objectives. They may or they may not, and typically they do not. Thus, it is a routine and very important point that activists and "movement professionals" are often moved by systematically different considerations from those common amongst peripheral supporters and passive sympathizers.

Individualism within the resource mobilization perspective has been most systematically expressed, however, not by the use of macro-economic models, but by the adoption of rational choice theory. The work of Mancur Olson (1965) was (and remains) a major inspiration in the development of this kind of theory, and his analysis of the free-rider problem provided a crucial justification for its rejection of any link between movement activity and the existence of grievances. Because of the free-rider problem, most of the perceived grievances and injustices in a given society will fail to gain expression through a social movement. A movement that seeks to articulate and remedy a grievance needs to act collectively, and will arise only where the opportunity for collective action exists; but such opportunities will be very rare because, according to Olson, free-riding, and not collective action, is almost invariably the rational strategy. To argue in this way, however, raises the opposite problem. Why is there any movement activity at all? Why do not independent individuals free-ride all the time?

The importance of these questions and the difficulty of answering them have long been recognized. Some resource mobilization theorists have regarded them as insoluble in a strict rational choice framework. Thus, Anthony Oberschall, in his seminal discussion of *Social conflict and social movements* (1973), cited both evidence and Olson to support the view that independent (isolated, atomized) individuals are not disposed to act collectively. But he went on to argue that many individuals are *not* independent, that they are tied into communities and associations and act as participants in social networks. These are the individuals who are most likely to become mobilized as social movement members and to act collectively to further movement objectives.

Oberschall dealt with the free-rider problem by dropping the independence postulate of individualism and looking to social ties and affiliations. In doing so he took a promising course that many others were able successfully to follow. But others again remained true to individualism, in the form of a rigorously formulated rational choice theory, and sought to account for movement activity on that basis. This has been an extremely valuable exercise in the empirical application and testing of theory, to the extent that there is probably no better place to go to appraise the merits of the rational choice approach than to the extensive literature in this area. How far the approach is vindicated in this literature is, however, another matter.

To vindicate Olson's rational choice approach it is necessary to make out movement members as ER individuals, and movement action not as genuine collective action but as individually rational action. Olson himself suggests three ways of explaining away *prima facie* cases of collective action: the group involved may be extremely small; or coercion may be operating; or private (selective) benefits may be associated with "collective" action, benefits that make that action individually profitable. Clearly, although the first two possibilities might be relevant in a few particular cases, only the third promises to be of any general significance. What then are the private incentives that might induce an individual to participate in a movement? And why is it that these incentives have to be provided by the movement, and cannot be obtained more cheaply by other means?

No doubt leaders, entrepreneurs and prominent activists in social movements may look forward to eventual private gains, if, that is, they are not already being paid for what they do. Prominent participants may sustain a claim to a position of power, influence and high remuneration should the movement eventually come to enjoy a measure of success. Nor is there any obvious alternative route to such rewards. But this does nothing to solve the problem of rank and file participation. Ordinary membership of most social movements does not even offer the opportunity of reductions for private health insurance or a special discount on the next new car as trade union membership sometimes does. All the potential benefits of rank and file movement membership would appear to be collective ones. Why then is there an ordinary membership at all? It is true that the ordinary movement supporter expends much less on her involvement than the devoted activist does, and hence that much weaker selective inducements will suffice to account for her participation. (The way that movement participation may involve highly variable individual costs has been beautifully systematized by Granovetter (1978) in his "threshold model" of movement recruitment.) But this does not alter the basic point: if membership is costly at all, then some account is necessary of why the cost is paid. It is important to recognize that collective movement action may be sustained by large numbers of tiny individual contributions each representing only a very small concession to the collective good, but this is not a vindication of rational choice theory.

There is no individual material benefit generally associated with rank and file membership of a social movement. Even Zald & McCarthy (1987a), with their strongly "economic" orientation, refer to subscriptions to movements as "conscience money", and rational choice theorists should likewise be prepared to give reality best at this point. However, the individualist, rational choice approach has the status of a paradigm for many theorists, and rather than give it up they have tended to stretch its concepts beyond the realm of their legitimate application. Olson himself provided a model here when he suggested that "social" as well as material or financial incentives may inspire collective action, and that "social incentives must be analysed in much the same way as monetary incentives" (Olson 1965: 61). This claim has already been considered and rejected in Chapter 3, where it was shown that the system of what Olson calls "social incentives" operates in a way quite different from any system of economic reward, and that its existence is inconsistent with the tenets of rational choice theory, and indeed with individualism generally (Ch. 3: pp. 77–84). This conclusion, however, is not generally accepted, and analyses of movements in terms of selective "social" incentives are still reckoned to lend support to the individualist approach.

Perhaps the best way of indicating the enormous respect the individualist, rational choice approach enjoys in this context is to cite its use by two sociologists who actually have significant reservations about it. Friedman & McAdam (1992) suggest that recruitment to social movements is individually rational action induced by "identity incentives". Social movement organizations offer recruits a "collective identity" that serves as a sufficient individual inducement to secure their membership. Activists within the organization design an associated identity as a consumer good for purchase by the subscriptions of members (Friedman & McAdam 1992: 164). It is important that the identity fits with the self-image of potential recruits. A balance has to be struck: narrowly specialized movement objectives will resonate with the self-images of only a few potential recruits, but broad and many-faceted objectives will increase the number of cases where there is a clash with a recruit's self-image. With astute product design, however, an attractive and widely desired identity can be produced and purchasers will flock in.

How should this account be evaluated? Let us not quibble with the treatment of activists and movement professionals, or the possibility that they may regard the relatively uninvolved supporters whose cash is none the less needed as so many consumers. Perhaps it is especially tempting for activists in the professional direct-mail social movement sector to think in this way as they seek to get their mail-shots right. Certainly, individual subscribers in this sector have only so much to subscribe, and professionals have an interest in ensuring that it comes to their movement rather than another. Moreover, it is clear that many subscribers in this sector regard their modest financial contributions as the only form of support they are prepared to extend to movement causes (McCarthy 1987: 59–64). But are these subscribers actually consumers, purchasing collective identities?

The claim is that, in purchasing individually desired identities in a "rational" transaction, movement subscribers accidentally and incidentally finance movement collective action. There is however a difficulty here, and Friedman & McAdam draw attention to it. It takes the form of a fundamental criticism that has long stood against Olson's entire selective incentive account of collective action: why do not rational individuals purchase selective incentives separately and hence more cheaply, instead of buying them in a package that involves paying for collective action as well? In the present context this translates into the question: why do not people simply adopt identities, say as greens or feminists, without bothering to pay the subscriptions of joining associated movements or movement organizations? Friedman & McAdam rightly note that this is "a form of free-riding that is virtually impossible to overcome" (1992: 167).

Why then should we accept that this virtual impossibility is none the less achieved? Not because of the force of the rest of the argument. Consider how it goes. We are asked to accept that potential recruits have self-images according to which they are genuinely desirous of the just treatment of other people as well as themselves. We are also asked to accept that the existence of these self-images has consequences for action, that people engage in costly activities because of them, that, for example, they join social movements and thereby provide the resources for collective action those movements otherwise would not receive. But we are then asked to reject the authenticity of those self-images. People act not as those self-images would suggest, but rather out of self-interest as purchasers of identities congruent with the images. Why must we accept this? Solely, it would seem, to avoid acknowledging the existence of altruism. When individuals subscribe to movements, it must be that self-interest is involved, that a private incentive exists, that an altruistic self-image brings about altruism only at one remove, via the purchase of a congruent collective identity as an individually desired consumer good.

This is the kind of catch-all "economic" discourse that would helpfully suggest that Christ really wanted to be crucified. It reflects undue deference to individualism, not the inherent potential of that approach itself. The "merit" of references to selective incentives is that they save the phenomena for individualism. They allow collective action in social movements to be redescribed as individually rational actions. As ever with such approaches, however, they thereby create, and leave unresolved, the problem of why rational, independent, calculative, well informed individuals are so grossly mistaken in their knowledge of themselves. This is a price that is often paid to maintain individualism and rational choice as universal sense-making systems of discourse: to account people rational they are assumed to be deluded.[3]

6.2 Beyond instrumentality: new social movements

Resource mobilization theorists have produced an extensive, empirically detailed and densely interconnected literature that serves as a rich resource in the checking and testing of many different kinds of social theory. None the less, individualism, particularly in the form of rational choice theory, is the only fundamental theoretical approach that has been systematically used and developed by resource mobilization theorists themselves. And this has led them into confrontation with the problem of collective action. Since this problem has already been shown to be insoluble within an individualistic framework, it is unsurprising that efforts to give an individualistic account of social movement collective action have proved unsatisfactory. Brief reference has been made to the suggestion by Friedman & McAdam that individual desire for collective identity is a private incentive sufficient to account for movement participation. It is interesting to compare this account of collective identity with an alternative that does not seek to remain within an individualist framework:

> Collective identity is an achieved definition of a situation, constructed and negotiated through the constitution of social networks which then connect the members of a group or movement. This process of definition implies the presence of cognitive frames, of dense interactions, of emotional and affective exchanges. What holds individuals together as a "we" can never be completely translated into the logic of means–end calculation, or political rationality, but always carries with it margins of non-negotiability in the reasons for and ways of acting together. (Melucci 1992: 244)

For Friedman & McAdam, even though their concern is with recruitment and mobilization, the social movement itself is a given, a taken-for-granted pre-existing factor in their account. Activists in this given movement are strongly contrasted with supporters-subscribers, but both activists and subscribers operate in terms of individual rationality. The identity sold by the former to the latter is a transferable package capable of appropriation and use beyond the context of the movement as a private possession. In contrast, for Melucci, that a movement exists and remains constituted is something in constant need of understanding as a contingent accomplishment: its being is its becoming; its becoming requires collective effort. In making this effort, members are conceived of as peers and no strong division is made between activists and supporters. The effort of movement constitution itself is not reducible to means–end individual calculation. And what is constituted remains intrinsically a collective accomplishment, incarnate in social interaction and no more removable from the context of that interaction than minds are removable from brains.

It is arguable, particularly in view of the fact that these conflicting accounts have been based on familiarity with different movements, that their different definitions of "collective identity" are both tenable, and that the term refers to different things in the different accounts. Nevertheless, it is Melucci who speaks of identity in the generally recognized sense, and who encourages the deeper sense of curiosity about its emergence. And it is Melucci, by acknowledging the limited scope of rational choice approaches from the beginning, who points to a route around the problem of collective action.

Melucci is one of a number of European writers on social movements who have the resources of Marxism ready to hand, who have been influenced by its concepts and analyses, and who write with a strong awareness of its practical failure. The idea that identity and solidarity must be generated in practice, through interaction and through struggle against external agencies, is a routine one for them, and the question of whether persistent collective action that persistently fails can none the less be instrumentally oriented and rational is all too easy for them to ask. It is against this background that theories of the rise of the "new social movements" have evolved, and by reference to this background that much of the difference between these theories and contemporaneous theory in the USA is best understood.[4]

The greens, the women's movement and the gay rights movement are among the many routinely cited examples of new social movements. They are said to contrast with the class-based movements typical of Europe in the nineteenth century. These last were movements with large aims beneficial to majorities in their host populations: the franchise and full political equality in a democratic society; the right to organize in the pursuit of economic objectives; the right to legal protections and full equality under the law. But the older movements succeeded and these objectives were substantially achieved. And the new social movements recognized the achievement and were happy to live with its consequences. They acted not to attain democracy, but within it, in a way that both accepted and took account of its existence. This is said to be the key to their distinctive character. The older movements had to mobilize the power to press political change upon a recalcitrant system. They had to maximize their resources by organization and hierarchical coordination, and use them to challenge the state. The maximum possible level of recruitment was required, implying a universalistic ideology with a clearly articulated statement of very general aims or values, and an all-embracing vision or myth of the course of social change. But the new movements could learn to live with the state and the not completely unsatisfactory democratic political and administrative structures associated with it. Nor had they any longer a need to maximize coercive power. They were free to turn to civil society to advance narrower causes, by bringing them to public notice, engaging in persuasive argumentation on their behalf, and claiming not power and submission but space and toleration. What mattered was not wholesale social transformation but the piecemeal defence of particular threatened groups or lifestyles, and the empowerment of those whose chosen way of living had hitherto been pressed upon by needless regulations and restrictions. Thus, movement objectives became cultural and communicative rather than "political" in a narrow sense. Movement action became not just restricted in scope but self-restricted. And movement ideologies swung correspondingly away from the articulation of a universally applicable concept of *value* toward the celebration of *difference* (Jordan 1994).

There is a great disparity of style between this European work and the American material previously alluded to. Whereas the latter is suffused with empiricist ideals, much of the former expresses a commitment to the success of specific movements, and is happy to select for study only those that are considered "historically significant". A European study may be interested above all in the "emancipatory potential" of a movement (Habermas 1987, Tourraine 1981, 1985) when an American one would be asking how on earth its participant members manage to find the time. There is no doubt that for insight into the full range and variety of movements and movement organizations the American literature is the place to go. And it also gives the better sense of the diversity of movement objectives: how on the one hand they may imply vast social and political upheavals and involve members in a life or death struggle; and how on the other they may be nothing more than the passing whims of suburbia, collectively expressed in very weak and diffuse interaction networks, but swept up and amplified by movement professionals using mail-shots.

Even though the two approaches have now had time to influence each other, the stylistic gulf remains. So, for example, when Snow et al. (1986) take up the theme that movement objectives are socially negotiated cognitive institutions and not aggregates of the objectives of individual movement members, they give it a characteristic stylistic twist. Their empirical, ethnographic approach leads them to note objectives that any European study would surely pass over; that some individuals may join movements, for example, on hearing of the "many pretty girls" therein (Snow et al. 1986: 473). And with similar empirical thoroughness they reveal how the social negotiation of movement objectives is by no means always an authentic negotiation between peers. Sometimes it is expedient flexibility by activists, who seek to "hook" new recruits through engaging with their personal interests. Thus, to cite a hypothetical example, a member of a rural arts and crafts society must not be surprised to receive a mail-shot that explains that, just like her, the British Nazi Fellowship has a deep and genuine interest in high-quality leatherwork and invites her involvement in a movement that thus effectively addresses one of her own individual concerns. Again, then, for a

162

sense of the many different ways in which objectives may be negotiated and the many different motivations that may inspire the negotiations, the American literature may be preferred.

But if that literature is descriptively and ethnographically the more impressive, the selectivity of the alternative European perspective gives it a specific theoretical interest. It is characteristic of the "important" new social movements focused upon in Europe that they seek to bring about not radical changes in the political system but diffuse cultural change running through the whole of civil society. This means that their activities are oriented toward the communication of messages rather than to the mobilization of forces or threats. And this in turn has important consequences for *collective action*, which is now no longer purely a matter of getting some technical task done, or achieving a specific extrinsic objective. The business of making claims for a form of culture or way of living is not something independent of participating in the culture or engaging in the way of living. Indeed, it may be that to live authentically in a certain way is the best endorsement of that way of living. To be sure, in the context of a movement the forms and meanings of a way of living may be intensified, dramatized and given peculiarly apposite forms of symbolic expression, as the living becomes as it were a message about itself to the wider context, and a claim for acceptance and recognition by that context. In the context of a movement, living is at the same time more than living; it is acting collectively in relation to wider objectives. But, precisely because of this, the collective action in question is no longer pure instrumentality; it can "no longer be completely translated into the logic of means–end calculation".[5]

In an invaluable review, Cohen (1985) suggests that European accounts of new social movements point the way to a solution of the problem of collective action. She begins by emphasizing how collective action that is performed purely as the means to an extrinsic end can never be understood as the outcome of individually rational calculations. All efforts in this direction fly in the face of principle. But the new theories have adopted an "identity-oriented" paradigm to account for movement action, not the instrumental or "strategic" paradigm characteristic of resource mobilization theory. According to the new paradigm, collective action is devoted to the creation and re-creation of collective identities, the contestation of cultural frames and definitions with other collectives, the invention of cultural forms and their display through expressive symbolism and theatrical presentation. Action of this kind has intrinsic value and significance to the individual who enacts it, and does not have to be accounted for by reference to consequences, externalities or extrinsic considerations. Hence no collective action problem arises in relation to it.

Cohen uses a classification of kinds of action drawn from Habermas to elaborate her point. According to Cohen, Habermas identifies five action types: teleological, strategic, dramaturgical, normatively-regulated and communicative.[6] Teleological and strategic actions are carried out purely as means to ends: action is teleological when an extrinsic purpose is furthered by taking account only of physical states of affairs, and strategic when it is also necessary to take into account what other people are independently deciding to do. Resource mobilization theory assumes that movement activity is made up entirely of these two purely instrumental kinds of action. In contrast, the "identity-oriented" paradigm interprets movement activity by reference only to the other three categories: it is dramaturgical in that it expresses subjective feelings, desires and experiences, normatively regulated in that it conforms to agreed norms or rules, communicative in that it is designed to bring about agreement in rules and meanings and to sustain it as an (ever-changing) consensus. Dramaturgical, normatively regulated and communicative forms of action are not purely instrumental. They have intrinsic value, so that their own nature will account for their enactment.

It may seem that the collective action problem is now disposed of: movement collective action is all of the intrinsically significant kind and done for its own sake. Cohen, however, rejects this simple solution. To deny the importance of instrumental or strategic action in social movements would, she says, be to confuse them with cults or contemplative communities. By definition social movements are oriented to extrinsic objectives. Within them, collective action of both extrinsic and intrinsic value will be found, action that is instrumentally oriented and action that is expressively or dramaturgically oriented. Both the American and European approaches throw light on how movements operate, and the need is to combine them.

Cohen is surely correct to press the argument in this direction. But one consequence of this is that the collective action problem rears its head yet again. If there are collective instrumentally oriented activities in the context of social movements, it does not account for their existence to note that there are dramaturgically oriented activities running alongside them. Indeed the problem remains, however mixed together the various actions or action orientations may be: the collectively instrumental dimension of movement activity cannot be accounted for simply by reference to its non-instrumental dimension. It might perhaps be accounted for, however, if a systematic generative connection could be shown to exist between the one dimension and the other.

6.3 Social movements and status groups

All accounts of social movements agree upon their intimate association with social networks, although that association is accounted for in a number of different ways. One explanation is that recruitment is facilitated by contact with an existing member and will consequently tend to follow the linkages provided by existing social networks. This is accepted wisdom. But it is also suggested that the social support available to members of networks may encourage their *continued* participation, and that where that participation involves high costs, in the form for example of personal danger, social ties may have a very considerable importance (McAdam 1986). Case studies suggest that "affinity groups", in which small numbers of individuals offer each other strong social support, are capable of extremely "costly" forms of collective action on behalf of movements (Gamson 1992).

The most radical formulation of the association is provided by Melucci (1985), who proposes to *replace* the concept of "social movement" with that of "movement network", defined as "the network of groups and individuals sharing a conflictual culture and a collective identity" and including "the network of 'informal' relationships connecting core individuals and groups to a broader area of participants" (1985: 798–9). What initially prompts us to refer to "a movement" is a system of collective action, but in so speaking we imply the existence of a unitary object "to which one attributes goals, choices, interests, decisions" (ibid.: 793). Thus, Melucci suggests, we overlook the plurality of meanings and orientations associated with the action system, and the problem of understanding how they are related one with another. When we abandon the presupposition of "a movement" and look to the action system, we find underlying it "a network of small groups submerged in everyday life which require a personal involvement in experiencing and practicing cultural innovation. They emerge only on specific issues, as for instance the big mobilizations for peace, for abortion, against nuclear policy, etc." (ibid.: 800). Participation in these submerged, often invisible, movement networks may be part time and sporadic, but it none the less represents an essential underlay to highly visible eruptions of collective action.

All this implies the plausibility of an interactionist theory of social movements that accounts for their output of collective instrumentally oriented action by reference to the informal interactions between participants. The conjecture must be that networks are associated with social movements because the collective action definitive of such movements will emerge only from the patterns of interaction that define social networks. If this is so, then networks of interaction are not merely associated with movements but necessary constituents of them. A general account of how interaction engenders collective action has already been set out in section 3.3 above, along with the reasons for regarding it as irreducible to individualism. And the account has already been used to understand the collective actions of status groups in the previous chapter. The next step must be to attempt to extend that account to social movements.

Let us recall the key points of the theory set out and applied earlier. Mutual symbolic sanctioning is held to be what instigates collective action, and such sanctioning is regarded as in need of no special explanation. In an interacting collective, members will sanction the collective good simply by giving expression to their thoughts. "Social pressure" or "social encouragement" will be part and parcel of communication itself and its existence will demand understanding only to the extent that communication itself demands understanding. All that will need particular attention is the matter of which collectives individuals know themselves to be members of and which collective goods they will sanction. Where one distinct collective good is sanctioned, it is necessary to postulate a setting for communication in which only one collective identity finds expression. And it is necessary to identify what induces members to remain in that distinctive setting subject to its distinctive sanctions and rewards. In the case of status groups, Max Weber identified the means by which such a setting was established and the factors that induced members to remain within it. A distinctive lifestyle identifies members to each other, offers positive social and cultural incentives to participation in interaction, and provides the setting for such interaction. Restrictions upon social intercourse clear a crucial area of interaction "not subservient to economic or any other purposes" for communication with members only, so that conceptions of the collective good of members are the only conceptions encountered, the only basis for negotiating the collective good of the group. The constitution of a special honour of membership creates a dimension of sanctioning wholly at the disposal of members themselves and available for the task of sanctioning their distinctive collective good.

It is generally agreed that interactive settings exist in which members of social movements may also sanction their distinctive collective good. But how are these settings achieved and sustained, and how far can Weber's account of status groups serve here as a model for understanding social movements? Crucially, social movements, like status groups, do encourage distinctive lifestyles. As far as lifestyle is concerned, there is a parallel between status groups and social movements – or at least those movements with large objectives and high levels of activism. Again, it is clear that the members of most social movements, like those of status groups, engage in a restricted social intercourse, although there is a significant difference here between the two. Status groups seek to exclude, and hence must place prohibitions upon those seeking to join them, whereas movements seek recruits and find themselves with a restricted social intercourse because those with whom they differ have no desire to join them. None the less, the outcome is identical in both contexts: a restricted social intercourse exists. Finally, there is the special honour of membership, which clearly exists in social movements, but in a slightly different form from how it manifests itself in status groups. Again because of concern with recruitment, the lack of honour accorded outsiders cannot be associated with any unchangeable characteristic they possess and must be associated with some deficiency that movement membership will remedy. Thus, a common way of expressing contempt for outsiders will be in terms of their lack of knowledge or insight. Initiation into the movement may provide these things. And a movement member given recognition and standing as the possessor of collectively sustained insights is in the same position as the group member given honour as the possessor of collectively sustained status, and in particular is vulnerable to a distinctive form of collective sanctioning of just the same kind.

Thus, both status groups and social movements generate their essential output of collective action in much the same way. Both sustain activity oriented to their own distinctive good by mutual interaction in the context of a restricted social intercourse. But in social movements the role of

SOCIAL MOVEMENTS

interaction and social intercourse is even more clear and evident than it is in status groups. In the latter, only a little of the output of collective action feeds back into the task of the (re)constitution of the group itself. Most goes to the securing of monopoly profits for individual members, who incur correspondingly large exit costs if they leave or are ejected from the group. Hence, even though it is the social intercourse of the status group that makes possible its entire operation as an economic unit, individual members need feel no *positive* involvement in that intercourse, and any given individual may actually continue to participate in it purely for material gain, generating collective action purely to avoid negative sanctions from fellow members. Odd as it may sound, members of status groups may be engaging in purposeless social intercourse for only very specific purposes, interacting with others who may be competitors (as Weber points out – see Ch.5 p. 131) or, for that matter, enemies. In a social movement, on the other hand, participation at the grass roots normally yields no material gain, and there are no exit costs of a material kind associated with leaving. Looked at in purely material terms, members pay a price in collective action in order to belong. Hence, if incentives to movement participation must be either material benefits or factors related to lifestyle and social intercourse, it is evidently the latter that are operative. The crucial importance of social intercourse is thus quite unequivocally apparent in the case of social movements: only this will account for recruitment and the retention of members.

The important similarities between status groups and social movements have been neglected by social theorists. Even the names of these social formations have been chosen to imply a false contrast between them. Status groups are things; they are parts of the status quo, naturally "there", needing no effort to sustain and no explanation. But social movements are processes; movements move, the moving takes effort, the effort needs explanation. We have now moved away from this misconceived contrast by recognizing both the normality of social movements and the work needed to sustain status groups. But for theoretical purposes what is needed is a complete inversion of the old perspective. The intrinsically valuable dimension of action in both "groups" and "movements" must be given theoretical priority. The extrinsically valuable instrumentally oriented collective action that both produce must be recognized as secondary and derivative. Theoretical understanding must begin with the restricted context of social intercourse maintained in both "kinds" of collective. In such a context, where the instrumental dimension of action has low priority and social exchanges are in no way "subservient" to instrumental considerations, communication and interaction can be freely varied and modulated to encourage the thinking and acting of the collective good. According to who is attracted into this sphere, specific conceptions of the collective good will be negotiated and constructed. According to the intensity of mutual symbolic sanctioning in this sphere, a supply of action for the collective good will emerge.

Where there is a network of social intercourse it may be thought of as analogous to the engine of a car, turning over with the clutch disengaged. Power is latent in the engine as it idles purposelessly, implicit in the relationship of its many parts and components. When the clutch is let out, the power is drawn off and appears as the performance of work. So, similarly, a network of social intercourse may exist, ticking over, putting out only enough power to keep itself constituted, like the idling car engine puts out power to pump its own cooling water and send sparks to its own plugs. But the potential for extrinsically useful work is also there in the network, waiting to be drawn upon. In the case of a status group it is used to exclude and monopolize. In the case of a social movement it is used to incite social change or to increase recruitment and the availability of resources – for it is only where collective action of these kinds is apparent that we speak of a social movement.

The theoretical value of this reorientation is obvious: in allowing us to perceive sameness where previously there was pure difference, it promotes that generalization of perspective which is a major task of theory. But the reorientation is richly suggestive as well in more specific ways. It implies that a social movement might metamorphose into or even at one and the same time *be* a status group, and vice versa. And it prompts the question as to why collectives use their potential for collective action in systematically different ways. One thought here is that actions reflect opportunities, that the difference between movements and status groups is largely one of opportunities. Members of status groups are usually in a strong position relative to external powers and able to exclude many of them from opportunities without prohibitive costs; nor do they find the powers and capabilities of such excluded powers so significant that productive alliance with them is preferable to their exclusion. Members of a social movement on the other hand are likely, at least initially, to be too weak to implement profitable exclusionary strategies, or indeed any successful collective action at the expense of significant outside powers, and accordingly must look to increase their capacity for collective action by recruitment.

It is also worth bearing in mind that there are social networks that make very little actual use of their potential for collective instrumental action. They are content to operate as the idling car engine does, acting instrumentally only to the extent necessary to remain constituted. Many of these are conventionally referred to as "religious" groups or movements. James Beckford (1985) has described how individuals may move from one context of social intercourse to another, sometimes from their family circle to the esoteric world of a "cult", for no identifiable extrinsic reason and hence presumably purely for a change in lifestyle and in the intrinsically valuable quality of lived experience. Beckford classifies new religious movements according to their mode of "social insertion" into the wider context. Some simply serve as *refuges* for members, making no active effort at recruitment but accepting those who are drawn to the social intercourse of the movement, whether on an occasional basis or as a complete way of life. Others remain inwardly oriented save that they actively recruit members with the promise of *release* from their existing problems or difficulties, or with a vision of the *revitalization* of society that will ensue when most of its members are drawn into the movement and internally transformed by it. But even these more actively proselytizing movements maintain a domain of social intercourse that is the more or less exclusive preserve of members only, and that is often recognized by members and enemies alike as the key to whatever success in recruitment the cult or movement enjoys.

Purely expedient collective action cannot exist without a basis in interaction, but ordered networks of interaction can exist without expedient extrinsic objectives: one can have the engine without its power, but not the power without the engine. Thus, our understanding must begin with interaction and move to instrumentalities, begin with the sacred and move to the profane. This suggests, further, that "purely religious" mobilizations may serve as important precursers of potent collective action (Zald & McCarthy 1987b). Participation in religious activities engenders co-ordination and religious organization. Religious organization, being organization for no extrinsic end in particular, becomes organization for every extrinsic end in general. Where there is social intercourse there is the possibility of all kinds of expedient collective action; where there is religion there is social intercourse. Certainly, it is the case historically that coming together for social intercourse in a "religious" context has been the prelude to potent political action: this was true of action by disenfranchised working people in nineteenth-century England, by black people in the twentieth-century USA, and further recent examples may readily be found in Eastern Europe.

Needless to say, the point of this discussion has not been to contrast "religious" and "social" movements.[7] There is an obvious continuity between the one and the other as they are conventionally identified. And indeed it is worth asking whether reference to "religious" movements might not be dispensed with altogether for theoretical purposes, and the phenomena so labelled considered simply as movements like any other. Although the ubiquitous use of the term "religion" is an important social fact, its reference is so exceptionally problematic and extraordinarily variable that the grounds for its transplantation into the vocabulary of social theory need to be given particularly careful scrutiny.

What the discussion did seek to emphasize was the fundamental theoretical importance of communication and interaction in social networks and hence the plausibility of the account of the genesis of collective action first presented in Chapter 3. At the same time, the discussion has lent support to many of the claims of the theorists of the new social movements. However, precisely because there is agreement on these theoretical points, it is necessary to disagree with these theorists on matters of history. Because of the essential role of interaction in movements, and because the collective good furthered by a movement is whatever specific collective good is sanctioned in its particular interaction network, it is hard to see how a genuinely distinctive universalism can be associated with older movements. And because formulations of the collective good must invariably be negotiated achievements produced in interaction networks, it is hard to see how older movements could have been any less concerned with culture and communication than are new ones. Theorists of new social movements have managed to identify many of the features necessary for the operation of social movements generally, to the extent that it is hard to accept that there is anything significantly new about the specific movements that have interested them. This is a thought that will be developed further in the next chapter.[8]

7

Social classes

7.1 "Class" in social theory

There is no way in which all the many and various uses of "class" in social theory can be adequately considered here. It is widely used to refer to categories of individuals defined by their "economic" situations or interests, in which role it is not always clearly distinguished from "status". In particular, it is used in Britain to refer to occupational groupings, and indeed the "classes" defined by Her Majesty's Registrar General, devoid of any theoretical rationale though they be, probably represent the conceptualization most widely employed by British sociologists. But "class" is also recognized as an actors' category and employed to describe affiliations and conceptions of stratification current amongst people themselves. And some theorists have used the term performatively, in an attempt to create social classes as class-conscious collectives through the very process of making reference to their existence.

Given all the diversity, it is necessary to simplify, and this can be done by asking if "class" has any distinctive uses, where other notions current in the social sciences will not serve.[1] This implies an evaluation of "class" in the traditions deriving from Marx and from Weber, both of whom had a central and distinctive role for the "class" concept. In these traditions: "First, classes are large-scale groupings. . . . Secondly, classes are aggregates of individuals rather than 'social' groups. . . . Thirdly, the appearance of classes presupposes the dissolution of the personalised ties of fealty or obligation characteristic of feudal society, and their replacement by 'impersonal' relationships of a contractual kind. . . . Finally, classes are nominally 'open'" (Giddens 1979: 84). All that needs to be added to this summary of the basics of "class" is that individuals of the same class will of course be those similarly placed in the "relationships of a contractual kind". They will be to this extent in a similar "economic" or "socio-economic" situation to those in the same class, and in a different one from individuals in other classes.[2]

In the Marxian tradition, members of different social classes differ in their relationship to the means of production. In a capitalist society, where there is a free market in labour and a securely established institution of private property, the key division is taken to be between those who own the means of production and those who own only their labour power. In the Weberian tradition, individuals with the same economic opportunities are said to be in the same "class situation", and Weber seems usually to mean by an "economic opportunity" a chance for gain available in the market place: Weber tends to treat "class" as a meaningful concept only in market, i.e. capitalist societies.[3]

When social theorists place individuals in the same category, it is usually in the belief that their situation affects them in the same kind of way, so that they are disposed (potentially) to act in the same kind of way. A common basis for their action is assumed, a common set of incentives to action. This is the case when individuals are categorized by class. Individuals of the same class, by virtue of the similarity of their economic situations, are considered to have some common interests that may dispose them to act alike. In particular, it is assumed that class interests dispose to joint action. Individuals with such interests are likely to come together, organize and act in order to further them. A class as an aggregate of interest-sharing individuals is potentially a body of organized interest-furthering members, and a potent source of collective action. This was the view of both Weber and Marx. But Weber was content to take class as just one potential basis for collective action, and one that might or might not become actual, whereas Marx insisted that, in the long term, class was overwhelmingly the most important basis for collective action and that in due course it would be actualized.

Marx took it as a matter of empirical fact that interests engendered organization and collective action and cited historical evidence, some of it generated personally, to show that class interests had been *de facto* of overwhelming importance in engendering social change via this route. The emergence of capitalism was a matter of the members of a socioeconomic category with common interests becoming an organized interest-furthering collective. The contemporary activities of workers were understood by Marx as a part of an analogous long-term development.

That human beings would act, and in due course act collectively, to further their interests was something Marx regarded as empirically clear. What concerned him rather more was why class interests should predominate. For he was perfectly willing to admit that individuals would always have a variety of other interests. And even when considered simply as workers or capitalists he was well aware that they could be tempted to take account of other than class interests: as competitors for jobs or markets, individuals of the same class might have opposed interests and act against each other; as joint beneficiaries of a particular producing enterprise, individuals of different classes might ally and act against competing producers. Indeed, Marx was ready to allow that such interests might have priority in the short term. And there is nothing in his position to suggest that other interests, such as concern us more today, might not similarly have priority in the short term: (status-linked) interests related to gender, or ethnicity, or nationality could readily take on an immediate predominant importance without conflict with Marx's views.

In the long term, however, according to Marx, class-related interests were bound to become all-important. First of all, in capitalist societies, with private property and the free market in labour at the core of the economic-institutional order, the opposition of capitalists and workers was, as it were, structurally built in. Secondly, and crucially, Marx's analysis of the dynamics of capitalist economies convinced him that the intensity of this opposition would inexorably increase: a constant increase in class conflict would be a consequence of the ever-growing immiseration of the exploited proletariat and the allegedly unrelenting fall in the rate of profit to capital. With hindsight, however, few theorists find themselves any longer able to accept the "immiseration" thesis or indeed Marx's economics generally, and many reject the associated long-term vision as teleological and based upon an arbitrary and implausible metaphysics.

If, as we should, we accept this judgement, then we should dismiss the Marxian view of the long term.[4] As for the short term, Marx and Weber are in agreement: class interests are bases for collective action that may or may not become actual. In so far as it does become actual, Marx and Weber offer a general theoretical scheme to account for its emergence:

(a) situation $\rightarrow$ interests $\rightarrow$ organization $\rightarrow$ action

This is a different scheme from that used in earlier chapters to account for collective action in status groups and social movements. The earlier scheme was:

(b) interaction $\rightarrow$ organization $\rightarrow$ interests $\rightarrow$ action

For the most part Marx's social theory implies scheme (a). Weber also used (a) in his discussion of class, but something close to (b) in his discussion of status groups. He evidently believed that both schemes were possible. One way of considering whether "class" has a distinctive significance is to evaluate the explanatory power of scheme (a). For clearly, if class-related interests can engender collective action according to that scheme, then "class" is irreducible to "status" and becomes an important concept in the explanation of social change.

7.2 Individualism, interactionism and class action

In both the Marxian and Weberian traditions class interests dispose individuals to action. Class action is latent in any social order because class interests are associated with all social positions and are liable to become part of the awareness of their individual occupants. The problem for both traditions is to understand when and how the interests are recognized, how they are weighted against other interests, and how their potential as incentives to action becomes actual.

From the individualist perspective, however, the very idea that a class interest may dispose an individual to act is called into question. The nub of the issue is (yet again) the free-rider problem. Action for the good of a class is collective action: the benefits of such action will accrue to all members of the class alike. No individual member will find it advantageous to incur personal costs by performing it, and hence no ER individual will perform it. Better, they will reason, to let someone else do it.

Mancur Olson addresses his analysis of *The logic of collective action* (1965) directly against Marx: "class action will not occur if the individuals that make up a class act rationally" (Olson 1965: 105). Because of the free-rider problem, the "rational" worker will leave it to others to promote organization, to go on strike, to press for the support of the state apparatus and the implementation of class legislation, to take up arms for the Revolution. There is no individual incentive to do any of these things.

The argument represents a problem for Olson however, much more

175

than for Marx,[5] because all these things seem actually to have occurred. It needs to be shown how individualistic social theory can be squared with historical studies of what is generally identified as class conflict. Fortunately, there are now impressive studies available that seek to do just this. There can be, of course, by definition, no empirical historical studies of class action from a rigorously individualistic perspective. But John Bowman's account of *Capitalist collective action* (1989) is a fine example of individualism, and the mine-owners who feature in his study of the American coal industry have all the attributes normally required to be regarded as members of the capitalist class.

Bowman's study is too extensive to be summarized here, but a good sense of its general approach can be conveyed by considering just the part that deals with bituminous coal-mining between 1880 and the outbreak of the First World War. The mines in this period were the property of a large number of small owners, each of whom acted as an independent employer, paying wages in the normal way and disposing of product on the open market. Demand for the product naturally varied over time and there were periods when it fell so far as to force price-cutting in an effort to maintain sales, price-cutting that, even when accompanied by corresponding cuts in wages, resulted in mines running at a loss.[6]

At such times, the owners were wont, through the voice of their trade association, to recognize the nature of their difficulty and call for an adequate price for coal; they had an obvious common interest in price maintenance and would all have gained from the creation of a cartel. This, however, they failed to do, as an individualist would have predicted, because the cartel required collective action by large numbers of individuals. Whatever other owners did, it was rational not to join the cartel. The more owners who did support the cartel and agree to hold back some of their product from the market, the higher the coal price would go, and the higher the profit for everyone in the cartel. But, at every level of support, even more gains would be made by the owners who remained outside and slightly undercut the cartel to sell every pound of coal they could produce. Thus, it was in nobody's interest to join the cartel. And nobody did join. Everybody took a free ride. There was no cartel. Nobody gained anything. The analysis set out in section 1.4 was vindicated and its predictions verified.

So far, the study merely confirms familiar experience. Capitalists bring their products to the market place. Where they are present in numbers, they are unable to co-operate with each other to further their shared interests as producers and suppliers. They fail to further their collective good, to the great good fortune of the rest of us as consumers. The phenomenon is known as market competition and, while it should perhaps be cited more to combat various theories of class solidarity, it was certainly well known to Marx, who lost little sleep over it. In Bowman's study, however, we find that the mine-owners, themselves well aware of all this, were by no means willing to rest content with it. They saw clearly that their tragedy was the product of their individual freedom of action. And, accordingly, they sought somehow to constrain themselves, to restrict their freedom of action to their mutual advantage.

The owners' attempts to create a cartel were, of course, a part of this very strategy. Individual owners sought to commit themselves to a price-fixing agreement, recognizing that to restrict their actions by conforming to the agreement would be to the collective good. But conformity to such an agreement was not enforceable; the owners had no power to press it upon each other. Freely they were forced to act, and their freely chosen actions were a cause of damage to themselves. Accordingly they looked beyond themselves for sources of constraint; they sought an *external* power, a Hobbesian sword as it were, which might remove their freedom to their own greater good. The three powers they turned to are wonderful symbols of the important routes to a solution of the problem of capitalist collective action available in modern societies.

First of all the owners turned to local and federal politicians, recognizing the power of the state as a possible source of constraint. If a minimum price for coal could be legislated, owners would be saved from their own lamentable inclination to undercut each other and their collective good would be furthered. If minimum conditions of health and safety were legislated, some mines would be permanently disadvantaged by the increased costs and forced to close, again furthering the collective good. Accordingly, the owners lobbied for legislation, but none too successfully. Anti-trust considerations were apparently taken seriously at this time, and legislators tended to maintain and intensify competition rather than restrict it. The state was apparently more than a mere "committee of the bourgeoisie". The owners were forced to look elsewhere.

Their next hope lay in the railway company, which was the monopoly owner of the means of coal transportation. Unfortunately, while the railway had the power to regulate the production of coal, it had no interest in doing so, or rather no interest in doing so in ways advantageous to the mine-owners, and so this approach also proved to be fruitless. Monopoly ownership would come to play an immensely important role in sustaining sectors of the capitalist economy, but did not do so here.

The external power that did eventually ameliorate the owners' problems was the *mine-workers* and their trade union organization. High wages raised owners' costs, and if made a permanent feature of the economic context would induce the most marginal producers to close down. With inelastic demand, the remaining producers would secure higher prices more than sufficient to cover their increased labour costs. Thus, although it was in no individual owner's interest unilaterally to increase wages, a binding wages agreement was a collective good for the owners. And such an agreement would indeed be binding if the strike power and disruptive capacity of organized labour lay behind it. Thus, it was in the interest of the owners collectively to encourage a strong union, facilitate its activities, enter into agreements with it, and support the extension of its power into those competing mining areas which were not yet unionized. As for the union, it proved willing to put up with higher wages and to tolerate the "hearty support" of the employers for its efforts to extend its organization and strengthen its powers. According to Bowman, in Ohio, Pennsylvania, Illinois and Indiana, an agreement of operatives and the union in 1898 "ensured the union-enforced organization of the coal industry which endured with greater or less success for the next twenty-five years" (Bowman 1989: 107).

As one owner was later to write in the trade journal, *Black Diamond*, "the United Mine Workers of America, as a body, have forced the operations of the various competitive fields into one large combination" (Bowman 1989: 108). The power of the workers organized the capitalists and freed them once more to make a profit. And when the profits of those same capitalists were threatened by the competition of non-unionized mines in other states, the workers went forth, in the shape of extraordinarily tenacious and courageous union leaders, to organize and unionize the competing workforce. In the eyes of a West Virginia mine-owner this was "Pennsylvania and Ohio operators – sending the union to action . . . the miners are being used as tools by the operators in competitive states"(ibid.: 120).

Thus the mine-owners were saved from their own rationality by their workers. In this case, as predicted by individualism, the mine-owners were not able themselves to act collectively to further their "class interests". Instead of co-operating with fellow members of their class, they chose initially to free-ride. They acted as rational, self-interested, independent individuals. And yet there are problems here. First of all, the owners *did* act collectively, albeit very weakly: they constituted and sustained a trade association; they lobbied legislators; they negotiated as a body with their workers.[7] And secondly, when they were forced to act for their own collective good, it was by the collective power of their own workers. Whence came this power? In a sense it came from their union, but whence came the union? Where else but out of the collective action of the workers? Evidently, what was impossible for the capitalists was possible for the workers. Considered in this way, Bowman's case history will actually serve to call into question the whole basis of the individualistic approach.

It is a matter of history that coal-miners in the United States engaged in prolonged and intensive collective action in the course of forming unions and labour organizations and in providing them with the necessary support. There is no doubt that this was costly action. Miners risked loss of livelihood and even loss of life itself in the course of it; not a few did lose their lives in what was often a violent struggle. Bowman himself has no hesitation in acknowledging all this; indeed he records his admiration for the collective action of the miners, although it is no part of the objective of his work to chronicle it. But it is hard to see how this extremely costly action can be understood from the perspective of an individualistic social theory.

Why then did the miners manage to achieve a far more intense and effective output of collective action than the owners? An obvious conjecture, in the light of the discussion in earlier chapters, is that different interaction conditions characterized the two groups. Miners work long hours together in conditions of close proximity and strong interdependence. And not only do they work closely with fellow miners, typically they work *only* with fellow miners. Moreover, the need for a considerable concentration of labour underground typically leads to a concentration of miners' dwellings above ground, and hence in many cases to a differentiated social network, a demarcated community, a shared and distinctive culture. As a consequence, frequent interaction with fellow miners is obligatory; the interaction *de facto* excludes outsiders; the costs of exiting from the interaction are very high. These are the very conditions that status groups seek to sustain as a basis for successful collective action. No such conditions appertain, however, for mine-owners. They are not thrown together by the nature of their work. They are not obliged to live together or in close proximity. They need pay no great price for removing themselves from social intercourse with their fellows. Small wonder then that owners' ability to engender significant collective action is correspondingly limited.

The argument, of course, is pure conjecture and must remain so. Bowman's concern is with the mine-owners. He tells us something of the collective action of the miners but nothing of their conditions of life. None the less, what is recorded elsewhere of those conditions does add plausibility to the conjecture. And there are other studies that can take the present argument forward, including studies of British mining communities where the role of interaction conditions is a familiar motif. In David Gilbert's *Class, community and collective action* (1992), for example, a comparison of two very different locations is used to make an argument very close to that above. In the Notts coalfield, mining developed in areas that were already highly populated, engaged in other industries, and socially organized in various cross-cutting ways. Miners took homes in existing developed communities, which sometimes became mining towns but rarely miners' towns. Their communal life was forged with families from a variety of other occupations and their particular economic interests were but a part of the many and various interests that received attention in their communities. In this context, miners' collective action was relatively weak. This was the region of moderation and conciliation, of the emergence of the Spencer union (and eventually of the rejection of the strike instruction from the National Union of Mineworkers in 1984). It is contrasted with South Wales, with its remarkable capacity for communal solidarity and intense, sustained collective action. And, here, interaction was more frequent, homogeneous, obligatory and isolated, as a consequence of the social geography of the region.

Mining in South Wales expanded in a hitherto sparsely populated area where the terrain had ensured that even agriculture was little developed. "The Valleys" in the floors of which the pits were sunk were remarkably narrow and steep-sided, which led to a distinctive pattern of settlement. Small villages became strung along the valleys like the beads along a necklace, each surrounding a pithead. Few expanded beyond the size where all the inhabitants would know each other and sustain social relationships with each other. And the same physical constraints that limited size also tended to isolate the villages from each other and discourage mobility between them. Finally, these same features of small size and isolation discouraged settlement by anyone other than mine-workers; company officials, managers and "middle-class" members of the wider

society tended to live elsewhere. In these *de novo* communities, consequently, social interaction was internally homogeneous and externally
insignificant owing to isolation. Miners in dense proximity were obliged
to engage in frequent interaction with each other without the realistic
probability of withdrawal or of alternative forms of social relationship.
And it was just these villages that later became the *sine qua non* of labour
solidarity and discipline in the mining industry. In the disputes, strikes
and lockouts that later came to constitute their history, they proved to be
remarkable for their capacity to engender collective action and to suffer
its costs.

Gilbert's study does not merely confirm a relationship between interaction and collective action; it offers insight into how the one gives rise
to the other. How does life become ordered in a newly established mining settlement, such as that of Ynysybwl in South Wales to which Gilbert
devotes special attention? First of all, a network of social relationships
begins to develop, and institutions and organizations that give pattern
and coherence to social intercourse. The pub, the school and the chapel
quickly come to prominence, and all alike mark the evolution of a distinct form of culture (a form, as it happens, clearly designed in opposition to dominant external social and cultural forms). Above all, the
chapel emerges as the focus of social life and the organizational centre
for collective responses to a whole range of practical needs and exigen-
cies. Interaction, it would seem, engenders a degree of organization, and
the organization takes place prior to any specific narrow end or objective
to which it might later be directed. Later, the union lodge will take the
place of predominance initially held by the chapel – an organization oriented to a specific interest will supplant a general-purpose one – but the
sequence serves as a nice symbol of the relationship of social organization and social interests. Perhaps it serves also as a symbol of the priority
of social intercourse over instrumentally oriented action. Be that as it
may, it is clear which of the two schemes set out earlier is operative
here; it is the second:

(b) interaction → organization → interests → action

Because of the social homogeneity of the Welsh villages (of
Ynysybwl) the organizations that evolved out of this process were
responsive to and indeed incorporated a common notion of the collective
good, which allowed a clear and consistent encouragement and sanction-

ing of collective action to occur. In Notts, where there was more hetero-geneity amongst interacting individuals, communities and organizations evolved that embodied more diverse and conflicting conceptions of the collective good and were less easily moved to act in furtherance of one factional conception of that good. In neither case did given economic interests determine how people organized themselves. Shared economic interests emerged and became salient only after interaction determined by other factors had engendered community and organization, and even then they were locally defined interests whose furtherance was sanctioned as the good of a specific interacting collective. This last point is indeed given considerable emphasis by Gilbert. The collective action of the Welsh miners during strikes and lockouts was sometimes unleashed as part of a national dispute, but it remained community-based and primarily oriented to the collective good of the local interacting community. Local interests tended to take priority when they conflicted with the interests of the region.

Gilbert's study is exemplary in its combination of theoretical concerns with empirical and historical investigations, and its conclusions are, at least for one reader, entirely convincing. It leaves little doubt of the inadequacy of individualistic accounts in this context, and explains collective action in what fundamentally are interactive terms. But in doing this it treats the miners' collective action not as "class action" in an abstract sense but as the action of specific communities of people furthering their particular collective good. The action in question is accounted for by the scheme previously used to explain the collective action of status groups and social movements and no role is found to exist for the alternative explanatory scheme traditionally associated with a distinctive conception of class.

7.3 Classes, status groups and communities

The treatment of "class action" as the collective action of status groups is an increasingly common strategy in modern social theory. An important contribution to this development has been made by Frank Parkin (1979), whose concern, above all, has been to understand class action and class conflict in an empirically reputable way. Exploitative class action occurs, according to Parkin, when a collective, operating along the lines of a Weberian status group, successfully achieves a closure that excludes others from goods or resources. In the case of bourgeois groups, the key exclusionary criteria are possession of *property* and/or possession of *credentials*. On the basis of the former, outsiders are excluded from entrepreneurial opportunities and the possibility of engaging in the most profitable forms of investment. On the basis of the latter, the most rewarding occupational positions are monopolized. This successful exclusionary and monopolistic activity serves to define in turn a class of exploited outsiders, in Weber's terms a latent negatively privileged status group, who seek to act as a group themselves in order to usurp the goods and privileges they are being denied. On this account of class conflict, nothing special is credited to the means of production or to the opportunities available in the market, or to the relationship of any individual to them. No fundamental difference is admitted between class action and collective action based on ethnicity or religious affiliation or any other basis for status differentiation. No case is made for the priority of usurping actions by workers over exclusionary actions whereby one group of workers deprives another such group of goods and opportunities. And no theoretically significant difference between "class" and "status" is identified.

Another seminal contribution here has been made by Randall Collins (1986). He agrees with Parkin that class action is a species of status group action, but is still more iconoclastic in the conclusions he draws from this.

> The existence of status groups does not eliminate class conflict. Rather, it provides the specific form in which it takes place. It is not usually possible for all the members of a Marxian class – essentially reifications of the abstract factors of production in economic theory – to act together as a unified group. Status group organization . . . is the natural form in which economic interests can act socially. This model of stratification, then, cannot be determined by mere relationship to the means of production; the actual form of that relationship is itself the result of specific social processes. (Collins 1986: 129)

Thus, if Collins is correct, Weber on status groups does not merely help us to understand class action, he requires us fundamentally to redescribe it. Weber's theory of status groups implies a rejection of Marx's understanding of class, and even of Weber's understanding of class. The whole history of modern capitalist society has to be seen in a new way. It is no longer a history of class conflict, or even a history of shifting conflicts with a tripartite basis of class, status and power. It is the history of economic conflict based on status group action, in effect a "*series of monopolizations*" (Collins 1986: 129). Collective economic action is action to create, defend, exercise, extend, oppose or destroy a monopoly. It is to be understood in terms of status group affiliations and the collective good of status groups, as described in Chapter 5 above.

Let us review the advantages of treating *prima facie* instances of class action as forms of status group action. First of all, as both Parkin and Collins emphasize, the consequent descriptions allow a direct comparison of economic position with ethnicity and other criteria as bases for collective action, and make all kinds of such action intelligible in the same way, in terms of a single scheme. Secondly, as Collins in particular emphasizes, they take explicit account of the fact that putative instances of class action are always associated with more narrowly defined groups or networks and are typically actions for the good of their particular members. Thirdly, and this is something that neither Parkin, nor Collins, nor even Weber himself sufficiently recognizes, the redescription of class action as status group action is at the same time a way of understanding its basis and hence accounting for its existence. One does not have to accept Olson's criticism of Marx in order to recognize that the rationale for class action in Marx is problematic. Rendered instead as status group action, the action in question, however extended, can be understood and explained as instrumentally oriented collective action sustained on the basis of restricted social intercourse. Such an explanation, moreover, has the additional virtue of bridging any alleged gap between macro and micro theory.

Status group theory is not, however, the only body of theoretical work with these merits. Similar advantages accrue if class action is redescribed as social movement action – just as we should expect given the arguments made earlier in Chapters 5 and 6. Craig Calhoun (1982) has used the insights of social movement theory to redescribe "class action". He has taken a special interest in the history of the "classic" period of the industrial revolution in England, i.e. the period 1780–1840, and has documented how the collective action of workers in that period was quintessentially *local* action, bounded and circumscribed and oriented to the circumstances of a particular place. As a result, like Collins, Calhoun stresses that "it is not usually possible for all the members of a Marxian class to act together". But Calhoun makes even more of the point than Collins does. A Marxian class, according to Calhoun, is something that extends through the entire system of production. It exists at the same level as capital. It is not manifested in local eruptions, but only in activities that involve an entire delocalized social formation. According to Marx, a class has no specific boundary; not even the boundaries of the state itself serve to bound and define it. But writers in the Marxian tradition have forgotten this, and described any eruption of collective action by workers as class struggle. This is illegitimate and confusing: "It is as weak to describe workers' struggles caught within the bounds of locality – in Oldham alone, say, or even all of Southeast Lancashire – as comprising 'class struggle' as to describe the local industrial organization as comprising (rather than reflecting, or being shaped by) capitalism" (Calhoun 1987: 51-2).

The nub of the error is that *class-based* collective action is being confused with *community-based* collective action. And the difference obscured by the error is a vital one because strong collective action is intelligible precisely as the product of developed communal ties. The nature of community is both systematically defined and extensively exemplified in Calhoun's work. In itself, a community is no more than a network of social relationships in a particular space or region that are internally stronger and more numerous than those connecting the network with the outside. For given individuals however, experience of community varies in intensity and inclusiveness:

> Structurally an individual becomes more deeply woven into a web of relationships and they become a part of his established premises of action. This happens as relationships become dense within a social field (so that activity in each involves a considerable range of others as an implicitly relevant public), as relationships become multiplex (so that each involves many purposes and qualities of bond) and as relationships become systematic (so that each has its existence, not independently, or voluntarily, but rather as part of a differentiated set of relationships each of which preserves the others, as in kinship). This is community. (Calhoun 1982: 233-4)

Why is it that strong community is the basis for strong collective action? Calhoun offers a great range of reasons, most of which relate to the dense and bounded network of social relationships in communities. These relationships allow rapid mobilization for collective action when the occasion arises. They allow for the ready application of social pressure against free-riders, or alternatively for the sanctioning of such deviants by the withdrawal of social relationships. And, less directly, differentiated, dense social relationships lead to a shared and differentiated culture, a shared tradition, in which the individual thinks as part of the collective and identifies herself as a member of the collective. When this is the case, the collective good is not cognitively differentiated from the individual's good, and is enacted as part of the maintenance of that individual's identity (Calhoun 1991).[8]

Because theories of social movements, including resource mobilization theories, have been an important point of reference in his work, Calhoun is particularly aware of the problematic character of collective action and very much concerned to account for its existence. Accordingly, he attends very carefully to the way in which collective action is facilitated by and emerges from the social relationships of community. The consequent explanation of collective action is again consistent with scheme (b) above, in which it is not given socio-economic interests but interaction and organization that are inceptive. And it is consistent too with the approach of the "closure" theorists. Like Randall Collins, Calhoun studies large-scale processes in the evolution of industrial capitalist societies while constantly attending to the particulars of local social relationships. As with Collins, his work serves to refute the claim that any gap or disjunction exists between micro and macro-theory in the social sciences. And, again as with Collins, the overall development of modern capitalism has to be reconceptualized if the results of his work are accepted.

In Calhoun's view of the industrial revolution in England, the emergence of a working class organized at the national level is associated with a move from strong to weak collective action. The early stages of industrialization, in the half-century from 1780, had the effect of putting pressure on the ways of life of workers in established traditional communities. They responded vigorously, sometimes violently, with strong and direct forms of collective action against the new forms of capitalist industry and the state and local power that supported it. The consequent agitation, with accompanying riots and outbreaks of Luddite destructiveness, have been extensively chronicled. But these were not, in Calhoun's view, instances of class action. They were produced by radical populist social movements based upon the local solidarity of traditional communities. They expressed the radical conservatism of artisans, craftsmen, traders and skilled home-workers, even sometimes small employers, responding to a perceived threat to a traditional way of life.

At this time the increasingly numerous factory workers and the inhabitants of the rapidly expanding urban areas were deeply involved in the creation of new communities, communities that would be of ever-increasing importance as the century proceeded. But even as these communities were forming, the need to oppose capital on more than the local level was becoming increasingly recognized, and appropriate organizational means were being developed in both political and economic spheres. Chartism and trade unionism grew into movements that linked together communities of workers throughout the length of the land and presented an organized opposition to a similarly extensively organized capitalism. And as these movements gained support, "class consciousness" became increasingly evident in the form of theories of class conflict articulated by workers themselves, their allies and their enemies. But even as the organization of workers became increasingly coextensive with the organization of capital, the intensity of the collective action directed by the one against the other declined. By the 1850s capitalism had stabilized in Britain. And as the rapid growth of communications and infrastructure further facilitated the organization of workers through the second half of the century, their political stance moved strongly in the direction of reform, the encapsulation of conflict, the search for compromise.

Why did this occur? Because, says Calhoun, workers threatened by capitalism were being replaced by workers who were part of capitalism. The way of life of the "conservative radicals" was dying out, and the new factory workers saw no fundamental threat in the system as such. Moreover, the new workers were increasingly living in loose association with each other, rather than close community, and engaging in industrial confrontation through unions and delocalized organizations based upon associational ties, weak bureaucratic social relationships that while not unable to generate effective collective action, were unable to sustain action of high intensity and great individual cost. As workers more and more came to live not in dense networks of multiple communal relationships but in loosely constituted networks in which associational ties figured increasingly large, they found themselves unable, as well as disinclined, to press themselves into highly costly collective action, and more inclined to support reformist policies through party and union and to negotiate with employers and politicians only too willing to offer the olive branch of compromise.[9]

Calhoun's insistent contrast of community-based and class-based collective action and its exemplification in the context of nineteenth-century English social history are obviously contestable. But if they are accepted they raise at least two questions of great theoretical importance. First of all, the thesis discussed in Chapter 6, of the recent emergence of new kinds of social movement, is (again) put in doubt. The contrast between earlier class-based movements and modern particularistic movements looks artefactual when many of those earlier movements are redescribed as "radical conservative" local movements bent upon the defence of particular communities. And the alleged movement away from "strategic" to "identity-oriented" objectives in "new" social movements is called into question if the preservation of a traditional lifestyle was what the defence of community then entailed, as Calhoun suggests.[10]

Secondly, despite the contrast with "community", "class" in Calhoun still refers to a bounded, networky (status) group, wholly comparable with all the other such groups that make their presence felt in the democratic politics of industrial societies.[11] And the strength and incidence of "class" collective action is still made intelligible in terms of the distribution of social relationships and the nature of social interaction rather than by reference to a distribution of given socio-economic interests.[12] Unsurprisingly, when class is seen through the filter of social movement theory much the same conclusions emerge as when it is seen in terms of the theory of status groups. In the last analysis, Collins and Calhoun lead us to see the world in much the same way.

7.4 "Class": what use?

If the argument made so far is correct, then social theory loses nothing by dispensing with "class": it has no distinctive role to play, and the work it has done hitherto would be done as well or better by use of other concepts. The role of social linkages, organization and mutual social control has been emphasized in the understanding of putative class action, which has effectively made it visible as a form of status group action based on "economic" membership criteria.[13]

The argument may seem strange in one respect: it proceeds by emphasizing factors that have always been given prominence by theorists of class themselves. Marx famously stressed the importance of physical proximity, social relations and political organization in converting a class from a mere economic category into a self-aware, socially cohesive entity, and the same theme has been addressed again and again in later Marxian discussions of class consciousness and class struggle. Weber made an explicit distinction between "class situation" and "social class", which is "the totality of those class situations within which individual and generational mobility is easy and typical" (Weber 1968: 302). And his clear intention was to bridge the gap between class as a mere aggregate of individuals with similar opportunities and class as a connected social formation with some degree of unity. Nor is there any shortage of more recent attempts to bridge the gap between class as an "economic" category and class as a socially aware and ordered collective.

The importance of this literature and its many insights goes without saying, but this by no means amounts to an argument for the importance of "class". It is necessary to continue to ask what distinctive role "class" can be given, which is close to asking how far similar interests, associated with similar class positions or situations, can be shown to have an explanatory role. Note that Weber's concept of "social class" is defined in a way that makes no mention of similar class situations and/or shared interests. It refers to nothing more than a domain of easy mobility. Any such domain, extending across any class situations, however diverse, however different, constitutes a social class. Rigorous use of this Weberian concept might extend the use of the word "class", but would at the same time diminish the importance of the concept "class" as traditionally understood. It would move the basis of explanatory theory away from given interests toward interaction and social relations, precisely as a move from "class" to "status" serves to do.

It is hard to see what justification there can be for use of the "class" concept, other than the conviction that similar given economic interests somehow prompt the evolution of coextensive organized groups and the incidence of collective action. "Class" is associated with a particular explanatory scheme: situation → interests → organization → action. But no plausible account exists of how given interests engender organization and action as this scheme implies, and historical studies point to the superiority of an alternative scheme, the scheme associated with the concept of status set out earlier. The use of "class" as a key *theoretical* concept should thus be discontinued.

Having said this, it is necessary immediately to add that it does not amount to the wholesale dismissal of core ideas in the work of two of the greatest of all social theorists. Nor does it even imply the redundancy of their thoughts on economic interests. What it does imply is that some of their ideas might have been better extended in slightly different directions. Recall how Marx's analysis of production derives from the economists' concepts of "capital" and "labour" as universally required inputs into the process. In the particular conditions of capitalism, capital was privately owned and labour freely marketed; the institutions of private property and the labour market were fully developed, deeply entrenched and strongly protected. Thus, returns on capital routinely flowed to its owners and payment for labour routinely passed to its providers. There was, however, a "surplus" from production that might have gone either to capital or to labour but in fact went to capital. This surplus, which to the extent that it went to the one could not go to the other, was the symbol and the enduring basis of an opposition between capital and labour, an opposition that would operate as a significant influence upon action, whether or not individuals recognized its existence or acknowledged its importance explicitly. Note how theory can move along these lines, this far, without reference to social classes.

What then happens in Marx and the subsequent Marxian tradition is that this opposition is further transformed into the opposition of sets of individuals, the members of different social classes. In flowing to different social locations, wages and profits are assumed to flow to distinct, mutually exclusive categories of persons. And each person so categorized is assumed to have in consequence a well-defined class interest with the inherent potential, in the last analysis, to orient her actions. The imagination is thus illicitly drawn on to envisage a conflict of interest defined between categories of persons. Capital and labour are reified,[14] as is often pointed out, as the Marxian classes of capitalists and workers, bourgeoisie and proletariat; and the players are thereby created to play the parts in a forthcoming drama of class struggle. No doubt Marx was well aware that his account of "two great camps" was false as he wrote it, but expected it to become more and more accurate in the long term as the consequence of changes (to which he sought to contribute) that would increasingly polarise individuals along class lines. But social change has not continued in this direction. Instead of the last handful of capitalists struggling on alone, vainly attempting to consume unaided the mind-boggling surplus of a vast, mechanized, technologically awesome, productive system, it has occurred to them to ask the workers to lend a hand. "Surplus" is now incarnate in wage packets, and flows of returns on capital now irrigate very large areas of society, albeit very unevenly.

190

And indeed the possibility of carefully tailoring the social distribution of returns on capital as political expediency dictates, of exploiting it as a means of social stabilization and control, is now both widely recognized and successfully acted upon. In this changed context, in which "class", originally inapplicable, has failed to become applicable, it must be asked whether the reification that it represents should not be reversed. The reification conflates theoretical problems of group formation with those concerning the institutionalized basis of calculative action: undo it and it is possible to abandon Marx's account of the evolution of collective action while retaining his insights into the pervasive economic significance of institutional arrangements.

From this perspective, the key insight in Marx is that private property and the alienability of labour have become entrenched as enduring features of capitalist societies, along with a whole range of associated and derivative patterns and practices. These things are crucial and distinctive institutions of capitalism. On the account of institutions proposed earlier in chapter 2, they may be understood as ubiquitous, all-pervasive elements of the extended distributions of self-referring knowledge that constitute capitalist societies. They are institutions that, like all institutions, exist by virtue of being known to exist. Calculations made on the basis of their existence constitute the phenomena that confirm their existence. Such calculations have increasingly permeated the industrial societies that Marx described, so that their premises have increasingly become recognized as definitive features of its institutional landscape, crucial elements in sustaining the gigantic self-fulfilling prophecy that is a capitalist society. It is true that even deeply entrenched institutions of this kind do change; indeed change is their normal state. The central institutions of capitalism have systematically changed since Marx, with the continued rise of the joint stock company and "impersonal possession" (Scott 1985, 1986), and the ever more pervasive role of the institution of money and the system of finance capital: "money in its modern form is surely the most implacable collective representation people ever imposed on themselves" (Lee 1994: 406).[15] But such change does not occur at a rate sufficiently rapid to disrupt those calculations that both rely upon the existence of the institutions and keep them in existence.

Analyzed in this way, the opposition of capital and labour will express itself not in an isomorphous opposition of classes, but pervasively and profoundly through being taken account of, over and over again, in the calculations and calculative actions of all kinds of groups, collectives and organizations. The opposition will not imply a given distribution of interests, but exist as a ubiquitous factor bearing upon diverse reckonings of interest. In a capitalist society, all kinds of circumstances and accidents of history may result in the emergence of extended status groups, or movements, or networks of members who recognize themselves as sharing specific collective interests and who seek to further them. But among the features of the social context that account for those collective interests emerging and being recognized will be the entrenched institutional features emphasized by Marx. Members themselves will recognize them as givens of their situation and act on the basis of their being there. Knowledge that they are there will both condition calculations of what actions further interests and, perhaps more important, condition the collective cognitive processes that lead to the emergence of recognized definitions of what are shared interests and which have priority. For, to have an interest in a state of affairs is to recognize it as being *en route* to something desired or sought after. And for members to determine what is *en route* to the fulfilment of all their various wants requires them to take cognizance of the social circumstances of action, and the problems and the opportunities presented by the existence of what present themselves as enduring institutional arrangements.

To deal with the problem in this way recognizes the truly profound importance of those features of capitalist societies described and analyzed by Marx and Weber, and the fact that the opposition between capital and labour in such societies is material to all kinds of calculations of interest and forms of conflict. But to accept that something is of pervasive importance in conditioning the calculations of groups, networks or collectives is not at all the same as accepting that it can account for the emergence of them or that it may serve as the template for the overall pattern they will eventually manifest. It is this last assumption that is implied by distinctive theoretical uses of the concept of class; the assumption is incorrect.

8

Administrative hierarchies

8.1 The command model

At the opposite extreme from the status group lies the administrative hierarchy. Although both make claims against outsiders, a position in the former signifies equality with peers, whereas a position in the latter signifies difference expressed as rank. In formally democratic societies of equal citizens, status groups are most readily accepted as repositories of expertise, whereas hierarchies are widely perceived as essential devices for the organization and co-ordination of action.

In the familiar conception of a hierarchy as a chain or a pyramid, decisions by persons or offices "high" in the system take priority over those "lower down" in determining how the capacity for action of the whole will be employed. Co-ordinated, concerted action is achieved, and conflicting, self-destructive actions are avoided, by routine acceptance that some judgements will override others as the basis of what is done. Those "high" in the system possess the capacity to act through the bodies of others, and those "lower down" put the corresponding capacity at the disposal of their "superiors".

The existence of hierarchies of this kind implies, of itself, neither enduring relationships of domination and subservience nor systematic inequalities in the ability to exercise power. The co-ordination made possible by the creation of hierarchy may be in the individual interest of all involved. Hierarchy may voluntarily be constituted, on the spot and temporarily, by the unconstrained action of those involved, to hunt, for example, or to fish or to climb. Members may actively seek subordinate rather than superordinate positions in such ad hoc hierarchies, and find no difficulty resuming normal equal relationships once the task at hand has been accomplished. Thus, when we look at the semi-permanent bureaucratic hierarchies of modern industrial societies and note how they make social power differentially available, we should take care not to conflate the evaluation of those systems with an evaluation of hierarchy *per se*.

The accepted starting point for any study of the system of established bureaucratic hierarchies is, of course, the work of Max Weber. In a famous passage, he identified six key characteristics of modern bureaucracies: their confinement to a specific area of jurisdiction; their constitution as offices arranged so that "lower" offices are supervised by "higher" ones; their reliance on files; their use of trained officials; their insistence on full-time working; and their obligation to operate according to abstract general rules (Weber 1968: 956–8; see also 220–1). As usual, Weber provided a cautiously formulated ideal-typical account based on actual cases, but a consistent theoretical vision is unmistakably present in the passage, a vision moreover that is entirely consistent with that implicit in all of his scattered but extensive writings on bureaucracy.

Ever-present in Weber's discussions is the conception of bureaucracy as a vast instrument, something analogous to a machine or mechanism. What the instrument does, its "regular activities", is assigned as the duties of officials; and the authority to give the commands that result in the discharge or enactment of the duties is given to other officials, for use strictly according to rule (Weber 1968: 956). Thus, just as an officer on the bridge of a ship may pull levers and thereby bring about a swing in the rudder or an increased output from the engine, so an authority in a bureaucracy may issue a command and thereby bring about the execution of a "regular activity" by someone lower down the system. And, just as a secure connection exists between the lever on the bridge and the ship's rudder or engine, so a secure connection exists between the command of the authority and the action elsewhere of the underling. In the case of the bureaucratic authority and the subordinate, the connection is secure because both are oriented to rules: the authority commands the enactment of a rule and the underling enacts it just as commanded.

The bureaucratic hierarchy resembles an instrument or mechanism not only in its determinate internal operation but also in its necessary dependence upon externalities. Bureaucratic hierarchies are not self-sufficient systems. Unlike other social formations, they are externally designed to serve external purposes, just like instruments or machines. They need external resources, just as machines need fuel. And most important of all they need external directives. It is true that an official discharging a duty is generally doing so at the command of an internal authority, a senior official in the same hierarchy. But that official will herself be acting upon instructions and according to rules. The hierarchy constitutes a chain of command, and individual officials transmit commands down it; they act as passive agents, as relayers of instructions originating above them. The chain of command ends with someone who inserts commands into the top of the system, who is not bound by its internal rules. Just as an instrument or machine operates according to the direction of its operator, who is external to the machine mechanism itself, so must the bureaucracy operate under external direction to serve external ends.

Weber very much took for granted that a bureaucracy was an administrative instrument at the disposal of an external controller. He stressed the difference between a bureaucracy *constituting* power (for external use) and a bureaucracy possessing the power that it constituted (Weber 1968: 991). Emphatically, the former did not imply the latter: just like a waterfall, the bureaucracy could supply power without possessing any. Weber drew a famous distinction between power as the probability of implementing one's own will, even against resistance, and authority as the probability of being obeyed. The official within the bureaucratic machine had authority, in that her commands would probably be obeyed if correctly and legitimately issued. But she had no power; her commands were the commands she had to give and were not a matter of "will" or choice or discretion as far as she was concerned. The controller of the bureaucratic machine, in contrast, had power as well as authority: she could choose commands to implement her will, and they would probably be obeyed.[1]

On the other hand, Weber sought to make a strong contrast between the power of the controller of a modern bureaucracy and wholly arbitrary power. The controller had to choose from a range of commands set by "the rules". Obedience to her commands depended on their consistency with "the rules", so that arbitrary and whimsical use of the bureaucracy in the manner of a despot was impossible. "The rules" were constitutive of the bureaucratic mechanism and set limits on its possibilities just as the parts of a machine set limits upon what the machine can do: the army bureaucracy would not routinely arrange political assassinations any more than the lawn-mower would routinely trim the hedge. (Weber's death in 1920 came after turbulent times but well before the advent of the Third Reich and the Second World War.)

Weber considered that modern bureaucracies were particularly successful in achieving a "rigorous mechanization" of administration based upon a reliable conformity to rules. He offered no systematic theory of the basis of that conformity and related it to a number of different factors, including belief in legitimate authority and the moral qualities of officials. But it is clear that the peculiar reliability of modern systems is related to their distinctive means of monitoring and control, to the situation in which officials work that is, more than to their "inner" individual qualities. Weber stressed four factors that made for an especially reliable administrative system: the isolation of official tasks; their "more or less exhaustive" specification by rules; the surveillance of their performance; and the availability of appropriate sanctions.

The key to the isolation of the official is her occupancy of an office within a purpose-built permanent system of such offices. The relationship between these offices is specified by impersonal rules. In so far as the rules define the command system of a "monocratic bureaucracy", links with the immediate superior and immediate subordinates will be the only normal and appropriate ones. The office-holder, in thus being defined as a relay in the chain of command, is at the same time cut off from the rest of the system of offices, which is revealed only through the stream of instructions from above that finds its way into the office and the related stream of records from below of instructions carried out. The office-holder is thus presented as very close to being an atomized individual in the context of the system, with all the vulnerability to control which that implies.

Even more important, however, is the isolation of the work of the office-holder from the world outside of work. It is characteristic of modern bureaucracy that what officials do in their offices should have no connection with the activities and social relationships of their private worlds or indeed any other "external" activities. In the office they carry out their only form of paid work, and do so using knowledge and skill distinct from that employed elsewhere. There is a complete separation of "the bureau from the private domicile of the official and . . . official activity from the sphere of private life. Public monies and equipment are divorced from the private property of the official. This condition . . . is found in public as well as private enterprises; in the latter . . . even [the office of the entrepreneur at the top] is separated from the household, business from private correspondence, and business assets from private wealth" (Weber 1968: 957).

The significance of this isolation and insulation of the system of public administration is, of course, now everywhere recognized. It means that the particular nature of what is done is typically of no significance to those who do it: what is being done has no bearing upon specific, personally involving and emotionally charged concerns within the private realm, and because work lacks extrinsic significance in this sense it is experienced as devoid of intrinsic significance as well. It is purely work to be done, meaningful only for other lives; that it requires one kind of action rather than another engenders little in the way either of pleasure or of pain. And this means that what is done may be effectively controlled by means of weak sanctions and incentives; because doing A or not A is a matter of indifference in so far as the acts themselves are concerned, a very modest external sanction will suffice to determine which act is performed. Thus may a tax officer, for example, for a very modest inducement be moved to bring ruin to any number of individuals, with no more involvement in their fate than the lawn-mower has with that of the lawn.

This separation of the public and the private allows the realization of what it is tempting to identify as the key principle of action of modern societies, the principle that is at the very core of bureaucracy but that is also clearly evident elsewhere: a truly remarkable amount may readily be obtained from people, provided that one expects and requires only a very little of them. Just how much may be obtained on this basis is evident, for example, in parts of Zygmunt Bauman's (1989) study of *Modernity and the holocaust*. And the principle continues to lie at the heart of our institutional arrangements, the secret of our current success.

Once the separation of bureaucratic activity is accomplished, a variety of internal control systems will suffice to ensure its appropriate operation: instructions may be conveyed, their execution appraised, and rewards and sanctions imposed by many different means. But Weber wishes to identify the means characteristic of developed Western bureaucracies as the most conducive to reliable, disciplined, predictable and elaborately detailed administration. Action oriented to impersonal rules is that much more predictable than action oriented to personal pronouncements: where action is oriented to "general rules, which are . . . more or less exhaustive", and the "reduction of modern office management to rules" (Weber 1968: 958) is thereby achieved, a very high level of predictability follows. Where files are kept, they allow a level of detailed surveillance otherwise beyond contemplation. Where reward takes the form of a salary that can be trusted to continue in the long term, the consequent "steadiness" offers the optimum basis for reliable administration.

Of course, bureaucracies that make extensive use of impersonal rules, files and monthly salaries are not possible in all social contexts. They require a literate population and a money economy. But, where they are possible, they arise and spread, just as new technology spreads, by virtue of their "technical superiority". In these bureaucracies all the desirable features of systematic administration "are raised to the optimum point" (Weber 1968: 973). On this basis their growth is to be looked for in any kind of society capable of sustaining them. But with capitalist market economies they have a particular affinity, which extends beyond mere need: "Bureaucracy develops the more perfectly, the more it is 'dehumanised', the more completely it succeeds in eliminating from official business love, hatred, and all purely personal, irrational and emotional elements which escape calculation. This is appraised as its special virtue by capitalism" (Weber 1968: 975). (It goes without saying that the analogy between the early Marx on the worker and Weber on the official is very close. The basis of the tragic vision of the latter is, formally speaking, hard to distinguish from the basis of the romanticism of the former. Indeed, the key arguments to follow in this chapter could equally well have been ordered around a discussion of the former topic.)

So much then for the basic elements of the command model. As is typical with Weber, it represents an ingenious synthesis of the empirical and the ideal, hard to evaluate from either perspective since it claims neither general descriptive adequacy nor formal theoretical rigour. Although in the present context our interest is in the command model as theory, it is worth recalling some of the well-known empirically based criticisms that have been advanced against it, since empirical failings may be useful pointers to theoretical weaknesses.

First of all, Weber's stress on their "technical superiority" is often held to be incompatible with the manifest ineffectiveness and unreliability of modern bureaucratic organizations. This, of course, is a criticism of long standing, such long standing that it actually precedes Weber's work and is reflected in an earlier meaning of bureaucracy as inefficient and needlessly elaborate administration. It is also a criticism that merits some suspicion in that it is associated with pro-"market", anti-regulation polemics. But the criticism is more broadly based than this; indeed, the doyen of modern "Weberian" sociologists, Randall Collins (1979, 1986), identifies the higher layers of bureaucratic structures as part of the "sinecure sector" of the economy, in which groups of insiders monopolize "cushy number" occupational positions.

Moreover, Collins does not merely point to inefficiency, which could easily be accounted consistent with the properties stressed by Weber: reliability, stability and rationality. He suggests that "overmanning" and "feather-bedding" result from the failure of the hierarchy to act as a reliable instrument, from the ability of bureaucrats to elude control and act on their own behalf. This is a conclusion now amply supported by the many case studies of "bureaucratic politics" wherein bureaucrats are revealed as intensely concerned with their own internal rewards and satisfactions, with empire-building and the diversion of resources to themselves, with undermining or destroying organizational elements that stand against their own internal bureaucratic interests.[2]

What evidence of this kind suggests is not only that the "disciplined mechanism" of the modern bureaucracy turns over much more slowly than it could and does far less than it might, but also that what it does do is liable to be done not in the guise of an instrument serving the interest of another but with its own interests very much to the fore. It could be, of course, that even this might be reconciled with the content, if not the spirit, of Weber's account, that even the most superior administrative machines have their limitations and inadequacies, which must be tolerated because there is nothing better. But again, empirically informed commentary has long suggested that there is something better, that the administrative machinery can be substantially improved not by tinkering on the basis of the Weberian conception but by transforming it, notably in ways that diminish the extent of the control exerted from "the top" of the hierarchy.

For as long as they have existed, studies of bureaucratic hierarchies have noted the existence of local autonomy in the lower reaches. General organizational rules may be adapted to local circumstances, or overlooked, or even systematically disregarded. They may constitute an incomplete basis for a decision-making influenced additionally by external pressures and commitments, and/or consultation and co-operation with peers, and/or local knowledge and custom. They may prove not after all to be "exhaustive", so that even junior officials are forced to make judgements and choices, to act as powers rather than authorities. The observation that local autonomy exists prompts the thought that it may after all be a positive virtue not a defect, that administration may be the better for it. So it may be said that local knowledge is needed to further the specific local objectives bureaucracies face, objectives that remain unknown to those at the top. Or local modifications of rules may be said to reflect local needs, in circumstances where "the rules" as they stood would be disasters if routinely applied. Following on again from this, the logical next step is to offer theories and conjectures as to why modifications to the command model may sometimes actually improve administration.

In a justly famous case study, Burns & Stalker (1961) suggested that strictly hierarchical, "monocratic" bureaucracy, the kind regarded by Weber as "the most rational known means of exercising authority over human beings" (Weber 1968: 223), was seriously deficient in adaptability and flexibility. As such it was suited to the administration only of stable routinized activities.[3] A better system for the administration of innovating and changing systems was one rich in "horizontal" ties that allowed information exchange and the taking of knowledgeable collective decisions by subordinates at the expense of the reliability of vertical control and surveillance. More recently, policies involving a weakening of vertical control have been advocated as general desiderata of good administration. The devolution of decision-making down the system is increasingly recommended without qualification. And the "delayering" of administrative structures is seen as an associated strategy that as well as realizing the cost-savings of devolution also has its own specifically administrative advantage in bringing the "top" and "bottom" of the hierarchy into closer proximity. The consistently advanced justification of all these strategies – the sacrifice of "vertical" to "horizontal" connections, the devolution of decision-making, the delayering of the administrative hierarchy – is that they deal with problems of information-handling intrinsic to the Weberian conception, wherein the controller of the machine is liable to chronic information overload.[4]

Finally, it is worth considering how far devolved power and discretion may be necessary even in the normal, day-to-day operation of bureaucratic administration. One of the things that studies of bureaucracies suggest is that their "normal" operation may not be "normal" at all, that what is considered normal and routine may in actuality scarcely ever appertain. The superior may be on leave or ill; the office regime may be in the midst of an update; the case in hand may represent a lapse from the rules by the office forwarding it, perhaps the office of a superior; the relevant file may be missing. In these (normal) circumstances, routines are routinely departed from and rules are cheerfully disobeyed "in the letter" to be followed "in the spirit"; the "disciplined mechanism" apparently abandons a little of its discipline so that the work gets done.

8.2 Impersonal rules

To return from the inordinate complexities of substantive studies to the simplicities of theory, if the command model is indeed seriously inadequate, what are the theoretical flaws that make it so? Many of them derive, or so it will be argued here, from Weber's view of the role of rules. The use of impersonal rules permits, according to Weber, the "rigorous mechanization" of administration. It allows commands to be relayed down the hierarchy and carried out with the full reliability conventionally attributed to a machine. The links between the trained officials who constitute the administrative machinery may reliably be constituted by rule, and so too may the link between the machinery and the (untrained) "master" who makes use of it. The "master" of such machinery is in possession of a maximally reliable instrument for the realization of his command.[5]

An individualistic notion of "rule", and of "command", is evident here: a rule can be followed by an individual acting independently. What a rule implies is an inherent characteristic of the rule itself and can be read off, as it were, by any individual who comes to inspect the rule. The sociological problem of securing obedience is merely that of ensuring that the real implications of rules are enacted. The achievement of a shared sense of what the rules imply is not addressed as a problem, because it is not conceived of as problematic. Weber evinces no sense of difficulty at all in relation to the matter of the understanding and interpretation of rules.

It is interesting in this respect to compare Weber with Hobbes. Both are strong rationalists, convinced of the value and the power of reason, and yet, for Hobbes: "the Interpretation of all Lawes dependeth on the Authority Sovereign; and the Interpreters can be none but those, which the Sovereign, . . . shall appoint. For else, by the craft of an Interpreter, the Law may be made to beare a sense, contrary to that of the Sovereign; by which means the Interpreter becomes the Legislator" (Hobbes [1651] 1968: 322). Whereas Hobbes understands that the correct application of

ADMINISTRATIVE HIERARCHIES

rules depends upon the authority of persons, Weber sees the one as a (desirable) substitute for the other (Weber 1968: 1028–9). Whereas Hobbes invokes power to solve the problems of social and of cognitive order, Weber takes the latter as given.

If the earlier discussion of rules in section 2.4 is correct, then Weber is fundamentally mistaken here. He is failing to recognize that nothing in the rule itself fixes its application in a given case, that there is no "fact of the matter" concerning the proper application of a rule, and that what a rule is actually taken to imply is a matter to be decided, when it is decided, by contingent social processes. Weber is treating something that needs to be examined and accounted for – what a rule implies – as something that needs no such examination and that can be taken for granted in accounting for other things. The consequent errors have profound and far-reaching implications. Thus, they force an immediate reappraisal of the nature of the sanctioning system in bureaucracies. This system, based on use of "the files", is said to possess an extraordinary efficacy: obedience is much more likely to be secured if a permanent trace of the relevant action exists, and its relationship to "the rules" can be scrutinized and sanctioned at leisure. But such a system cannot constrain any more strongly than "the rules" themselves, which amounts to a serious limitation if "the rules" do not constrain. Certainly, such a system, operating as Weber conceived of it, cannot prevent action described as "in accordance with the rules" that is not the kind of action "in accordance with the rules" that is wanted. And this kind of action is a major form of problematic action in bureaucratic settings, where officials facing external scrutiny and possessed of the choice of presenting what they have done as in accord with or divergent from required rules will rarely be in doubt that the former is the more expedient policy.[6]

It is true, of course, that officials cannot expect to escape censure merely by the rationalization of what they do. To present some perversion, with impeccable logic, as normal rule-following behaviour will by no means invariably protect its perpetrators. And indeed administrators are invariably aware of the limitations of logic-chopping and the need also to bear in mind what the powers that be "really want". But this is just to emphasize once more the need to relate rule-following to the authority of persons, and to recognize the constitutive role of that which Weber sought to eliminate from his enquiries.

The fact that a rule cannot be followed by an isolated individual is a point of fundamental importance. Because the command model is fundamentally inadequate in its account of rules, it will not serve *even as an ideal type*. Bureaucratic organization following the command model would seek to restrict social links and relationships and to press officials into an isolated and atomized condition. But to move in this direction is to weaken administrative capacity by fragmenting the *collective* foundations on which it must rest: total isolation and atomization imply total administrative incapacity. A thoroughly dehumanized, mechanized system of administration is both impossible to realize in principle and counterproductive as an ideal guide to practice.

Most of the criticisms of the command model made in the course of empirical studies are consistent with this general theoretical criticism and can be rationalized as particular instances of what it implies. All the particular accounts of the insufficiencies of "the rules", adaptations of "the rules" and deviation from "the rules" may be rendered as illustrations of the general point that "the rules" lack power and cannot explain the practice with which they are associated. The critics are entitled, of course, to resist what in some cases is a radical reformulation and generalization of what they have said, but the plausibility and significance of all the diverse empirically based criticisms of Weber are enhanced when they are perceived to be all of a kind in this way. Moreover, such a reformulation transforms the criticisms from accounts that implicitly sustain the model precisely by talk of its limitations and deficiencies into criticisms that genuinely call it into question.

What is the alternative to the command model? Clearly, such an alternative must avoid empowering rules and treating officials as atomized individuals. It should accept that bureaucracies are genuine social formations involving the social relationships necessary to sustain shared understandings and shared practices. Weber himself hints at the kind of model required when he notices that bureaucracy is invariably associated with *status* requirements, and that officials are very often both members of an external status group with a special honour and occupants of a specific social status by virtue of their position in the hierarchy. But Weber is strangely tentative and insecure in his treatment of this connection and fails to provide a convincing analysis of either its positive or negative implications.[7] Well equipped to analyze the status claims of bureaucrats in terms of credentialism, monopolization and bureaucratic politics, he none the less largely refrains from doing so.[8] Yet neither does he convincingly account for them in any other way. It was clearly his intuition that the connection of administrative hierarchy and status group was by no means entirely negative and extrinsic, but the basis of the intuition remains unclear. It can, however, be transformed into a plausible argument by connecting together his own work in the two separate contexts.

Status groups, with their networky patterns of interaction and their restricted social intercourse, sustain a distinctive lifestyle and an output of co-ordinated, instrumentally relevant collective action. Manifestly, their members achieve and sustain a shared sense of what is involved in following rules: they achieve an agreement in their practice. What a rule "in itself" cannot produce – a compelling indication of what it is to follow it in the next instance – can be produced by references to the rule in the context of the ongoing practice of the status group. Thus, members of a status group may serve as a reliable transmission and implementation system for instructions and commands that refer to rules, in that their interaction and the shared culture they thereby sustain constitute them as agents likely to apply rules in "the same" way. If a body of officials is to carry out tasks involving *distinctive* rules and practices, it may be expedient that they exist as a status group of peers as well as an administrative hierarchy. This may be brought about either by creating the group from members of the common culture, adding further "expert" elements to that culture in the course of a specialized training, or (as was common in "pre-modern" bureaucracies) by allowing an existing status group with a "suitable" form of culture a monopoly of administrative posts.

The way to an alternative general conception of administration to that provided by the command model is now open. If administration is the implementation of rules, then administrators must be constituted as a collective able to sustain a shared sense of what rules imply and hence an agreement in their practice when they follow rules. They must engage in social intercourse in order to sustain a shared organizational or administrative culture.[9] This is the essential basis of administration, the source of administrative potential, as it were. And if there is a concern to maximize administrative potential then there should be a corresponding concern for the richness of the organizational culture, its homogeneity, and its effectiveness as a basis for communication. With regard to maximally effective administration, blocks on communication are detrimental; problems of intelligibility are detrimental; so are information bottlenecks, or unduly long transmission paths, or other conditions that produce either overload or information starvation at decision-making points; so too is conflict of interests and objectives amongst administrators. Inverting these conditions suggests an administrative ideal of a densely connected network of interaction sustaining an agreement in practice based upon extensive, richly detailed shared understandings and judgements. The common image of the tree hierarchy should perhaps be complemented by that of the neural network.

Where a shared administrative culture exists, one possible form of administrative action (among many) is that wherein a rule is routinely followed in obedience to the command of a designated superior. In the command model, this is a "rigorously mechanized" procedure. On the new model, it is worth emphasizing yet again since the consequences are so far reaching, it is understood differently, as the matter-of-course continuation of a collectively exemplified practice of rule-following, a continuation particular to a given context and not intelligible as the "real" implication of the rule itself. On the new model, hierarchies are made of active agents, who sustain a shared sense of what rules mean by continually working to secure agreement in their practice. They have constantly to make judgements and decisions in the articulation of rules, just in order to remain at one in the matter of what the rules mean. They achieve *routine* administrative tasks not by imitating automata but by continually monitoring and if necessary adjusting their first "automatic" responses, in order to secure a collective uniformity as rules are applied. Were they to act separately, each putting forth their own immediate individual response to rule-related commands, the result would be the same – chaos and disruption – as is engendered by "work to rule" in all other occupational contexts.

The disempowerment of rules acknowledged in the move away from the command model implies a corresponding empowerment of those who follow rules. In the command model, only the "commander" is a power, in the precise sense of having both authority to command and discretion (choice) in what to command. Every subordinate may act with authority only by acting with complete obedience and doing precisely what is required; this is assumed to be a matter of acting as part of a mechanism, of acting as a passive agent, without discretion. But in the new conception every subordinate may authoritatively enact any of the innumerable possibilities that can plausibly be made out as consistent with rules and precedents. Hence when she does act authoritatively it must, *pro forma*, also be with discretion; even as a participant in a collective agreed in its practice, the subordinate counts as a power in her own right. Power (authority with discretion), accordingly, is no longer restricted to the apex of the hierarchy but is found at every point within it, and is expressed even in the most routine action involving only the most mundane judgement (Barnes 1986, 1988). And power is indeed *necessary* here because the routine application of a rule is *pro forma* the same kind of activity as its problematic or innovative or deviant application.

Having dwelt upon this point we can now move back and adjust our understanding of the operation of hierarchies as a whole. They contain officials skilled in the routine application of rules and thus *ipso facto* skilled in their improvisatory use, their creative use, their elaboration and adjustment in the course of use, even their competent misuse. All these activities become the same kinds of activity, involving the same kinds of skill and competence, when seen in the light of a correct understanding of the nature of rules and their relationship with the agents who apply them. Thus, an efficient control hierarchy will have the capacity effectively to accomplish a very wide range of tasks. It will be able to operate adequately in relation to routine activities. It will be capable of operating adequately when routine is disturbed and interrupted; indeed, this is little more than to repeat the first point because disturbance and interruption are part and parcel of routine activity. It will possess the (routine) flexibility and adaptability to administer change and introduce innovation. It will be able to improvise. (Note how the most highly trained and disciplined personnel are typically called upon for tasks requiring the greatest degree of on-the-spot judgement and improvisation.) It will be able to self-repair and self-reconstitute. Should the system fragment (as a military command structure may, for example, during battle), its parts will remain capable of some degree of independent action, since independent judgement and discretion are in any case routinely required at every point in the hierarchy.

These are powers far in excess of those possessed by a "rigorously mechanized" bureaucratic instrument. Yet, far from representing a gratuitous excess of administrative capacity, they merely represent powers that are required as a matter of course even for the most mundane administrative tasks. It is as well that these powers exist, because anything worth calling administration would be out of the question without them. And yet the mere existence of these powers does not solve "the problem" of administration, for there remains the question of whether or not they will be exercised. And indeed, if they are exercised there is the matter of whether they will be put to legitimate use, or directed instead to the pursuit of bureaucratic politics, for which purpose they are also ideally suited. It is worth recalling how the social intercourse of a status group allows it to generate a shared sense of its own collective good and a stream of collective action devoted to the advancement of it. Evidently the social arrangements for maximum administrative capacity need not be the same as those for maximum administrative subservience and may even be the opposite of them. For this reason they may appear to the "controller" of the bureaucratic "machinery" as far from ideal, and other arrangements may be preferred.

It is tempting to suggest that Weber's own account of bureaucracy is so obsessively concerned with the rational accountability and reliable subservience of administrators that it neglects to consider administration itself and gives no attention to the conditions of its successful accomplishment. Any attempt ruthlessly to implement the Weberian model through isolation, restricted communication, surveillance and efforts to enforce "more or less exhaustive" rules implies such an atomization of personnel as to make administration impossible. As noted earlier, moves in the direction of Weber's unrealizable model represent moves to ineffectiveness and weakened administrative capacity as the price of increased restriction and control. That this has not always been recognized as a matter of course is perhaps because bureaucratic hierarchies have so often been studied by researchers who adopt the viewpoint of the external "controller". The rider of a horse does not always understand that the bit and the harness function by *destroying* powers and capacities.

None the less, arguments somewhat of this kind are now routinely recognized in current accounts of bureaucracy, both by observers and practitioners. More and more there is an explicit acceptance that, throughout the hierarchy, administrators operate as irreducibly active agents with discretionary powers. It is now found more economical to accept the inevitable presence of some level of bureaucratic politics than to pay the exhorbitant costs of attempting to reduce them to zero. It is recognized that it may be cheaper to pay a potent administration the incentives to use its power appropriately than to bear the costs of forcing a hobbled and impotent administration to do so. Thus the relation between administration and those it serves is being reconceptualized not as one of command and obedience but more as one of exchange, bargaining and negotiation. And similar adjustments are occurring in the accounts given of social relationships within the hierarchy itself.

Sometimes these more recent accounts are presented as responses to real changes in the setting and practice of administration. It is said that the command model worked well for the stable, repetitive productive process characteristic of the nineteenth century, but failed as a means of controlling complex and rapidly changing processes. If the present account is correct, however, then the command model is fundamentally faulty and empirically unrealizable, so that the vicissitudes of its credibility must be accounted for in a slightly different way. In the nineteenth century, it is tempting to suggest, the relatively low capacity and inefficiency of bureaucratic arrangements conceived of as implementations of the command model did not matter. "Controllers" were most concerned with domination and disempowerment, both of the administered and of those in the "administrative machine". Possibly, like the Taylorists in the context of work generally, some of them were attracted by a mechanistic fantasy that represented a certain ideal of social order. Today, on the other hand, there is greater concern with administrative capacity and effectiveness, and a more relaxed attitude to domination, so perhaps it is this switch of priorities that has led to the credibility of the command model being eroded.

Coda: *en route* to the madhouse

It is now time to move away from technical concerns and to look once more, in this final section, at the value of social theory as myth. The focus this time will be the myth through which Weber expressed his tragic vision, the myth of the cage.[9] This envisages our future as one of ever-increasing, ever more pervasive rationalization, one where means–end reasoning and action oriented entirely to instrumental success become more and more important. In the present context we can think of it as implying the growth of administration, impersonal regulation and bureaucracy, to the extent that they become a stifling and intolerable burden. The myth is historicist and teleological and might on those grounds be described as an Enlightenment myth with a pessimistic twist. But this would be seriously misleading; for Enlightenment myth is characteristically dualistic – the separate opposed forces of good and evil conflict and one will be victorious – whereas the structure of Weber's myth is monistic, with good and evil inherent in the same actions. It is through recognizing the benefits of administration, and implementing it in the form of modern bureaucracy with its "technical superiority", that we enter the cage.

In the previous section, Weber's account of the internal structure of bureaucratic administration with its "rigorous mechanization" was rejected but not his insight into the separation of administrative systems and the impersonality and instrumentality of their orientation toward those they administer. As for Weber's claim that administration and instrumental relationships are likely inexorably to increase to oppressive levels, it can only be said that the myth of the cage has been one of the great enduring myths of social theory precisely because it has fitted uncomfortably well with so much accepted knowledge and current experience. Administration and bureaucratic regulation have grown and proliferated through all the various phases of industrialization in every kind of cultural and political context, and continue to do so unabated. The process does on the face of it appear inevitable: it proceeds indifferently under governments that favour it and governments that ostensibly oppose it and denounce it. Indeed, bureaucracy seems to thrive on opposition and resistance, springing forth the stronger, hydra-like, whenever it is pruned or cut down, which task has generally itself to be entrusted to some bureaucratic agency. And it does invariably seem to represent an increase in the impersonality and instrumentality of social relationships, now as much as ever, as is evidenced by the very facades of courtesy and concern constructed to conceal from those who are "administered", "managed" or "professionally served" the unpleasant truth about their position. In summary, the plot of Weber's myth appears still to be unfolding before our eyes, and with the appropriate appearance of tragic inevitability. Any attempt to dismiss or radically to modify Weber's tragic vision must therefore offer some plausible alternative account of these developments, of their significance, and of what they imply for the future.

There is no shortage of material that offers alternative conceptualizations of much the same social changes as those addressed by Weber. The work of Habermas (1984, 1987) is an obvious point of departure in that it provides a different form of myth, which is none the less a systematic extension and modification of Weber's own.[10] Habermas is at one with Weber in recognizing the continuing proliferation of bureaucratic administration and legal regulation, and agrees that this represents an extension of "zweck-rational" or means–end oriented action (an extension of "instrumental reason" and "purposive-rational action" as Habermas terms it) into more and more areas of social life. Nor does he fail to recognize the paradox that this apparently progressive development would, in its fullest and most comprehensive expression, be oppressive and stultifying. But Habermas none the less recoils from Weber's tragic vision, and reconceptualizes the myth of the cage in a normative social theory according to which instrumental reason becomes threatening and pathological only to the extent that it transgresses beyond its own proper and appropriate boundaries.

In capitalist societies, ubiquitous processes of social evolution and social differentiation have resulted, according to Habermas, in the emergence of separate subsystems of purposive-rational action with unusual degrees of autonomy. Both the economy, internally controlled and coordinated through the medium of money, and the system of political administration, internally controlled and co-ordinated through the medium of power, have achieved substantial independence of the "lifeworld" of shared, taken-for-granted understandings and common-sense knowledge.[11] However, these subsystems of purposive-rational action are now reacting back upon the lifeworld itself: they have begun to recast its activities in a wholly instrumental mould and to couple them also to control and direction via the media of money and power. This is adversely affecting those lifeworld activities that are functionally dependent upon social integration through values, norms and the consensus formation accomplished through communicative rather than instrumental kinds of action.[12] We are facing a "colonization of the lifeworld" that is unambiguously pathological and leads to conflict. One widespread manifestation of this conflict is the rise of new social movements, whose efforts at self-realization, cultural creation and the dramatic reassertion of the value of different forms of life are to be understood as attempts to defend the lifeworld against permeation and reconstitution by the media of money and power (Habermas 1987: 392).

Why though does the lifeworld come under threat of colonization? Under what force or pressure do "the imperatives of autonomous subsystems make their way into the lifeworld from the outside – like colonial masters coming into a tribal society – and force a process of assimilation upon it"? (ibid.: 355). The pressure derives, according to Habermas, from the continuing need to integrate and stabilize a capitalist social order that, being exploitative and unjust, can persist only if it generates an ever-increasing surplus to distribute to the masses as compensation payments. This pressure is felt in the autonomous subsystems, where money and power are used as steering media to co-ordinate actions in the course of system integration. As the cost of system integration increases and the need to sustain the growth and vigour of capitalism becomes more and more pressing, the autonomous subsystems embark upon the instrumentalization of the lifeworld itself in order to cope with the problem: individuals in their everyday lives are forced into roles as consumers vis-à-vis the economy and as clients of the welfare state and the range of state administrators and experts. The lifeworld is rationalized and instrumentalized under the pressure of the functional imperatives of system integration, to the extent that the very patterns of communicative action required to create and sustain the lifeworld are threatened with erosion.

This alternative to Weber may be analyzed and criticized from many different standpoints, but let us concentrate here wholly and entirely on the nature of theory as myth.[13] Habermas has constituted a myth with a different *form* from that of Weber: he has replaced a picture of tragic inevitability with one in which "system" and "lifeworld" can be given the roles of villain and hero in a dramatic confrontation. This permits a story of social change in which opposed forces of good and evil conflict with each other and there is at least the possibility that good will triumph.[14] But detailed examination reveals inadequacies in the construction of the story, of a kind that calls into question the dualism crucial to its role as myth.

Weber tells of the tragedy entailed by the triumph of a particular kind of social action, and relies accordingly on our willingness to recognize actions as being of one kind or another. His own classification (Weber 1968: 24) famously distinguishes the increasingly dominant "instrumentally rational" kind of action from "value-rational" action as well as from "traditional" and "affectual" kinds. Habermas uses a somewhat different taxonomy, which refers to "instrumental", "strategic", "normatively regulated", "dramaturgical" and "communicative" kinds of action (Habermas 1984: 85–6). But much more importantly, he also provides a clearer and more developed understanding of what it is for an action to be of a kind. Indeed his definitions of kinds of action remind us of the well-known but often forgotten difficulties entailed in referring to actions as of a kind. In Habermas's account, instrumental and strategic kinds of action (together referred to as "purposive-rational" or "teleological" kinds) are actions oriented to success, whether success in acting upon the physical world (instrumental) or success in a context where other people have to be taken account of as well as the state of the world (strategic). Normatively regulated action is oriented to norms and designed to accord with them. Dramaturgical action is oriented toward conveying an image of the performer to others. Communicative action is oriented toward the achievement of mutual understanding (Habermas 1984: 85–101). In every case it is evident that an action belongs to a kind not by virtue of any property or characteristic intrinsic to it, but always by virtue of how agents are oriented when they perform it. Nothing *in* the action makes it of a kind. This is a crucially important point.

Imagine that we seek to act instrumentally to shut a door. We can act in this way by recourse to innumerable behaviours. To shut a door does not restrict us to behaving in just one way. To be sure, it disallows an infinite number of ways of behaving, but it allows a similar number. (Think of how an instruction to choose an even number disallows an infinite set of possibilities, yet allows an infinite set.) Hence, in shutting the door it is open to us to orient our action in some further way, say dramaturgically, and to shut the door in some appropriate style or manner. Even here, though, say as we choose to shut the door aggressively rather than peaceably, innumerable possible behaviours remain available, and it remains possible to take account of still other orientations and frameworks in deciding how to behave – i.e. how precisely to act.[15]

The key point is that to act under one orientation does not exclude simultaneously acting under another or others. Strictly speaking, there are distinct kinds of orientation to action but not kinds of action *per se*. If we do speak loosely of kinds of action, sacrificing precision to convenience, as it were, then we have to recognize that these so-called kinds are quite different from the kinds of birds or plants or other paradigm cases that set our routine habits of thought about kinds. *The kinds of action thus referred to are not mutually exclusive.* Indeed, given that a number of orientations to action typically have relevance in any given social context, any particular action will normally be of several kinds at once. And this will be the case not just with physical actions like shutting a door but with speech-acts as well.

This is something that needs constantly to be borne in mind in the practice of social theory, where conventional descriptions of institutionalized social action rarely take account of the point. Consider, for example, how we routinely describe "the economy" as a "system of instrumental actions" and thereby forget how those actions amount to far more than that. Take a routine "instrumental" action in "the economy", the killing of a beast in an abattoir, for example. Such an action, in a modern abattoir, will indeed be highly efficacious and readily justifiable in terms of its instrumental success. However, it will also be normatively regulated, whether by this is meant oriented to externally imposed regulations, or oriented to informally established local rules and customs. Nor will the need for both instrumental efficacy and compatibility with norms preclude the possibility of a dramaturgical aspect to the action in question. Where then lies the difference between this (and let it be clear that the example is of a typical "economic" action) and an extreme case of "non-economic" action, such as, for example, the execution discussed in section 3.1. Was not this a paradigm of dramaturgical action? And yet the executioner was constantly oriented to a normative order as the action of decapitation was performed, nor is there any question but that the crucial action must be understood as instrumental, as a means, and its performance as oriented to success.

That the kinds of action are not mutually exclusive is a point that Weber failed to emphasize in his own typology, and this makes Habermas's more sophisticated discussion of immense value and importance. However, having emphasized that actions may be multiply oriented (and thus of several "kinds" at once), Habermas chooses to downplay this empirical possibility in his discussions of modern highly differentiated societies.[16] Here, he suggests, actions are predominantly oriented in just one way, not several, and actions oriented in the same way (i.e. of the same kind) increasingly cluster together. Thus, the autonomous subsystems of the economy and the polity are overwhelmingly constituted of actions oriented entirely and exclusively by instrumental and strategic considerations: "in modern societies economic and bureaucratic spheres emerge in which social relations are regulated only by money and power. Norm-conformative attitudes and identity-forming social relationships are neither necessary nor possible in these spheres" (Habermas 1987: 154). "Via the media of money and power, the subsystems of the economy and the state are differentiated out of an institutional complex set within the horizons of the lifeworld; *formally organized domains of action* emerge that . . . sheer off from lifeworld contexts and congeal into a kind of norm-free sociality" (ibid.: 307).

By postulating a differentiation of kinds of action and the clustering of actions according to kind, Habermas moves away from Weber to an account with a dualist mythical structure. This allows social theory to be presented as a drama, wherein clusters of instrumental and communicative action can play villain and hero respectively, in a plot of system versus lifeworld. This drama of "the colonization of the lifeworld" is the latest of a series of evolving, similarly structured accounts that Habermas has given of the threatening evil of rampant instrumental rationality and technocratic consciousness. Even more than any previous account, however, it accepts, indeed stresses, the positive value of purely instrumental action orientations in their proper place. The growth of system *per se* is no tragedy; indeed it is a benefit. It is system out of place that serves as villain and needs to be resisted. However, this basically optimistic dualist vision crucially depends upon an either/or strategy in the identification of kinds of actions and the existence of separable clusters of actions of different kinds.

It is not easy to reconcile these crucial requirements with substantive studies; in particular, the evidence suggests that so-called media-steered subsystems are replete with "lifeworld elements" (Baxter 1987). Studies of work, of the management and administration of work and of administration generally all leave little room for doubt that they consist in far more than strategic action, "steered" or otherwise. Indeed, as far as work is concerned, the evidence includes some of the finest achievements of a great tradition of empirical sociology, the one that has studied the workplace and workplace subcultures, and displayed them as very much more than "formally organized domains of action" – even if attention is confined simply to task performance in such settings. Again, with regard to administration itself, it is interesting to note what a vast range and extraordinary variety of images of organization and administration are now deployed in the descriptions of theorists, and how only a proportion of these are images of "formally organized domains" in Habermas's sense (Morgan 1986). And it is even more salient to note how many of these different images of organization may be used by administrators themselves as part of the business of constituting the orderliness of the enterprises in which they operate (Law 1994).[17]

However, whilst it is important in this context, where so much substantive work has been done, that theorists should be willing to confuse their thinking with the facts, it is important to note that fundamental theoretical problems underlie the issue, and that case studies and their findings will not suffice to resolve it. Thus Habermas himself recognizes that his position faces difficulties in the findings of case studies. He accepts, for example, that within what he characterizes as the "formally organized domains" of the media-steered subsystems, informal organization is also invariably found, and that " . . . the lifeworlds of members, never completely husked away, penetrate here into the reality of organizations" (Habermas 1987: 310–11). But his response to this criticism is a conservative and defensive one – a peripheral theoretical adjustment that allows the core of the theoretical position thus threatened to be retained unrevised. Habermas accepts that members in fact act communicatively and non-strategically in organizations, but insists that the crucial point is that they are not *forced* to do so: "They know that they can have recourse to formal regulations, not only in exceptional but in routine cases"(ibid.: 310–11). Thus, like Weber with his command model, Habermas falls back on empowered formal rules.[18] And, as before, the theoretical counter-argument must be that rules cannot be so empowered and that (communicative) interaction is all the time required to give them an agreed significance. Accordingly, in the media-steered subsystems, not only are "non-teleological" orientations to action possible (which is evident in their invariably being actual), they are also necessary (which is why they are invariably actual). Any rule-oriented system must be continually reconstituted interactively in the context of the system itself. The two kinds of action that Habermas seeks to decouple are necessarily coupled together. The output of success-oriented, instrumental action even of a bureaucratic hierarchy must be understood just as the collective action of a status group or social movement is understood. This is merely to recapitulate what was argued in section 8.2 above.

To summarize, Habermas's contrast of "system" and "lifeworld" fails because of fundamental flaws in the method used to construct it. And, accordingly, the myth of a sphere of media-steered regulation, bureaucratization and rationalization, which becomes a threat only when it embarks upon a "colonization of the lifeworld", should be discarded. In particular, the thought that there is in the sphere of work, or task performance, or the economy, a domain different and distinct from that of the lifeworld should be dismissed. What we find in this context is precisely lifeworld, albeit lifeworld that is increasingly of an impoverished and unpleasant kind. And to recognize that is to recognize the double-edged character of the rationalization of economic activity, and hence to move back into the ambit of Weber's tragic vision.[19]

The move to a strongly dualist framework evidently represents a false path forward from Weber. It does not, however, by any means represent the only available path. There are theorists like Adorno, with his nightmare of "the administered society", and Foucault, with his stunning evocations of ubiquitous normalization, who address the Weberian theme without any of the residual rationalist optimism apparent in Habermas. Indeed these theorists paint a picture of desolation more appalling even than Weber's own: with them, the "there is hope" sticker can be unpeeled from the rear windscreen of the motor-car.[20] Not that this has any relevance to the value of the work of these theorists. That resides above all in the monism of their theoretical vision. To put the point succinctly, what these theorists provide is an unwavering and undiluted recognition of the original sin that taints the instrumental orientation to action and lends a double-edged quality to all instances of means–end reasoning. They enrich, if that is the right word, Weber's own insights into the fundamental problems associated with "instrumental reason".

When we describe a piece of behaviour in terms that make it visible as instrumentally oriented action, we focus upon just a tiny sector of the expanding circle of consequences that flows out like a wave from the point of its enactment. The rest of the wave travels off into an unknown environment, both human and physical, wherein it is generally assumed that it will peter out. If we allow instrumentality to predominate in our discourse we shall create an entire cognitive order that is selective in this way. And if we allow ourselves to believe that the kinds of action recognized in that cognitive order cannot at the same time be other kinds, then we shall further reinforce that selectivity. Actions will then be referred to as nothing more than pathways to the locally expedient objectives that they are intended to bring about. It is hard to exaggerate the importance of this. The whole basis of the utilitarian "morality" practically universally acceded to today depends upon it: how could consequentialist moral rationalizations persist if we ceased to speak of "the" consequences of our actions? Even the most radically critical voices have to speak in this idiom. Recall Ulrich Beck (p. 107), referring with shuddering irony to "the side-effects" of economic production. As Beck's discussion makes clear, references to "the" side-effects and pollutions of a productive process involve selective perception just as much as references to "the" direct and intended effects do: all of these things are recognizable only against the backdrop of a cognitive order that in its very form, in the teleology and instrumentality incarnate in it, is revelatory of how profoundly we treat each other as means.

The monistic myths of modern social theory that warn of the dangers in this development are merely recent instances of a long chain of similar warnings. It is worth briefly turning to one of the earliest extant instances. In the *Oedipus Tyrannus* of Sophocles, the hero, confident in his rationality and unrelenting in putting it in the service of good ends, is thereby destroyed. It is Oedipus's trust in "instrumental" reason, his utter consistency, not just in following wherever it leads, but in taking it on where others might see no way forward or fear what they see, that results in his ruin – a ruin as comprehensive and all-embracing as the nature of his initial trust.

The *Oedipus Tyrannus* is a sociological masterpiece. Not only does it "anticipate" current dilemmas concerning instrumental reason; it also represents fundamental themes in the sociology of knowledge. For all that it is one of the most gripping of all dramas, nothing "happens" until the denouement (and even this was anticipated from the start by the watching audience). All the significant "actions" have happened years before: what the drama consists in is a re-assignment of action descriptions, a recapitulation and redescription of behaviour long past. That which was the slaying of an enemy and the taking of a wife becomes reconceptualized as parricide and incest. It is the revelation not of the error of the earlier action-descriptions but of their selectivity, and hence in this case their insufficiency, that produces the final catastrophe. Oedipus becomes aware of the "side-effects" of what he has done. The becoming aware is the drama. It is the extraordinary achievement of the dramatist that in this work catastrophe is catastrophe in knowledge; perceptions of catastrophe and catastrophe are not different things, but one and the same (cf. p. 110).

It is worth asking why so many social theorists have taken a deep interest in the myth of Oedipus, but only in Freud's version. Why do problems of neurosis, individual repression and infant sexuality attract so much attention, while the sociological themes addressed in the earlier version do not? Is it that the undifferentiated character of a culture that can set epistemology in the context of song, dance and poetry is hard to come to terms with? Or do "enlightened" theorists find it difficult to respond to a vision apparently even more pessimistic than Weber's, one that seems to encourage passivity and fails to "tell us what to do"? There is indeed a curious authoritarianism about some Enlightenment thought: theorists are expected to provide not a vision but a message, an assertion of what ought to be done, a set of instructions.[21] But a failure to issue instructions is not the same as an invitation to passivity. Thus, the myth of the self-destructiveness of instrumental rationality in the Sophoclean drama, wherein it is unparalleled in the generality of its formulation and the rigour of its presentation, was a positive contribution, by an experienced and involved practitioner, to practical reasoning and political wisdom. The nature of the contribution, however, was not so much words, or even arguments, as an offering of virtual experience. An audience could witness its movement, arrive at the final catastrophe, pass through to the other side, and reflect on the whole.

In the myth of Oedipus, the downfall of the hero is unrelated to any specific, local flaw or defect, any division of self, any tension between inclinations to good and to evil. The hero is a unity, brought low by the very capabilities and inclinations that raised him in the first place. He faces danger from his intrinsic nature as a rational agent. The danger increases as he gathers power. The acts through which he achieves his greatest power are the same as those whereby he incurs the greatest pollution. The whole form of the story is thus fundamentally incompatible with dualist myths, in which good and evil actions are separable and can be dealt with independently, or weighed on different sides of a scale. It is not incompatible, however, with the approach of a modern theorist such as Weber or Foucault. Foucault in particular makes a good analogy. In his vision of modern capitalist societies, control, regulation and normalization are so pervasive that any attempt to associate them with just one part of the whole seems misconceived. In Foucault's variant on the myth of the cage everyone is involved in the impersonal regulation and control of everyone else. Increasing bureaucracy is little more than the professionalization of practices already being competently performed by hordes of enthusiastic amateurs. We are all taking the road to rational lunacy together. And indeed, rather than merely being *en route* to the madhouse, we could well have already arrived.

Weber accounted for ever-increasing bureaucracy and regulation largely in terms of its "technical superiority", assisted perhaps by the inherent attractiveness of dehumanized rational calculation to capitalism (Weber 1968: 975). Habermas expresses a closely related view when he relates intensifying regulation and rationalization to the need to squeeze ever-increasing "compensation payments" out of a capitalist system. And indeed the ever-increasing supply of regulation is often put down to the economic "needs of capitalism", and not altogether unreasonably given that regulation has facilitated the organization and co-ordination of production, the integration of productive activity into the institutional structure, and a consequent economic expansion. But this is to make nothing of what Foucault emphasizes: the pervasiveness and ubiquity of regulation. Proliferating regulation and bureaucracy in modern industrial societies increasingly encompass activities not even remotely connected with increased production and economic co-ordination, and where there is a connection it frequently has consequences directly and even deliberately deleterious to them.

What might be the basis for a demand for regulation and impersonal administration present to some degree at every point in the social order? One hypothesis nicely extends the analogy with the Sophoclean myth. Regulation might be linked to empowerment. Suppose that, in all collectives, members seek to influence the behaviour of others in order to make those others parts of a benign, secure and predictable environment for their own habitation and exploitation. In present-day industrial societies there has been an ever-increasing empowerment of individuals consequent upon economic expansion. Economic expansion has been empowering both collectively and individually, so that the extent to which members impinge upon each other through their actions has continually increased, and the distance over which people affect each other physically has grown relative to the distance over which they directly affect each other socially and interactively. There is consequently an ever-increasing perceived need for the impersonal regulation of those anonymous distant individuals who none the less impinge upon life, and who will constitute a benign, secure and predictable environment only if they are regulated. This could now be the fundamental impetus to bureaucratization (as well, perhaps, as a source and inspiration of general conceptions of "the environment"). And if this is so, then, with everyone wanting everyone else to constitute the secure environment in which they shall be free, the moment of perfect freedom shall indeed be the moment that the cage door closes.[22]

As with the Athenian tragedian, Foucault has enjoyed honour and the attention of large audiences, but no general acceptance for his vision of the human condition. Indeed it is a part of the tragedy implicit in Foucault and the monistic mythical structure, which, however reluctantly, is given expression in his work, that his vision should not be accepted, or even understood. Foucault is the theorist of docile bodies in a normalized society: after his striking descriptions of what can be practised upon them, the constraints and intrusions that they are as likely to welcome as resist, it is hard to imagine that they would baulk at life in the cage. It would, after all, not be a disagreeable life. Regular visits to the toy shop would be a part of it.[23] And, given the innumerable different ways of expressing a docile conformity with even the most elaborate of regulatory requirements, life in the cage would be perfectly compatible with performance of the rites of the cult of the individual, with self-discovery, self-expression, and indeed self-obsession in general. Moreover, in cases of difficulty, Foucault does not forbear from pointing out that experts from the human sciences would constantly be on hand, with what is now a formidable range of therepeutic resources: from discourses for reassurance to electrodes for annihilation.[24]

It can be argued that Foucault's appraisal of the present-day human condition is a little one-sided (Habermas 1990: 290–1). Nor is it difficult to challenge him at the level of historical detail, and give comfort to those who see no merit in his vision with the conclusion that indeed it is false. But to reject Foucault on these grounds such as these is to proceed in a way that if rigorously pressed, would consign the whole of discursive social theory to the waste-bin. And, more important, it is to turn away from the core of truth in Foucault as myth. Among the insights in this core is that of the irreducibly double-edged character of instrumental orientations to action. This is perhaps the crucial insight in all the monistic myths of social theory, the unwelcome thought that they all seek to keep in the forefront of consciousness, in societies that would happily consign it to oblivion and increasingly administer to their own failures of forgetfulness with swathes of techno-babble and scientistic claptrap.

Let us, however, move back finally to empirical matters and prepare a conclusion of appropriate bathos. The generality of opinion is not going to move toward a tragic vision of social change. It is going to continue to accept that regulation is preferable to conflict, that a degree of impersonally administered constraint is "a price worth paying" for security.[25] And it is going to formulate its evaluation of regulation and administration in piecemeal, utilitarian terms – in terms of the supposed costs and benefits of particular instances or proposals.

It is, however, perfectly possible to formulate the problem of excessive regulation in narrowly utilitarian terms, and to identify conflicts of interest surrounding regulation that may give rise to it. These are not the conflicts between "two great camps" traditionally much beloved. Rather they are conflicts such as that between motorists and air-breathers discussed in section 1.4. Sociological theory would do well to give more attention to such conflicts; they seem destined to become of increasing importance and they exemplify particularly vividly the double-edged character of instrumentally oriented actions.

If we look at regulation as a collective action problem, the natural approach is to treat it as a collective good that is in danger of being undersupplied. But it may be that the structure of calculation in modern societies is now such that the situation in practice is the very opposite of this. In modern societies, the state is established as a given, taken-for-granted, "paid-for" supplier of regulation. It is pressed upon by groups of various kinds, including the memberships of social movements, which groups generate collective action to lobby, often successfully, for regulation for their particular "private" good. There need be no overall collective good associated with such regulation but there will invariably be an overall collective harm. Such harm, the harm of regulation itself, will, however, be very widely spread, and may be very small for any individual item. Typically, death by regulation is the death of a million cuts; and it may well be that any single cut is not just tolerable but even imperceptible. Thus, regulation may be massively oversupplied. It may become generally recognized as oversupplied, by sufferers who find themselves none the less unable to reduce it. It may even at some point begin to figure in the lists of significant health risks or underlying causes of death.[26]

Evidently, a pale shadow of Weber's tragic vision remains, even if the issues are considered in the very utilitarian framework that it calls into question. In this framework, a collective action problem is associated with the production of impersonal regulation: instrumental orientations in the context of state-centred industrial societies may lead to its over-production. Bureaucracy will then become a form of excessive pollution. And regulation will get to feel like a suffocating smog because that is what it will be. This raises interesting questions as to how far excessive regulation is inevitable and irresistible. Pollution, of course, is inevitable. Within any cosmology, any scheme for making sense of the world and ordering action within it, pollutions will be defined: the very business of the ordering and classification of an environment implies the construction of pollution. But given that environmental pollution can be controlled and kept in bounds, is there the possibility that so too, in the same way, can administration and regulation? If collective action is possible to limit the extent of insult to the environment, might it similarly limit the extent of insult to human dignity, at whatever point regulation becomes perceived as such an insult and in need of such limitation? And, finally, given that bureaucratic pollution is the normal outcome of attacks on environmental pollution, is there any sensible means of acting simultaneously against both? It is when facing questions like this last that the value of the monistic myths of social theory might in due course come to be more widely acknowledged.

Conclusion

The survey of theoretical resources with which this book began has now been supplemented with a review of some of the available materials on social formations and some of the specific theoretical interpretations of their activities. But the completion of this review is also the conclusion of an argument. The discussion in the second part of this book is offered as grounds for recognizing the plausibility of the theory advocated in the first part. The operation of social formations is held to be best understood in terms of an interactionist social theory. The expedient collective action essential to the persistence, and hence the existence, of social formations of the kind discussed must be based in continuing interaction. The instrumental is essentially dependent on the non-instrumental. It is the interaction of mutually susceptible, sociable human beings, rather than independent calculation or independent awareness of rules, that sustains the shared understandings and collective actions essential for the existence of the formations. This is the case even for the most rigidly ordered and specified bureaucratic hierarchies.

Clearly, to propose this particular theoretical perspective is also to propose that the various social formations differ from each other but slightly, as far as theory is concerned, and that there are no clear boundaries or discontinuities between them. All of them are constituted of similar kinds of social processes, which are organized and linked to each other in strikingly similar ways. This implies that theory could well benefit if it ceased to cluster work on different formations into different contexts and distinct literatures; the role of theory in pointing to sameness in an apparent difference, in extending the existing sense of sameness, would thereby be assisted.

But, if social formations are so similar, what is the basis on which they are actually distinguished from each other and considered to be significantly different? The answer must be that they are distinguished on pragmatic grounds, not primarily by theorists at all, but by members of the formations themselves and by those in the societies in which they exist who have to take account of them. In the first instance, it is ordinary members of societies who recognize, and thereby constitute the existence of, status groups, social movements, nations, hierarchies and so forth. Sociological theory piggy-backs on members' own knowledge in developing its own concepts and categories: the intersubjectively sustained categories of everyday knowledge of society are the prototypes for sociological theoretical categories, and much of the work required to sustain agreed applications for the theoretical categories is actually done by participants not theorists. Those extended, large-scale, orderly features of societies studied by macro social theorists should be recognized as being constituted as and through the knowledge of the participants in the societies in question. And it should be recognized further that the concepts and categories employed here by theorists are incompletely differentiated from and in a sense parasitic upon those of participants themselves. This need imply no criticism, but it can lead to serious problems if it is not accepted and explicitly taken into account. Many of the difficulties encountered in theoretical use of the concept of class have been related to this, and a good deal of the confusion encountered in this area has derived from differences of opinion on whether theorists' concepts should or should not be completely differentiated from those of members themselves.

Theorists and participants share, as it were, concepts such as "nation" or "social movement", or the various categorizations of statuses and status groups. Yet their attitudes to these concepts and perceptions of their utility are likely to be significantly different. Theorists will generally be aware of deficiencies in these concepts, and may lament their inadequacy as means of grasping the full complexity of the social order, even when they are well aware that no description of that order can be other than inadequate and incomplete. Participants, however, will employ the concepts as resources in constituting the social order, and may perceive no failings in them as resources, no reservations about the extent to which they simplify and thereby possibly misrepresent their social environment. Indeed, in modern, complex, differentiated societies, incompleteness and even oversimplification may become positively valuable features of bodies of knowledge, and participants may choose to act on the basis of knowledge deliberately simplified and far less richly structured than it easily could be. In modern societies, members often like to make use of small-scale maps of their social environment: they operate with motorists' maps let us say, occasionally with air-travel maps, only very rarely with walkers' maps. Thereby, they reduce the true complexity of experience, and yet still find it easy to co-ordinate with other people, if those others are using the same maps as themselves. And in simplifying their maps, and hence their actions, they simplify the social order itself – the social order that is represented in their maps. For social order just is the action people take on the basis of the maps they make. And the simpler social order is taken to be, the simpler it becomes.

Social order always remains, none the less, far more complex than any map of it can ever be. And all such maps are constructed on the basis of incomplete and hence unreliable experience of what is mapped. For the social theorist this must be disturbing, and for those who create the very small-scale maps that are macro social theory it must be especially so. In the writing of the second part of this book the salience of these points was inescapable, and for that reason it was often a threatening and demoralizing experience. Just a very few of the substantive fields currently of interest to sociologists are covered, and yet the materials available in each area are so extensive, so detailed and so complex that it is easy to despair of imposing any satisfactory form of order upon them, or of offering any generalizations that do not immediately prompt the recollection of some apparent exception or anomaly. Nor is it just the volume and complexity of findings or descriptions that are intimidating: even the "middle-range" theories used to make sense of materials within these different areas are so many and various that it is beyond the ability of one person to grasp them all and take proper account of them. No doubt everyone who indulges in theoretical generalization is prone to the same kind of disorientation as they move closer to the detail of what they are trying to understand. But for those, like myself, whose intuitions include a profound suspicion of strong rationalism, and who take shared knowledge to be constructed by means not of deductive but of inductive connections and linkages (however unsatisfactory), the intensity of the disorientation is perhaps especially strong. Certainly, I find it hard to quarrel with the urge to caution in theorizing characteristic of the social sciences in the English-speaking world, or with the familiar ideals concerning evidence and documentation to which insufficient attention has been paid in this book. Perhaps the most general forms of theorizing in the social sciences should always have something of an illicit quality, as a reminder of their problematic relationship to evidence, although that is not to say that they should not be engaged in at all.

The second part of this book is offered not just as illustration, but also as evidence, of the theory developed in the first part. It is perhaps worth recording that the theoretical conclusions did not precede work on the substantive materials, but to an extent evolved together with that work. It was a matter not of forcing materials into a preconceived mould so much as of finding that one approach, from the small number that can readily be constructed with the traditional resources of social theory, seemed to order the materials with fewer problems and anomalies than others. That was the subjective feeling. None the less the finished chapters do represent a selection and ordering of materials to make a specific case, even though they also seek to provide or to signpost some of the basic resources required to construct and evaluate alternatives. Serious engagement with alternative perspectives is of course essential to making a judgement of the merits of the one proposed here.

It will be clear from what has been said already that if what is proposed here is accepted it has many important implications, implications significantly different from those of the theories most commonly accepted in macro social theory and informally used in most of the substantive areas of sociology. In the rational choice theory, action is rationally calculated. What is claimed in this book is that such calculation is knowledge based and that knowledge is drawn from or developed from an existing accepted tradition. Thus, calculation is a form of conventional action, oriented to a tradition and implying the recognition of specific institutions and sources of authority. Again, in rational choice theory, the goals that calculators take into account are the goals of independent individuals, even if they imply altruism or regard for others. But it is suggested here that these goals, if such there are, will constantly vary and change with context and situation, owing to the susceptibility of individuals to others and to the evaluative significance of communications that specify and enjoin collective goods. This is a matter not of a fluctuation between egoism and altruism, but rather of quite specific, local, tangible states of affairs becoming "desired" because of their value to given collectives in particular circumstances. A particularly clear-cut clash with the postulates of individualism is exposed here: the claim is that what independent ER individuals would recognize as collectively desirable but individually undesirable may yet be individually desired after all by individuals who are precisely not independent.

In many other versions of macro sociological theory, action is understood as oriented to values or norms or rules. What is claimed in this book is that such action is thereby oriented to the continuing activities of other people, activities that are continually reinventing the tradition wherein orientation to norm or rule can ensue as practical action. With forms of theory that rely on norms or values, just as with rational choice theory, it remains impossible to understand individual actions without reference to the continuing social interaction that constitutes their context. Action, it might be said, is invariably social action, although given that anti-individualistic formulations of this kind are occasionally found threatening it is worth adding that in no way does this deny the powers, skills and capacities manifestly possessed by separate individuals.

The theoretical approach offered here can also be used to address a number of moral and evaluative issues, such as, for example, that of the desirability of a maximally inclusive civil society; and it would indeed be a source of satisfaction if it eventually found a use of this kind. But it has been my deliberate policy not to give any attention to such issues here, where a careful and detailed approach would not have been possible. There are impressive general arguments against a complete institutional and cultural separation of technical "sociological" issues and moral "philosophical" ones. But what applies to whole systems of activity or discourse does not have the same implications at the individual level. At this level, it may be more important to recall the criticisms, often expressed by Habermas, of forms of activity wherein " . . . rationality in the choice of means accompanies avowed irrationality in orientation to values, goals and needs" (Habermas 1971: 63). Many books and articles in sociology, especially in the English-speaking world, exemplify this contrast. Writers are strongly and explicitly partial in relation to currently controversial or highly visible value questions, but will not make the detailed, rigorous and systematic examination of such questions a part of the normal practice of their field. Instead we have the familiar experience of contributions that begin with a stark assertion of the personal "commitments" of the authors, continue with a sentence to the effect that sociology must necessarily be "value laden", and then immediately pass on to a detailed presentation of findings and technical analyses of their empirical significance and methodological reputability. This precisely amounts to a tacit acceptance that the solutions to moral and evaluative problems are simply matters of personal opinion. And I want to do nothing here that would in any way reinforce the assumption that this is a legitimate way of understanding moral and evaluative issues.

Notes

Chapter 1

1. Different texts offer differently formulated postulates. All make reference to rationality and goal-orientation, although these may be combined in the idea that human beings are utility-maximizers or that they are oriented to the optimal satisfaction of preferences. An assumption of independence is often implicit but is invariably present. References to self-regard or egoism may be insistent, or absent.
2. Coleman (1990) is the classic source for rational choice theory in sociology, but also relevant are Hechter (1987), Moser (1990), Abell (1991, 1995) Coleman & Fararo (1992) and for a critical analysis Hindess (1988). For game theory, see Binmore (1992). For rational choice Marxism, see Roemer (1982) and Carling (1991).
3. The example relies upon the false assumption that it is rational to vote. ER individuals ought not normally to vote at all. However, it may be that the individuals who do vote, whose intrinsic characteristics may later become better understood, are still going to be interested in co-ordination even though they are not ER individuals.
4. For an invaluable discussion of convention, see Lewis (1969), and, for insight into how we can get trapped into conventions less optimal than related ones, see Arthur (1984).
5. The original example of two-person co-operation as a problem facing two prisoners can be found in any standard text on game theory: for a number of presentations and commentaries, see Elster (1986). Part of the general interest of the dilemma for sociologists is that it provides one of the best means of coming to grips with the fallacy of composition, which illegitimately presumes that what is true of the parts of a whole will be true of the whole itself: rationality may invariably be the best policy for a single individual but it does not follow that it is the best policy for a group of individuals.
6. Axelrod's book (1984) is itself, however, open to criticism for looseness of argument, particularly in its later chapters where the assumption of egoism with

which it begins is often tacitly dropped.

7. Some game theorists believe that Axelrod's argument is false for any series of encounters of known length; for on the last encounter, given that it is known to be the last, defection is the only rational strategy, and hence so it must also be at the next-to-last encounter, and hence, by iteration, at the first encounter (see, for example, Hardin 1982). However, what, in this case, is to be made of the criminal sentenced to death within the following week, but told that she will not know the particular day of her execution. In this famous story, the criminal uses deductive reasoning like that above to conclude that she cannot be executed – and is greatly surprised to be taken and hung on the Wednesday. In controversies between deductivist and inductivist conceptions of "rationality", this book clearly inclines to the latter, although it is beyond its scope to show the relevance of inductivist theories of learning and inferring to sociological theory.

8. None the less, individualistic theorists occasionally deserve criticism for expedient equivocation here, taking credit for "successful" predictions at one point and stressing the difference between model and reality when prediction fails.

9. See, for example, Tversky & Kahneman (1981), Marwell & Ames (1981), Stich (1985), or for that matter Sherif (1936), Asch (1956), or indeed Coleman (1990), which is an admirable source of examples that create difficulties for its own postulates. There are also problematic mundane facts such as, for example, that in Britain hundreds of thousands of the present citizenry will take their own lives at some point. There is also now the national lottery.

10. Thus, in introducing a lengthy treatment of utility-maximization and profit-maximization models of consumer and firm behaviour in his (1990) textbook, Kreps merely follows accepted practice in noting: "Unhappily, rather a lot of data has been collected, especially experimentally, which falsifies the models we will employ" (p. 4).

11. Exchange is, of course, a far more complex process than simple cases of co-ordination or co-operation because it depends upon the existence of an institution of property. Conventional individualistic treatments presume the institution as given and stable, and to that extent are incomplete accounts of exchange. Moreover, it is arguable that general accounts of property and of money, the necessary backdrop to models of exchange, are strikingly inadequate in the individualistic tradition. Certainly, within the sociological tradition of rational choice theory, not even Coleman's extended treatment makes these institutions intelligible in individualistic terms (cf. Coleman 1990: Chs 3, 6, 10, 11).

12. There are many plausible reasons why the engineering of "free markets" may become an enduring political concern. Considerations of efficiency are commonly cited. But perhaps it is also partly because individuals in a free market act without co-ordination and the power associated with it. They exchange independently, which is the state in which their ability to affect the framework in which they operate is at a minimum. Looked at from the perspective of politics, a market may appear as an extreme case of divide and rule.

13. Wonderfully insightful analyses of these kinds of difficulty are offered by Simon (1957, 1982) and March (1978), who, in response, introduce concepts of

"bounded rationality", "satisficing" and "adaptive rationality", which are indeed of great utility. However, it is important to look below the surface of the vocabulary here. What are being referred to are forms of conventional behaviour, not rational behaviour in the usual sense.

14. An alternative is to stretch the notion of "rational action" to include action based on routinely accepted or tradition-derived knowledge (see Esser 1993). Theories are remarkably fluid entities, so fluid that they may metamorphose into each other, so fluid that it is never possible to say quite what they are – or even if they are (see Barnes et al. 1995).

Chapter 2

1. In a valuable review of functionalist theory in the social sciences, Elster (1984) criticizes practically all instances as defective by their own standards, and in particular in their neglect or mistreatment of feedback.

2. Talcott Parsons drew heavily on biology for his functionalism, being particularly impressed with the concept of dynamic equilibrium. It is indeed a richly suggestive notion for the social sciences because it implies that systems actively reconstitute themselves, that stability is the outcome of the work being done in them. This in turn makes it easy to reconcile functionalist theory with the idea of continual self-repair as a necessity for a persisting system. Nor is the phenomenon of social change difficult to deal with, since a shifting equilibrium point is now no more problematic than a static one. Indeed, dynamically equilibrated systems are typically in a state of long-term change: organisms age, climates change, ecosystems evolve and differentiate. Unfortunately this book lacks space to review functionalist theories of social evolution and differentiation.

3. There should be no need to document the standing of "health" as a constantly changing evaluative concept, in terms of which more and more conditions of body and mind seem to have become defined as "pathological" over time.

4. Parsons' functionalism is the underlying point of reference in this chapter, but the argument fastens upon just a very small number of key ideas, which are taken to be crucial to the entire complex structure of his thought. Other widely divergent accounts of that complex whole exist; see Alexander (1984) for a systematic overview.

5. See, for example, Morgan (1975). A thorough discussion of this topic would also have to make reference to the regrettable and unnecessary confusion caused by references in functionalist theory to arrangements that are "functional for the individual".

6. The impressive work of Niklas Luhmann (1979, 1982, 1986, 1989) is in itself enough to justify this point, although even here it is as well to be equipped with simple exemplars like the central heating system, and with that other great prophylactic against the side-effects of grand theory, large doses of detailed historical sociology and social history.

7. Functionalist sociology has tended to neglect the study of totalitarian systems, possibly for other than good theoretical reasons. One technical basis for this neglect, however, has been the assumption that intentional explanation makes functional explanation inappropriate, which last may address only arrangements that are not deliberately being perpetuated (see Elster 1984). There seems no good reason, however, why intentional accounts of social integration should not combine with functional analysis of system integration, or why accounts of system integration should not be at once intentional and functionalist (Rueschemayer 1986).

8. For Parsons, the interlocking of individual interests is "a brittle thing which comparatively slight alterations of conditions can shatter at vital points" ([1937] 1968: 404). Compare Durkheim: "There is nothing less constant than interest. Today, it unites me to you; tomorrow it will make me your enemy" ([1893] 1964: 204).

9. Because this is not a book about theorists, there is no need to discuss the flaws in Parsons' treatment of Durkheim.

10. This is an obvious point of attack for individualistic theorists seeking to rebut Parsons, but the opportunity it represents seems not to have been taken. Indeed, amazingly, in Coleman (1990), the bible of sociological rational choice theory, we find not a sense of conflict with Parsons' theory but a willingness casually to incorporate it into an individualistic approach (1990: 292–9). Nothing serves better to underline the theoretical incoherence in this formidable work.

11. Of course, norms may be formulated and exemplified ever more narrowly – nuclear weapons may be banned from vendettas – but the formal point continues to apply with each new reformulation. The argument remains important through the later discussion.

12. This does not imply that it is impossible to be honest when nobody is looking, any more than an analysis of language as a communication system implies that it is impossible to speak English in isolation. In the context of sociology, what is implied is that norms are paradigmatically collective accomplishments not to be reified as fixed entities with an independent existence. The argument is given by ethnomethodologists, as in Garfinkel (1967), Wieder (1974) and Heritage (1984), and by sociologists of knowledge as in Barnes (1982b) and Barnes et al. (1995).

13. Wittgenstein (1968) is seminal on following rules, and accounts the sociological importance of his work include Kripke (1982) and Bloor (1983, 1996). Bloor (1996) has a particularly lucid account of rule following, as well as references to the literature opposing the sociological account. See also McHoul (1986).

14. Any empirical similarity is formally a matter of analogy rather than identity. Similarity in empirical respects is irreducible to identity. And similarity is an *intransitive* relation: if A is similar to B, and B is similar to C, it does not follow that A is similar to C. Thus, norms specified in terms of empirical similarity would allow radical divergence of practice, and breakdown of linguistic accounting, if followed separately by independent individuals. Formally, this point is the crux of any argument against an individualistic account of following norms, including Parsons' account. The problem of transitivity is well covered informally

and implicitly in Wittgenstein (1968), and is given a thorough formal analysis in Hesse (1974). It is of course a standard topic in epistemology and philosophy of science.

15. From a strictly formal perspective: "no course of action could be determined by a rule, because every course of action can be made out to accord with the rule" (Wittgenstein 1968: 81 201). There is always some interpretation of an action, we might say, that makes it out as similar to what a norm requires.

16. "There is a way of grasping a rule which is *not* an *interpretation*" (Wittgenstein 1968: 81 201). "I obey the rule blindly" (1968: 85 219). This aspect of rule-following is overlooked in some forms of social theory.

17. Such capabilities, whether physical or mental, are of course normally the outcome of a training process.

18. "To think one is obeying a rule is not to obey a rule. Hence it is not possible to obey a rule 'privately': otherwise thinking one was obeying a rule would be the same thing as obeying it" (Wittgenstein 1968: 81 202).

19. "Following a rule is analogous to obeying an order. We are trained to do so; we react to an order in a particular way. But what if one person reacts in one way and another in another to the order and the training? Which one is right?" (Wittgenstein 1968: 82 206). Wittgenstein is clear that strong agreement in practice specifies rule-following unproblematically for practical purposes as custom, and that lack of any agreement means that we shall not be speaking of a rule at all. But there is little in Wittgenstein on imperfect agreement, or disagreement in a larger context of agreement.

20. Such disagreement, and the consequent search for agreement, will occur only against a continuing background of unproblematic agreement in practice. Without such a background, the communication essential to solve the local problem of disagreement would not be possible. This is why blind, unhesitating, matter-of-course rule-following in largely unproblematic agreement is essential.

21. This is not to assert that individual hang-ups, or inhibitions, or complexes, or whatever, do not exist or even that they cannot be incorporated into activities at the collective level. It is merely to suggest that they are not the basis of an ordered social life but rather among the problems encountered in the course of it.

22. Normative change accordingly cannot be planned and intended in Parsons' theory, although an evolutionary view based on random variation followed by selection in terms of "functional" fitness would be possible. Parsons (1966) did himself develop an "evolutionary" theory of social change and explicitly compared it with evolutionary biological theories. Of Parsons' theory, however, it has to be said that the merits of its biological "analogues" are conspicuously absent, and the notorious vices of undisciplined "evolutionism" are very much present.

23. Parsons' own attempt to introduce flexibility into a normative order involved postulating a hierarchy with specific norms at the bottom and general values at the top. His suggestion was that, in order to sustain general values, actors would adjust and modify more specific norms at need. This aspect of Parsons' account has not been addressed, because the problems raised concerning norms obviously

plague values as well and indeed are yet more obvious and easily addressed at that more general level. As with norms, values are part of the problem, not part of the solution. Parsons, however, thought otherwise, and indeed believed that commitment to general values could be so strong that it could cause problems in the course of social differentiation. The problems allegedly arise because values must become ever more general as differentiation proceeds: "generalization, however, often encounters severe resistance because commitment to the value pattern is often experienced by various groups as commitment to its particular content at the previous, lower level of generality. Such resistance may be called 'fundamentalism'" (Parsons 1966: 23). This appalling piece of theorizing has not altogether been transcended by current treatments of "fundamentalism", which topic seems to encourage all the least desirable traits in current social theory.

24. The literature of ethnomethodology is a wonderful source of material illustrating the way that individuals take account of the existence of norms as features of context but do not behave as if governed by them or stricken with guilt by them. See, for example, Wieder (1974) and Heritage (1984).

25. For an expanded treatment of this idea, preceded by another slightly different discussion of the themes of this last section, see Barnes (1983, 1988: Ch. 2).

Chapter 3

1. Any standard history of the period will serve as background if required. Note that Mary would be sovereign, not Elizabeth, if Elizabeth was "really" illegitimate and her father, Henry VIII, had not "really" divorced his first wife – given that he "really" had married her in the first place.

2. We are now encountering the more challenging version of Hobbes' problem with which this book began. Hobbes himself has some invaluable insights into this version of his problem.

3. See, for example, Durkheim & Mauss ([1902] 1963: 81–2) and the final chapter of Durkheim ([1915] 1976). Although Durkheim acknowledged functionality as a "side-effect" of the ordered products of interaction, the functionalist Durkheim seems for the most part to be the accomplishment of later theorists.

4. Goffman and, indeed, interactionism generally are reviewed in an extremely schematic way here. Strangely, even though this kind of theory is cited here as central to the whole macro sociological project, detailed analysis of its claims is not necessary; indeed, it could be counterproductive, because the crux of the argument is that *an* interactionist approach is needed, not that any particular existing approach is. For Goffman in rich detail, see Burns (1992), Manning (1992) and Smith & Travers (1995).

5. Scheff's discussion rightly points to the taboo laid upon explicit discussion of the deference-emotion system, and mutual susceptibility in general. There will surely be an important connection between this taboo, individualism and its popularity, and the cult of the individual in society (see also Barnes 1988: Ch. 5; 1990).

6. This implies a different account from Rawls (1987) of what sustains the interaction order.
7. See Chapter 2 n23.
8. "Mutual symbolic sanctioning" is a deliberately vague description, signifying how many different detailed accounts of what is involved could be compatible with the general argument here.
9. Could it be that the credibility and acknowledged scope of rational choice theory vary according to the strength of this taboo?
10. This is an analogy that it is almost impossible to push too hard. Most mutual symbolic sanctioning just is modulated breathing.
11. Unfortunately, Habermas's (1984) discussions of Goffman and Garfinkel reveal limitations of sociological vision that derive from his evaluative and philosophical concerns.
12. The journey around this circle ends only if and when the last increment of knowledge makes no difference to the behaviour of those who acquire it. Knowledge then sustains at the collective level the practice that makes it valid. The self-referential character of this knowledge is not discussed in this book, because it is a topic that gives rise to great difficulties (see, however, Barnes 1983, 1988). It is also useful to compare the argument with that of Lewis (1969), and to note the neglected remarks of Krishna (1971). Another route to recognition of the importance of the social stock of knowledge runs from the work of Alfred Schutz (Schutz 1962, 1964, Schutz & Luckmann, 1974, Berger & Luckman 1967) to Garfinkel (1967) and ethnomethodology. A beautifully lucid account of the treatment of knowledge and cognition in this tradition can be found in Heritage (1984).
13. Self-categorization theory goes far beyond those points plundered from it to suit the argument here, and many parts of it could be refuted without adverse effects upon that argument (see also Turner 1991, Reicher 1984).

Chapter 4

1. In fact the chapter concentrates on the second objective, and thereby avoids the need for a technical discussion of work in areas such as sociology of knowledge and ethnomethodology. These fields have thrived so well on their own concerns that a rich and difficult literature has come to surround them, to which it is hard to do any kind of justice in a brief space. Its theoretical importance, however, is arguably every bit as great as that of those earlier forms of micro sociology that the main body of theory long ignored, to its own great detriment.
2. The metaphor of frame and contents, although not intrinsically objectionable, is not favoured in current constructivist work because it may encourage the imagination to think of all the contents of experience, past, present and future, already divided and sorted by a grid, or already belonging in some given slot in a framework. In other words, the idea of a framework rightly conveys the notion of clas-

sifications as conventions, but creates some small danger of the conventions being reified.

3. See, for example, Pickering (1984), Collins (1985) and Knorr-Cetina (1981) in the sociology of (scientific) knowledge; Douglas (1970) in anthropology; Smith & Wynne (1989) on experts; Atkinson (1978) and Douglas (1967) for what is now classic work on suicide; Garfinkel (1967), Wieder (1974) and Cicourel (1974) for early studies in ethnomethodology and cognitive sociology.

4. A strikingly similar image is employed by Thomas Kuhn (1977) in his account of the acquisition of scientific knowledge. Kuhn too wants to convey a sense of the simultaneous involvement of nature and culture in knowledge acquisition.

5. Commentators take a great interest in the epistemological and evaluative significance of constructivism in sociology and continue to impute unfavourable implications to it, often charging that it expresses hostility to science and scientific knowledge claims. But many very different views of its implications exist among those who have adopted it (in so far as there is an "it"), as is clear from any detailed and scrupulous study of its literature. This, of course, does not prevent the production of other kinds of study, such as, for example, Murphy (1994).

6. Looking forward to the coda to this chapter, it should be said that the mythical structure of Beck's book is complicated. There are interesting analogies with Marx, whom Beck occasionally consciously parodies, but the book is not intelligible as a simple expression of Enlightenment dualism. A quick way of ascertaining this is to look at its humour.

7. This is one of many sentences in which Beck reveals his awareness of Douglas's theme that the environment you believe in is a product of the institutions you oppose (or support).

8. Thus Beck's book simultaneously offers a specific cosmology and a sociological theory of cosmologies and their credibility. The reader is offered insights into the basis of belief and is at the same time urged to a particular set of beliefs. DDT and other pesticides, for example, represent a "death threat" (1988: 42) – in contrast to other accounts in which the withdrawal of DDT from use is alleged to have killed many thousands of people. No doubt this combination of objectives is perfectly defensible, but it is beginning to lead to disquieting consequences in the social sciences. There are signs of a division of labour here wherein economists and individualistic sociological theorists associate themselves with establishment institutions and construct appropriate versions of the cosmos for them, while anti-individualistic theorists associate themselves with opposition movements and greenery. Thus we may more deeply institutionalize, in a far from ideal way, the divided expertise that Nelkin (1979) and others have so perspicuously analyzed.

9. This need not imply a narrow view of tradition. Let it rather encourage a broad view of knowledge, and in particular the thought that knowledge includes knowhow.

10. For accessible accounts of finitism, see Barnes (1982a, b), Barnes et al. (1995) and, as it is expressed in ethnomethodology, Heritage (1984).

11. Thomas Kuhn's (1970) account of the natural sciences also offers a relevant view

of tradition, which is especially insightful in the way it erases the contrast between the "routine" and the "creative".

12. Enlightenment thought needs for some purposes to be distinguished from the progressive and evolutionary thought characteristic of the English-speaking world at the same time. Strong rationalism is characteristic of the former and "reason" its central, if problematic, concept, whereas empiricism, the philosophical opposite of rationalism, suffuses much of the latter. This important distinction is neglected here.

13. This is beautifully captured in a quip by Hacking (1994: 25); who refers to the "Me rational, you Jane" argument. It is a form of argument that is still widely used.

14. See Popper (1959, 1969) for the key ideas of an important tradition in rationalist philosophy of science. One question that eventually came to be asked in this tradition, and could presumably be put also to Habermas, is whether or not the assumption of the value of rational criticism is open to rational criticism.

15. In thus parting company with the early Marx, Habermas allows the economy to become the legitimate domain for a purely instrumental orientation to action, and hence sees nothing tragic, in the way that Weber does, in the rationalization of work and task performance. This denial of Marx is necessary for Habermas's dualist myth of "the colonization of the lifeworld" discussed in the coda to Chapter 8.

16. There is no way of avoiding the conclusion that Habermas makes a terrible mistake here, and that it is Marx who is correct, in the last analysis, on this crucial issue.

17. It is clear also in Giddens (1990) how an understanding of tradition of a particular kind can structure a contrasted understanding of modern science, technology and expertise. Had these been the central subjects of discussion, it would have been necessary to take issue with Giddens's account of them, and to ask what evidence he had to offer in favour of them, since he makes no reference to any of the large amount of empirical work by sociologists on science, technology or expertise. Giddens (1994) has since extended his speculations, but continues indifferent to the need for any substantive support for them.

18. With regard to anthropological studies it is worth also asking how much "social change" would be visible, even in a modern "rapidly changing" industrial society, over the length of time of a typical piece of anthropological fieldwork.

Chapter 5

1. Weber sees class situation as an alternative basis for the organization of economic activity in the unique circumstances of modern "market" societies. However, both Collins' work discussed here and the arguments in the discussion of "class" in Chapter 7 suggest continuity between market capitalist societies and their predecessors and thus eliminate the problem of why capitalist societies should be

unique historically in this respect.

2. This argument is developed in Barnes (1992). The first two sections of this chapter represent a developed version of the material in that paper.

3. As a symbol of the importance of the point, recall Habermas's already cited characterization of instrumental action as "non-social".

4. In the context of the sociology of science, the seminal work of Robert Merton (1973) is in effect a study of peer control in the production of knowledge, where the peers are members of status groups. This indicates the quite extraordinary sensitivity and sophistication of which this very simple form of control is capable. See also Shapin (1994).

5. In the context of individualist theory, "the pursuit of self-interest" is a standard way of referring to egoistic activity designed to fulfil individual wants. But if one wishes to speak of *shared* interests, as many sociological theorists do, then a clear distinction between wants and interests is needed.

6. By no means all the theoretically important issues are touched upon in this section. For example, the extent of deference based on status distinctions and the basis of such deference need discussion, as do status emulation and status competition between groups. In general, the discussion is deficient in attention to phenomena involving outsiders.

7. Michael Banton (1983: 194–5) cites the case of Malaysia, where the Malay-dominated democratic government sought to reserve for Malays 80 per cent of civil service posts, 60 per cent of university scholarships, large tracts of land encumbered with especially low tax rates, and special access to business opportunities. The government also sought to make public discussion of these measures illegal. At the time, Malays were an economically disadvantaged majority vis-à-vis Chinese.

8. One of the weaknesses accepted to keep this book within reasonable bounds is omission of any theoretical discussion of the state.

9. An interactionist account will find it easier to deal with collective action in any given case than will individualism. This means that work such as, for example, that of Hechter (1983, 1987), which offers an individualistic rational choice account of nationalism, and of group solidarity generally, can be useful in the context of interactionist approaches as a limit (worst) case.

10. Even in the most bureaucratic of democracies the collective action of voting is none the less required, and it is perhaps worth adding that to walk down the road and vote is not the whole cost here: members must be willing to vote for representatives ready to tax and spend sufficiently to maintain the collective monopoly of the territory. It is important not to underestimate the contribution of collective action made by ordinary members of democratic polities and its crucial role in the routine operation of these polities.

11. The political community of the nation-state is one of the few extant social formations for which members will willingly risk death. Max Weber saw this political community as very closely analogous to normal forms of status group, but saw it none the less as distinctive because of its close association with warfare and the risk of death: "The community of political destiny, i.e. above all, of common

political struggle of life and death, has given rise to groups with joint memories which often have had a deeper impact than the ties of merely cultural, linguistic or ethnic community. It is this 'community of memories' which, as we shall see, constitutes the ultimately decisive element of 'national consciousness'" (Weber 1968: 903).

Chapter 6

1. For work particularly relevant to problems of definition, see Melucci (1989), Diani (1992), Diani & Eyerman (1992), Eyerman & Jamison (1991) and Lyman (1995).
2. Accounts of resource mobilization theory are legion. For a recent collection both illuminating and critical, see Morris & McClurg Mueller (1992). See also Zald & McCarthy (1987a), Tilly (1978) and Oberschall (1973).
3. Sometimes, not merely ignorance but irrationality may be imputed to keep actions rational. Thus, in developing his "economic approach to human behaviour", Becker (1976) spends some time asserting the irrationality of some "non-economic" efforts to explain that same behaviour. But there is no reflection upon those same efforts as anomalies for his own theory.
4. For discussions of new social movements, see Cohen (1985), Scott (1990) and Jordan (1994).
5. Gamson (1992) points out that a similar argument relating to authentic lifestyle and its significance as political action is made also by US theorists, and is, for example, very close to the important conception of "prefigurational politics" in Breines (1982).
6. There are problems with references to types of action, which Habermas himself emphasizes and which are discussed in the coda to Chapter 8 here. It is less problematic to speak of action orientations and of the analytic dimensions of patterns of action. However, as the final paragraph of this section implies, a more precise treatment of the issue would not change the conclusion arrived at.
7. A sustained effort to compare social and religious movements has been made by Hannigan (1990, 1991, 1993), who emphasizes the profound similarities between the two. Another way of recognizing their close connection is made available by Zald & McCarthy's richly illustrated discussion of "religious groups as crucibles of social movements" (1987b). It is obvious from these materials that an extremely close link has been recognized even by research that accepts an institutionalized separation of "religion" and "society" as foci of study. The possibilities of experimenting with an approach that ceases to make the distinction at all at the level of theory are obvious. Perhaps the absence of such approaches is another aspect of the reserve with which theorists treat Durkheim.
8. See also Tucker (1991) and Calhoun (1993, 1994), where case study materials are used to criticize the empirical implications of "new" social movement theory. Calhoun's charge that these theories are "historically myopic" (1994: 22) seems

wholly justified, and it is interesting to speculate on the cause of the myopia. Jordan (1994) is relevant here.

Chapter 7

1. The discussion here is confined to the use of "class" in the context of theory, as a concept for categorizing or grouping individuals or situations that individuals occupy. As well as the particular line developed in what follows, there is another widespread approach, which justifies theoretical use of "class" by predictive utility alone. For an admirably succinct criticism of this approach, see Scott (1994).
2. There is, of course, another, strongly Hegelian, strand in the tradition from Marx, which is not covered by the approach taken in this chapter.
3. Weber's accounts of "class" are readily accessible via the index of *Economy and society* (1968), and are a continuing resource for social theory. Marx's ideas on "class" are more difficult to document, and are usually approached through the vast secondary literature; see, however, Marx & Engels (1848).
4. A defence of the Marxian view of the long term none the less remains possible. Although most attempts are sterile exercises, an important exception is world systems theory (Wallerstein 1974, 1980), which adjusts the timescale of the theory to the *very* long term.
5. In the early Marx in particular it is made clear that, although individuals may be robustly self-interested and well able to see where their interests may lie, they are none the less wholly different in nature from the ER individuals of the economists: human beings "are atoms only in *imagination* – in *reality* [they are] not *divine egoists*, but *egotistic human beings*" (Marx & Engels 1846: 163). None the less, it is not altogether clear how Marx accounts for the collective action of "egotistic human beings".
6. The calculations imputed in the account that follows make sense as "rational calculations" only in the specific context. It is actually necessary to consider factors such as the inelasticity of demand for coal, the high fixed costs of mines, and the difficulty of selling them or the plant associated with them, to understand the strategies of the owners. Detail of this kind is provided in Bowman (1989).
7. The argument in this chapter should not be taken to imply that the position of numerous competing employers is invariably a weak one vis-à-vis their workers. There appear to be cases where such employers have taken effective joint action (see Wigham 1973).
8. Calhoun's argument here is very close to that of the self-categorization theorists discussed in Chapter 3 (p. 91).
9. Industrial conflict at this time may look intense and uncompromising from later vantage points, but it is important to keep in mind what a very strongly encapsulated and ritualized form of conflict the strike represents.
10. See also Chapter 6 n8.
11. From the perspective of the historian or historical sociologist, of course, it may

be perfectly legitimate to refer to extended, occupationally based status groups, with organizations built on associational ties, as classes, especially when members themselves so refer to them.

12. Extended classes in Calhoun's sense typically extend to but not beyond the boundaries of the nation-state, and it is plausible to suggest that organization and extension to this degree are precisely the product of the need to influence the state power. The more general implication of this thought is that the growth of capitalism and the growth of the nation-state are inseparable, and that "class formation" is simply unintelligible without reference to the state of the polity (see Giddens 1979, 1985, Mann 1988, Vogler 1985).

13. There have been a large number of theoretical discussions questioning the utility of the concept of class. Some of them are merely polemical and of little interest. Others suggest that social change is making older conceptions of class less readily applicable and in need of adjustment: Holton & Turner (1989: Ch. 6) is a good example, although it offers more than historical reflection. Others again evince theoretical dissatisfaction with "class" as normally conceived, and hence call the value of the concept into question, not merely as a help to the understanding of particular kinds of society or particular periods of history, but as a part of the conceptual structure of social theory. Pahl (1989, 1991) and Waters (1991) are among the contributions of this kind, as is the discussion here.

14. It is wholly misconceived to equate reification with inadequacy either in common-sense or in theoretical thought, if only because it is a necessity in some form in all thought.

15. Lee's extremely valuable and interesting paper offers arguments very close to those used here, but to defend rather than to call into question the theoretical utility of the concept of class. On one reading of the paper (see especially Lee 1994: 408), it comes close to equating class phenomena with the effects of the power of capital, and its dichotomous classification of individuals is an unnecessary appendage. For more on money and power as constituted in self-referring distributions of knowledge, see Barnes (1983, 1988).

Chapter 8

1. This point is given a particularly clear and insightful discussion in Albrow (1970: Ch. 3). See also Barnes (1986, 1988).

2. Some of the most insightful and penetrating accounts of bureaucratic politics relate to the US military (see, for example, Armacost 1969, Ball 1980, Beard 1976 and Sapolsky 1972).

3. The idea that the ideal control device depends on the activity to be controlled has been extended and developed in many directions, as well as being tested and "confirmed" in detailed investigations (see, for example, Woodward 1965, Thompson 1967, Lawrence & Lorsch 1967 and Perrow 1984). For a historical review of empirically based objections to Weber, see Albrow (1970). It is also

worth noticing the difficulty in characterizing bureaucratic control systems empirically. The now famous "new" bureaucratic techniques of the Japanese, for example, have been described both as devolving control and as intensifying it, and the proper description of particular examples remains controversial (Adler 1992).

4. See, for example, March & Simon (1958), Arrow (1974) and Galbraith (1977). Information overload is essentially the same problem as the one that creates the need for "bounded rationality" (see Chapter 1, n13).

5. It is important to recognize that the role of the machine here is a conventional symbol of reliability. Perhaps some of the aversion to mechanical analogies in the social sciences would be reduced if it was recognized that mechanisms could equally well be used as symbols of unreliability: "If we know the machine, everything else, that is its movement, seems to be already completely determined. . . . We talk as if these parts could only move in this way, as if they could not do anything else. How is this – do we forget the possibility of their bending, breaking off, melting, and so on? Yes; in many cases we don't think of that at all. We use a machine . . . to symbolize a particular action of the machine . . . the movement of the machine-as-symbol is predetermined in a different sense from that in which the movement of any given actual machine is predetermined" (Wittgenstein 1968: 77–8 193).

6. It is interesting to read Garfinkel's (1967) discussion of "Good organizational reasons for bad clinic records" from this perspective.

7. Consider, for example, Weber's comparison of status incentives and coercion as means of controlling officials (1968: 967–8). Weber has genuine difficulty showing why a regular salary and prestige should work better than enslavement and "prodigious use of the bamboo".

8. For a modern Weberian, the stimulus "status' evokes the response "monopoly", but one has to look to Randall Collins for an uncompromising application of this approach to bureaucracies. Weber himself stresses the positive value of status to bureaucratic operation, and expects "irrelevant" status distinctions to disappear from bureaucratic settings. Even his treatment of bureaucratic politics is marked by an extraordinary (ironic?) tenderness, as when he speaks of altruistic officials who "treat their official function from what is substantially a utilitarian point of view in the interest of those under their authority" (1968: 226).

9. The study of organizational culture is now an important research area with an extensive literature (see Martin 1992 and Turner 1990).

10. A great deal of Weber and his command model remains in Habermas. Moreover, his explanation of the growth and even the over-extension of instrumental systems presumes the efficiency and effectiveness of their mode of operation with much less equivocation than Weber.

11. Habermas's discussion of the lifeworld (1987: 113–52) is so complex that any brief specification of his concept inevitably falls short of capturing it.

12. With regard to norms and values, Habermas would appear to reject Parsons' idea that we lack discretion with respect to them, but retain his idea that they are externalities with clear significance and implications.

13. A properly critical attitude would encourage scepticism about the functionalism of the account, in which the "dysfunctional" is apparently explained as "functional"; about the relationship of "social" and "system" integration that is postulated; and about the evolutionism, which in many ways is analogous to that of Parsons, and is also explicitly linked to the theory of "moral development" of Lawrence Kohlberg (Habermas 1987: 174). Kohlberg's characterization of the most evolved form of morality as that wherein norms are judged in terms of general principles is formally very close to Parsons on the relationship of values and norms; Kohlberg's ideas deserve severe criticism both as description and even more as moral philosophy.

14. This mythical structure is not weakened by Habermas's willingness to distinguish good and bad lifeworlds and social movements. What is actually interesting about this last distinction in Habermas is how it is accomplished. It is very striking how, at the end of the vast complications of the *Theory of communicative action*, which leave no doubt of the difficulties associated with such matters, movements associated with peace and ecology are instantly and intuitively separated from movements for tax reduction, or against the siting of large technological projects close to middle-class neighbourhoods (1987: 394). Indeed, it is just this familiar contrast between vast theoretical development at the abstract level, and apparent absence of the content of the development at the level of application, that sustains much reasonable scepticism concerning the credentials of this kind of grand theory.

15. This point and its significance have already been discussed earlier in section 2.3.

16. Habermas may hold that two of the kinds of action, the strategic and the communicative, are mutually exclusive as a matter of psychology as it were: a person cannot simultaneously be oriented to success and to mutual understanding in an encounter with another (see Habermas 1984: 285–6 and, more significantly, 1982: 266). If this is so, then the position must be challenged. Indeed, a major theme of this book has been that ongoing interaction is typically at once success oriented and oriented to the maintenance of shared understanding – as in the crucial case of proposing a collective good and *ipso facto* sanctioning it.

17. It is hard to know which substantive materials are relevant here. If Habermas's account of systems is a kind of Taylorist vision, a conception of mechanized operations even more unequivocal than Weber's, then practically any case study of the relevant *subcultures* will count against it (Turner 1971). Case studies record situations where workers have some control over work rate, where managers are competing with each other for advancement, where managers or workers or both together are operating a racket, even where work is found intrinsically meaningful and satisfying; all these would count as anomalies for such a conception (Esland & Salaman 1980). Fortunately, however, Habermas himself recognizes the difficulties posed by substantive materials, so the problem can be passed over (see the immediately following discussion in the main text).

18. It is difficult to imagine how a rationalist account can avoid such an empowerment: this issue concerning rules is the crucial theoretical point in the social sciences where the perennial opposition of rationalism and empiricism crystallizes.

None the less, Habermas recognizes many of the points that can be used to argue for a finitist account of rules even if he does not himself proceed in that direction; see, for example, his account of literal meaning (Habermas 1984: 335–7).

19. What is strange here, particularly in a writer oriented above all to moral and ethical concerns, is how Habermas presents an extraordinarily dismal and depressing picture of the "steered systems", and yet at the same time appears to offer a positive evaluation of the differentiation of such systems, indeed a very highly positive one provided only that they remain in their proper place (see, for example, Habermas 1984: 72). But this is merely to reiterate what was said earlier in Chapter 4.

20. See, for example, Adorno & Horkheimer (1979), Adorno (1973) and Foucault (1977, 1980). Burns (1992) makes a valuable comparison between Goffman and Foucault as macro-theorists of normalization. It is arguable, of course, that neither Foucault nor even Adorno moved to a completely tragic position, that they left the sticker in the glove compartment.

21. This can be run back into the context of the origin of Enlightenment thought. Karl Mannheim (1953: 143) notes the comments of the conservative Justus Moser on Enlightenment authoritarianism: "Moser clearly recognized the spiritual affinity between the centralizing bureaucracy and the enlightened monarchy, and saw the essence of despotism in its wanting to force everything by means of a few rules."

22. References to "everyone" as sources of actions judged by theorists to be undesirable are invariably regarded with some suspicion because they can easily be converted into imputations of responsibility and blame of a kind that threatens the usual moral contrasts of dualist myth. In the context of dualism, the only routinely accepted way of acknowledging the ubiquity of undesired actions is to treat them as the result of system externalities pressing on persons rather than of persons themselves directly. It is interesting to note how, in Foucault, as undesirable actions are recognized as being more and more ubiquitous, as the transition from dualism to monism occurs, so the individual human being disappears from theory altogether.

23. Further to the previous note, recall that consumerism is insistently accounted by Habermas as something the system inflicts on its individual members.

24. Robert Pirsig records that the intense electro-convulsive therapy to which he (or his fictional hero) was forcibly subjected was technically known as "Annihilation ECS" (Pirsig 1976: 84).

25. Why indeed should it be inclined to do anything else? It is not possible to solve the problems that arise from the way that we now constitute the environment for each other by advocacy of a return to "community" – whatever that may mean. And in any case, perhaps regulation is preferable to community. The remark of a colleague with expertise in this area is worth mentioning here: "When I hear the word 'community', I think of witchcraft."

26. One of the attractions of cost–benefit analysis is the opportunity it provides for making ingenious causal connections. Too many safety regulations for air or train transport can be cited as the cause of road accidents. Prohibition can be assigned the costs of poisonous hooch and Al Capone.

Bibliography

Abell, P. 1991. *Rational choice theory*. Aldershot, England: Elgar.
—1995. Sociological theory and rational choice theory. In *The companion to social theory*, B. S. Turner (ed.). Forthcoming.
Adler, P.S. 1992. The learning bureaucracy. *Research in organizational behaviour* **15**, 111–94.
Adorno, T. 1973. *Negative dialectics*. London: Routledge & Kegan Paul.
Adorno, T. W. & M. Horkheimer 1979. *Dialectics of enlightenment*. London: Verso.
Albrow, M. 1970. *Bureaucracy*. London: Macmillan.
Alexander, J. C. 1984. *Theoretical logic in sociology. Vol. 4, The modern reconstruction of classical thought: Talcott Parsons*. London: Routledge & Kegan Paul.
Armacost, M. H. 1969. *The Thor-Jupiter controversy*. New York: Columbia University Press.
Arrow, K. J. 1974. *The limits of organization*. New York: W. W. Norton.
Arthur, W. B. 1984. Competing technologies and economic prediction. *Options* **2**, 10–13.
Asch, S. 1956. *Studies of independence and conformity*. Washington, DC: American Psychological Association.
Atkinson, J. M. 1978. *Discovering suicide: studies in the social organization of sudden death*. London: Macmillan.
Axelrod, R. 1984. *The evolution of cooperation*. New York: Basic Books.
Ball, D. 1980. *Politics and force levels: the strategic missile program of the Kennedy administration*. Berkeley: University of California Press.
Banton, M. 1983. *Racial and ethnic competition*. Cambridge: Cambridge University Press.
Barnes, B. 1982a. *T.S. Kuhn and social science*. London: Macmillan.
—1982b. On the extension of concepts and the growth of knowledge. *Sociological Review* **30**, 23–44.
—1983. Social life as bootstrapped induction. *Sociology* **17**, 524–45.

—1986. On authority and its relationship to power. In *Power, action and belief*, J. Law (ed.). London: Routledge.

—1988. *The nature of power*. Oxford: Polity.

—1990. Macro economics and infant behaviour: a sociological treatment of the free-rider problem. *Sociological Review* **38**, 272–92.

—1992. Status group and collective action. *Sociology* **26**, 259–70.

—1993. Power. In *Theories and concepts of politics: an introduction*, R. Bellamy (ed.). Manchester: Manchester University Press.

—1994. Cultural change – the thought-styles of Mannheim and Kuhn. *Common Knowledge* **3**, 65–78.

Barnes, B., D. Bloor, J. Henry 1995. *Scientific knowledge: a sociological analysis*. London: Athlone Press.

Bauman, Z. 1989. *Modernity and the holocaust*. Oxford: Polity.

Baxter, H. 1987. System and life-world in Habermas's theory of communicative action. *Theory and Society* **16**, 39–86.

Beard, E. 1976. *Developing the ICBM; a study in bureaucratic politics*. New York: Colombia University Press.

Beck, U. 1988. *Risk society: towards a new modernity*. London: Sage.

Becker, G. 1976. *The economic approach to human behavior*. Chicago: University of Chicago Press.

Becker, H. S. 1963. *Outsiders: studies in the sociology of deviance*. New York: Free Press.

—1970. *Sociological work: method and substance*. London: Allen Lane.

Becker, H. S., B. Geer, E. C. Hughes, A. L. Strauss 1961. *Boys in white: student culture in medical school*. Chicago: University of Chicago Press.

Beckford, J. A. 1985. *Cult controversies: the societal response to the new religious movements*. London: Tavistock Publications.

Berger, P. & T. Luckmann 1967. *The social construction of reality*. Garden City, NY: Anchor.

Binmore, K. 1992. *Fun and games: a text on game theory*. Lexington: D. C. Heath.

Bloor, D. 1983. *Wittgenstein: a social theory of knowledge*. Oxford: Blackwell.

—1996. *Wittgenstein: rules and institutions*. Forthcoming.

Bowman, J. R. 1989. *Capitalist collective action: competition, cooperation, and conflict in the coal industry*. Cambridge: Cambridge University Press.

Breines, W. 1982. *Community and organization in the new left, 1962–1968: the great refusal*. New York: Praeger.

Burns, T. 1992. *Erving Goffman*. London: Routledge.

Burns, T. & G. M. Stalker 1961. *The management of innovation*. London: Tavistock Publications.

Calhoun, C. 1982. *The question of class struggle*. Chicago: University of Chicago Press.

—1987. Class, place and industrial revolution. In *Class and space*, N. Thrift &

P. Williams (eds). London: Routledge & Kegan Paul.

—1991. The problem of identity in collective action. In *Macro–micro linkages in sociology*, J. Huber (ed.). Beverley Hills, Calif.: Sage.

—(ed.) 1992. *Habermas and the public sphere*. Cambridge, Mass.: MIT Press.

—1993. "New social movements" of the early 19th century. *Social Science History* **17**, 385–427.

—(ed.) 1994. *Social theory and the politics of identity*. Oxford: Basil Blackwell.

Carling, A. 1991. *Social division*. London: Verso.

Carrier, J. G. 1995. *Gifts and commodities*. London: Routledge.

Cicourel, A. V. 1974. *Theory & method in a study of Argentine fertility*. New York: Wiley.

Cohen, J. L. 1985. Strategy or identity: new theoretical paradigms and contemporary social movements. *Social Research* **52**, 663–716.

Coleman, J. S. 1988. Freeriders and zealots: the role of social networks. *Sociological Theory* **6**, 52–7.

—1990. *Foundations of social theory*. Cambridge, Mass.: Harvard University Press.

Coleman, J. S. & T. Fararo 1992. *Rational choice theory: advocacy and critique*. Newbury Park, Calif.: Sage.

Collins, H. M. 1985. *Changing order*. New York: Academic Press.

Collins, R. 1979. *The credential society*. New York: Academic Press.

—1981. *Sociology since midcentury. Essays in theory cumulation*. New York: Academic Press.

—1986. *Weberian sociological theory*. Cambridge: Cambridge University Press.

—1988. *Theoretical sociology*. New York: Harcourt Brace Jovanovich.

Commons, J. R. 1959. *Institutional economics*. Madison: University of Wisconsin Press.

Davis, J. 1993. *Exchange*. Milton Keynes, England: Open University Press.

Diani, M. 1992. The concept of social movement. *Sociological Review* **40**, 1–25.

Diani, M. & R. Eyerman 1992. *Studying collective action*. London: Sage.

Douglas, J. 1967. *The social meanings of suicide*. Princeton, NJ: Princeton University Press.

Douglas, M. 1970. *Natural symbols*. London: Barrie & Jenkins.

—1992. *Risk and blame*. London: Routledge.

Douglas, M. & A. Wildavsky 1982. *Risk and culture: an essay on the selection of technological and environmental dangers*. Berkeley: University of California Press.

Durkheim, E. [1893] 1964. *The division of labour in society* (English translation G. Simpson 1933). New York: Free Press.

—[1915] 1976. *The elementary forms of the religious life*, 2nd edn. London: Unwin.

Durkheim, E. & M. Mauss [1902] 1963. *Primitive classification*. London: Cohen & West.

Elster, J. 1984. *Ulysses and the sirens*. Cambridge: Cambridge University Press.

—(ed.) 1986. *Rational choice*. Oxford: Basil Blackwell.

Esland, G. & G. Salaman (eds.) 1980. *The politics of work and occupations*. Milton Keynes: Open University Press.

Esser, H. 1993. The rationality of everyday behavior: a rational choice reconstruction of the theory of action by Alfred Schütz. *Rationality and Society* **5**, 7–31.

Eyerman, R. & A. Jamison 1991. *Social movements*. Oxford: Polity.

Foucault, M. 1977. *Discipline and punish*. New York: Pantheon.

—1980. *Power/knowledge: selected interviews and other writings*, C. Gordon (ed.). Brighton, England: Harvester Press.

Friedman, D. & D. McAdam, 1992. Collective identity and activism: networks, choices, and the life of a social movement. See Morris & McClurg Mueller (1992).

Furnival, J. S. 1948. *Colonial policy and practice: a comparative study of Burma and Netherlands India*. Cambridge: Cambridge University Press.

Galbraith, J. R. 1977. *Organizational design*. Reading, Mass.: Addison-Wesley.

Gamson, W. A. 1992. The social psychology of collective action. See Morris & McClurg Mueller (1992).

Garfinkel, H. 1967. *Studies in ethnomethodology*. Englewood Cliffs, NJ: Prentice-Hall.

Giddens, A. 1979. *The class structure of the advanced societies*, 2nd edn. London: Hutchinson.

—1985. *A contemporary critique of historical materialism. Vol. 2, The nation-state and violence*. Oxford: Polity.

—1990. *The consequences of modernity*. Oxford: Polity.

—1994. Living in a post-traditional society. In *Reflexive modernisation*, U. Beck, A. Giddens, S. Lash. Oxford: Polity.

Gilbert, David. 1992. *Class, community, and collective action: social change in two British coalfields, 1850-1926*. Oxford: Clarendon.

Goffman, E. 1952. On cooling the mark out: some aspects of adaptation to failure. *Psychiatry* **15**, 451–63.

—1961. *Encounters: two essays on the sociology of interaction*. Indianapolis: Bobbs-Merrill.

—1963. *Behavior in public places: notes on the social organization of gatherings*. New York: The Free Press.

—1967. *Interaction ritual: essays on face-to-face behavior*. New York: Doubleday.

—1969. *Where the action is*. London: Allen Lane.

Granovetter, M. 1974. *Getting a job: a study of contacts and careers*. Cambridge, Mass.:Harvard University Press.

—1978. Threshhold models of collective behavior. *American Journal of Sociology* **83**, 1420–43.

—1985. Economic action and social structure: the problems of embeddedness. *American Journal of Sociology* **91**, 481–510.

Habermas, J. 1971. *Towards a rational society*. London: Heinemann.

—1981. New social movements. *Telos* **49**, 33–7.

—1982. A reply to my critics. In *Habermas: Critical debates*, J. B. Thompson & D. Held (eds). London: Macmillan.

—1984. *The theory of communicative action. Vol. 1, Reason and the rationalization of society*. London: Heinemann.

—1987. *The theory of communicative action. Vol. 2, Lifeworld and system: a critique of functionalist reason*. Oxford: Polity.

—1989. *The structural transformation of the public sphere: an inquiry into a category of bourgeois society*. Oxford: Polity.

—1990. *The philosophical discourse of modernity*. Oxford: Polity.

Hacking, I. 1994. Paul Feyerabend, humanist. *Common Knowledge* **3**, 23–8.

Hannigan, J. A. 1990. Apples and oranges or varieties of the same fruit? The new religious movements and the new social movements compared. *Review of Religious Research* **31**, 246–58.

—1991. Social movement theory and the sociology of religion: toward a new synthesis. *Sociological Analysis* **52**, 311–31.

—1993. New social movement theory and the sociology of religion. In *A future for religion? New paradigms for social analysis*, W. W. Swatos, Jr. (ed.). London: Sage.

Hardin, R. 1982. *Collective action*. Baltimore, Md.: Johns Hopkins University Press.

Hechter, M. 1983. *Microfoundations of macrosociology*. Philadelphia: Temple University Press.

—1987. Nationalism as group solidarity. *Ethnic and Racial Studies* **10**, 415–25.

Heckathorn, D. 1989. Collective action and the second order free-rider problem. *Rationality and Society* **1**, 78–100.

Heritage, J. 1984. *Garfinkel and ethnomethodology*. Oxford: Polity.

Hesse, M. B. 1974. *The structure of scientific inference*. London: Macmillan.

Hindess, B. 1988. *Choice rationality and social theory*. London: Unwin Hyman.

Hirsch, F. 1977. *Social limits to growth*. Routledge & Kegan Paul.

Hobbes, T. [1651] 1968. *Leviathan*. C. B. Macpherson (ed.). London: Penguin.

Holton, R. J. & B. S. Turner 1989. *Max Weber on economy and society*. London: Routledge.

Jordan, T. 1994. *Reinventing revolutions: value and difference in new social movements and the left*. Aldershot, England: Avebury.

Kornhauser, A. 1959. *The politics of mass society*. Glencoe, Ill.: Free Press.

Knorr-Cetina, K. D. 1981. *The manufacture of knowledge: an essay on the constructivist and contextual nature of science*. Oxford: Pergamon Press.

Kreps, D. M. 1990. *Game theory and economic modelling*. Oxford: Clarendon Press.

Kripke, S. A. 1982. *Wittgenstein on rules and private language: an elementary exposition*. Oxford: Blackwell.

Krishna, D. 1971. "The self-fulfilling prophesy" and the nature of society. *American Sociological Review* **36**, 1104–7.

Kuhn, T. S. 1970. *The structure of scientific revolutions*, 2nd edn. Chicago: University of Chicago Press.

—1977. Second thoughts on paradigms. In *The essential tension*. Chicago: University of Chicago Press.

Kuper, L. 1974. *Race, class and power: ideology and revolutionary change in plural societies*. London: Duckworth.

—1977. *The pity of it all: polarization of racial and ethnic relations*. London: Duckworth.

Law, J. 1994. *Organizing modernity*. Oxford: Blackwell.

Lawrence, P. R. & J. W. Lorsch 1967. *Organization and environment*. Cambridge, Mass: Harvard University Press.

Lee, D. J. 1994. Class as a social fact. *Sociology* **28**, 397–415.

Lewis, D. K. 1969. *Convention*. Cambridge, Mass.: Harvard University Press.

Lockwood, D. 1964. Social integration and system integration. In *Explorations in social change*, G. K. Zollschan, & W. Hirsh (eds). London: Routledge & Kegan Paul.

Luhmann, N. 1979. *Trust and power*. New York: Wiley.

—1982. *The differentiation of society*. New York: Columbia University Press.

—1986. *Love as passion: the codification of intimacy*. Cambridge, Mass.: Harvard University Press.

—1989. *Ecological communication*. Chicago: University of Chicago Press.

Lyman, S. M. (ed.) 1995. *Social movements, critiques, concepts, case studies*. London: Macmillan.

McAdam, D. 1986. Recruitment to high-risk activism: the case of freedom summer. *American Journal of Sociology* **82**, 64–90.

McCarthy, J. D. 1987. Pro-life and pro-choice mobilization: infrastructure deficits and new technologies. See Zald & McCarthy (1987a).

McCarthy, J. D. & M. N. Zald 1987. Resource mobilization and social movements: a partial theory. See Zald & McCarthy (1987a).

McHoul, A. 1986. *Wittgenstein on certainty and the problem of rules in social science*. Toronto: Toronto Semiotic Circle.

Mann, M. 1988. *States, war and capitalism*. Oxford: Basil Blackwell.

Mannheim, K. 1952. *Essays on the sociology of knowledge*. London: Routledge & Kegan Paul.

—1953. Conservative thought. In *Essays on sociology and social psychology*.

Oxford: Oxford University Press.

Manning, P. 1992. *Erving Goffman and modern sociology*. Oxford: Polity.

March, J. G. 1978. Bounded rationality, ambiguity, and the engineering of choice. *Bell Journal of Economics* **9**, 587–608.

March, J. G. & H. A. Simon 1958. *Organizations*. New York: Wiley.

Martin, J. 1992. *Cultures in organizations*. Oxford: Oxford University Press.

Marwell, G. & R. E. Ames. 1981. Economists free ride, does anyone else? *Journal of Public Economics* **15**, 295–310.

Marx, K. [1844] 1961. *Economic and philosophical manuscripts of 1844*. Moscow: Foreign Languages Publishing House.

—[1883] 1974. *Capital: a critical analysis of capitalist production*. London: Lawrence & Wishart.

Marx, K. & F. Engels [1846] 1947. *The German ideology*. New York: International Publishers.

—[1848] 1952. *Manifesto of the communist party*. Moscow: Progress Publishers.

Melucci, A. 1985. The symbolic challenge of contemporary movements. *Social Research* **52**, 789–816.

—1989. *Nomads of the present: social movements and individual needs in contemporary society*, J. Keane & P. Mier (eds). London: Hutchinson Radius.

—1992. Frontier land: collective action between actors and systems. In *Studying collective action*, M. Diani & R. Eyerman (eds). London: Sage.

Merton, R. K. 1973. *The sociology of science*. Chicago: University of Chicago Press.

Molotch, H. 1990. Sociology, economics and the economy. In *Sociology in America*, H. Gans (ed.), ASA Presidential Series. Newbury Park, Calif.: Sage.

Morgan, D. H. J. 1975. *Social theory and the family*. London: Routledge & Kegan Paul.

Morgan, G. 1986. *Images of organization*. Newbury Park, Calif.: Sage.

Morris, A. D. & C. McClurg Mueller (eds) 1992. *Frontiers in social movement theory*. New Haven, Conn.: Yale University Press.

Moser, P. K. (ed.) 1990. *Rationality in action*. Cambridge: Cambridge University Press.

Mullins, P. 1991. The identification of social forces in development as a general problem in sociology: a comment on Pahl's remarks on class and consumption relations as forces in urban and regional development. *International Journal of Urban and Regional Research* **15**, 119–26.

Murphy, R. 1994. The social construction of science without reality. *Sociology* **28**, 957–74.

Nelkin, D. (ed.) 1979. *Controversy: politics of technical decisions*. London: Sage.

Oberschall, A. 1973. *Social conflict and social movements*. Englewood Cliffs,

NJ: Prentice-Hall.

Olson, M. 1965. *The logic of collective action*. Cambridge, Mass.: Harvard University Press.

Pahl, R. E. 1989. Is the Emperor naked? Some questions on the adequacy of sociological theory in urban and regional research. *International Journal of Urban and Regional Research* **13**, 709–20.

—1991. R. E. Pahl replies. *International Journal of Urban and Regional Research* **15**, 127–9.

Parkin, F. 1979. *Marxism and class theory*. London: Tavistock.

Parsons, T. [1937] 1968. *The structure of social action*. New York: Free Press.

—1951. *The social system*. London: Routledge & Kegan Paul.

—1956. The American family: its relations to personality and to the social structure. In *Family socialisation and interaction process*, T. Parsons & R. F. Bales (eds). London: Routledge & Kegan Paul.

—1964. Social structure and the development of personality: Freud's contribution to the integration of psychology and sociology. In *Social structure and personality*. London: Free Press of Glencoe.

—1966. *Societies: evolutionary and comparative perspectives*. Englewood Cliffs, NJ: Prentice-Hall.

—1967. Durkheim's contribution to the theory of integration of social systems. In *Sociological theory and modern society*. New York: Free Press.

Perrow, C. 1979. *Complex organisations: a critical essay*. New York: Random House.

—1984. *Normal accidents*. New York: Basic Books.

Pickering, A. 1984. *Constructing quarks: a sociological history of particle physics*. Chicago: University of Chicago Press.

Pirsig, R. 1976. *Zen and the art of motorcycle maintenance*. London: Corgi.

Popper, K. R. 1959. *The logic of scientific discovery*. London: Hutchinson.

—1969. *Conjectures and refutations: the growth of scientific knowledge*. London: Routledge & Kegan Paul.

Rawls, A. W. 1987. The interaction order *sui generis*: Goffman's contribution to social theory. *Sociological Theory* **5**, 136–49.

Reicher, S. 1984. The St. Pauls riot: an explanation of the limits of crowd action in terms of a social identity model. *European Journal of Social Psychology* **14**, 1–21.

Reisman, D. 1990. *Theories of collective action*. London: Macmillan.

Rock, P. 1978. *The making of symbolic interactionism*. London: Macmillan.

Roemer, J. 1982. *A general theory of exploitation and class*. Cambridge, Mass.: Harvard University Press.

Rueschemayer, D. 1986. *Power and the division of labour*. Oxford: Polity.

Sapolsky, H. M. 1972. *The polaris system development: bureaucratic and programmatic success in government*. Cambridge, Mass.: Harvard University Press.

Scheff, T. J. 1988. Shame and conformity: the deference-emotion system. *American Sociological Review* **53**, 395–406.

—1990. *Microsociology*. Chicago: Chicago University Press.

Schelling, T. C. 1960. *The strategy of conflict*. Cambridge, Mass.: Harvard University Press.

Schumpeter, J. A. [1911] 1961. *The theory of economic development*. Oxford: Oxford University Press.

—1942. *Capitalism, socialism and democracy*. New York: Harper.

Schutz, A. 1962. *Studies in social theory. Collected papers*, vol. 1. The Hague: Martinus Nijhoff.

—1964. *Studies in social theory. Collected papers*, vol. 2. The Hague: Martinus Nijhoff.

Schutz, A. & T. Luckmann 1974. *The structure of the lifeworld*. London: Heinemann.

Scott, A. 1990. *Ideology and the new social movements*. London: Unwin Hyman.

Scott, J. 1985. *Corporations, classes and capitalism*, 2nd edn. London: Hutchinson.

—1986. *Capitalist property and financial power: a comparative study of Britain, the United States and Japan*. Brighton, England: Wheatsheaf.

—1994. Class analysis: back to the future. *Sociology* **28**, 933–42.

Shapin, S. 1994. *A social history of truth*. Chicago; Chicago University Press.

Shapin, S. & S. Schaffer. 1985. *Leviathan and the air pump*. Princeton, NJ: Princeton University Press.

Sherif, M. 1936. *The psychology of social norms*. New York: Harper.

Simon, H. A. 1957. *Models of man: social and rational*. New York: John Wiley.

—1982. *Models of bounded rationality*. Cambridge, Mass.: MIT Press.

Smelser, N. 1962. *Theory of collective behavior*. New York: Free Press.

Smith, G. & A. Travers 1995. Erving Goffman, his project and program. University of Salford. Forthcoming.

Smith, R. & B. Wynne (eds) 1989. *Expert evidence: interpreting science in the law*. London: Routledge & Kegan Paul.

Snow, D. A., E. B. Rochford, S. K. Worden, R. D. Benford 1986. Frame alignment processes, micromobilization and movement participation. *American Sociological Review* **51**, 464–81.

Stich, S. P. 1985. Could man be an irrational animal? Some notes on the epistemology of rationality. In *Naturalising epistemology*, H. Kornblith (ed.). Cambridge, Mass.: MIT Press.

Stinchcombe, A. L. 1992. Simmel systematized: James S. Coleman & the social forms of purposive action in his *Foundations of social theory*. *Theory and Society* **21**, 183–202.

Taylor, F. W. 1911. *Scientific management*. New York: Harper & Bros.

Thompson, J. B. & D. Held (eds) 1982. *Habermas: critical debates*. London: Macmillan.

Thompson, J. D. 1967. *Organizations in action*. New York: McGraw-Hill.

Tilly, C. 1978. *From mobilization to revolution*. Reading, Mass.: Addison-Wesley.

Touraine, A. 1981. *The voice and the eye*. Cambridge: Cambridge University Press.

—1985. An introduction to the study of social movements. *Social Research* **52**, 749–88.

Trevarthen, C. 1989. Signs before speech. In *The semiotic web*. T. A. Sebeok, & J. Uniker-Sebeok (eds.). Berlin: Mouton de Gruyter.

—1988. Universal cooperative motives: How infants begin to know the language and culture of their parents. In *Ethnographic perspectives on cognitive development*, G. Jahoda & I. Lewis (eds). Beckenham, Kent: Croom Helm.

Trevarthen, C. & K. Logotheti 1987. First symbols and the nature of human knowledge. In *Symbolism and knowledge*, Cahiers de la Foundation Jean Piaget No. 8, J. Montangero (ed.). Geneva: Archives Piaget.

—1989. Child culture: genesis of cooperative knowing. In *Cognition and social worlds*, A. Gellatly, D. Rogers & J. Sloboda (eds). Oxford: Oxford University Press.

Tucker, K. 1991. How new are the new social movements? *Theory, Culture and Society* **8**, 75–98.

Turner, B. A. 1971. *Exploring the industrial subculture*. London: Macmillan.

—(ed.) 1990. *Organizational symbolism*. Berlin: Walter de Gruyter.

Turner, J. C. et al. 1987. *Rediscovering the social group a self-categorization theory*. Oxford: Basil Blackwell.

—1991. *Social influence*. Milton Keynes, England: Open University Press.

Tversky, A. & D. Kahneman 1981. The framing of decisions and the rationality of choice. *Science* **211**, 453–8.

Vogler, C. M. 1985. *The nation state: the neglected dimension of class*. Aldershot, England: Gower.

Wallerstein, I. 1974. *The modern world system*, vol. 1. New York: Academic Press.

—1980. *The modern world system*, vol. 2. New York: Academic Press.

Waters, M. 1991. Collapse and convergence in class theory: the return of the social in the analysis of stratification arrangements. *Theory and Society* **20**, 141–72.

Weber, M. 1968. *Economy and society: an outline of interpretive sociology*. Berkeley: University of California Press.

White, H. C. 1981. Where do markets come from? *American Journal of Sociology* **87**, 517–47.

Wieder, D. L. 1974. *Language and social reality*. The Hague: Mouton.

Wigham, E. 1973. *The power to manage*. London: Macmillan.

Wittgenstein, L. 1968. *Philosophical investigations*, 3rd edn. Oxford: Basil Blackwell.

Woodward, J. 1965. *Industrial organizations*. Oxford: Oxford University Press.

Zald, M. N. & J. D. McCarthy (eds) 1987a. *Social movements in an organizational society*. New Brunswick, NJ: Transaction Books.

—1987b. Religious groups as crucibles of social movements. See Zald & McCarthy (1987a).

—1987c. Social movement industries: competition and conflict among SMOs. See Zald & McCarthy (1987a).

Index

INDEX

UNIVERSITY OF WOLVERHAMPTON
LIBRARY

Contents

Chapter 1
Being the best

It was Saturday, and the first football practice of the season had begun. Max and Zoe were excited.

"Wow, Max," said Zoe. "You're so good at dribbling. I'm rubbish at it!"

"You're not that bad, Zoe. You only knocked over five cones," Max said.

Zoe frowned. "There were only five cones to start with!"

"Okay, team," called Coach. "Line up for toe touches!"

Zoe watched as Max did the exercises perfectly. During her turn, Zoe's foot slid off the ball. She fell onto the grass.

"You are the best at everything, Max," Zoe said with a sigh.

"No, I'm not," Max replied.

"You do the best round-offs. You're the fastest reader. And you're the best at football," Zoe said.

"Well, you do the longe

headstands, and you're way

better at maths," Max said.

"I suppose

so," Zoe said.

Coach blew

his whistle

again. "Time for running

practice!" he said.

"At least I'm good at

running," Zoe said.

"I'm not," said Max. "I'm always the last one."

Zoe and Max lined up for the running.

"Ready, steady, GO!" Coach yelled.

Chapter 2
A long shortcut

Max ran hard. He had to keep up with Zoe.

They had to run all the way round the pitch. It was a really long way!

Max was sweating, and his legs were really tired. Worst of all, he was in last place.

Zoe led the pack. She sped past the first goal. Max ran towards it too.

Coach had said, "No cutting in front of the goals."

But Max was so tired. And he hated being last.

He looked over his shoulder. Coach wasn't looking. This was his chance.

Max ran in front of the goal. He caught up with the other runners.

"Hey, you cheated!" yelled a boy behind him.

The race ended. The boy who came in last told the coach that Max had cheated.

"Is that true, Max?" asked Coach.

Max kicked the dirt. "Yes. I didn't want to be last," he said.

"Shortcuts don't work, Max," said Coach. "The only way to get better is to practise. Run another lap."

Max did, all by himself.

"I wish I was a good runner," he thought.

"Game time!" called

Coach.

Everyone chased after the

ball. Max couldn't keep up.

He didn't kick the ball once.

He was too tired.

Chapter 3
No quitting

After practice, Max went

to Zoe's house.

"I'm going to quit

football," Max said.

"Don't quit," Zoe begged.

"You're really good at

dribbling and toe touches."

"Well, if I could run like you, maybe I'd stay," he said.

"I can run, but I can't do the other stuff," she said.

Max thought for a minute. "How about you help me, and I'll help you?"

"Good idea! We'll be way better by next Saturday," Zoe said as she gave Max a high five.

So Max and Zoe ran races
and practised dribbling.
They worked hard every day.

They did lots of different
drills. Sometimes they put
toys all over the garden and
ran round them.

By Friday, Max ran faster and breathed easier. Zoe was able to do toe touches without falling.

On Saturday at practice, Coach said, "Better running, Max! Better dribbling, Zoe!"

"Let's keep practising at home, okay?" whispered Max.

"Yeah. We'll get better than better. We'll be the best!" Zoe whispered back.

"Pretty soon we'll be football stars!" said Max. Race you across the field."

"You're on, Max!" Zoe said.

About the author

Shelley Swanson Sateren is the award-winning author of many children's books. She has worked as a children's book editor and in a children's bookshop. Today, as well as writing, Shelley works with primary-school-aged children in various settings. She lives in Minnesota, USA, with her husband and two sons.

About the illustrator

Mary Sullivan has been drawing and writing all her life, which has mostly been spent in Texas, USA. She earned a BFA from the University of Texas in Studio Art.

Glossary

cheated to act without being honest, in order to win a game or get what you want

dribble to move a ball while running, keeping it under your control

goal a frame with a net into which you aim a football

headstand the act of holding yourself upright on your head with the help of your hands

round-off an act similar to a cartwheel that ends with both legs finishing together at the same time

quit give up doing something

shortcut a shorter or quicker way

Discussion questions

1. Max cheated during the running challenge. His coach made him run another lap. Do you think the coach's punishment was fair? Why or why not?

2. Have you ever cheated or wanted to cheat? Discuss your answer.

3. Max wasn't good at running, so he wanted to quit football. Have you ever wanted to quit something that was hard for you? Explain your answer.

Writing prompts

1. Think about something you want to get better at. Make a list of three things you can do to make that happen.

2. Max and Zoe helped each other become better football players. Write about a time when you helped a friend.

3. Max and Zoe like football. Write three sentences about your favourite activity.

Football challenge

Zoe and Max made up their own exercises to get better at football. You can do your own challenges, too!

What you need:

- a safe space for running, such as a garden
- two footballs or two stuffed animals
- a tape measure
- a timer
- paper
- pencil or pen

What you do:

1. Put one ball or stuffed animal at one end of your garden. With the tape measure, measure out 5 metres. Put the second ball or animal at the other end.

2. Jog at a slow speed between the two balls or animals. Jog back and forth five times.

3. Next, raise your knees high when you run. Run back and forth five times. Now you are warmed up.

4. Now get a friend to time you as you run as fast as you can between the balls or animals. Speed back and forth five times.

5. Record your time so you can see how you improve each time you do this challenge.

6. When you finish, make sure you rest and drink some water.

The fun doesn't stop here!

We have lots more Max and Zoe adventures for you to enjoy!

Discover more books and favourite characters at **www.raintree.co.uk**